Pull Up a Chair

Pull Up a Chair

The VIN SCULLY STORY

CURT SMITH

Potomac Books, Inc.
Washington, D.C.

Copyright © 2009 Potomac Books, Inc.

Library of Congress Cataloging-in-Publication Data
Smith, Curt.
  Pull up a chair : the Vin Scully story / Curt Smith. — 1st ed.
      p. cm.
  Includes bibliographical references and index.
  ISBN 978-1-59797-424-0 (hardcover : alk. paper)
  1. Scully, Vin, 1927– 2. Sportscasters—United States—Biography. I. Title.
  GV742.42.S38S65 2009
  796.092—dc22
  [B]
                                                                                2009012779

Printed in the United States of America on acid-free paper that meets the American National Standards Institute Z39-48 Standard.

Potomac Books, Inc.
22841 Quicksilver Drive
Dulles, Virginia 20166

First Edition

10 9 8 7 6 5 4 3

To Olivia and Travis,

who nightly pull up a chair

"**What baseball is to America,**

Scully is to baseball."

—Doug Gamble, *Orange County Register*

CONTENTS

ACKNOWLEDGMENTS

AN EDITOR ONCE TOLD A FRIEND, "Remember that you're not writing *the* book. You're writing *a* book." This is not *the* book about arguably America's greatest twentieth century sportscaster. It is *a* book—surprisingly, the first—about Vincent Edward Scully.

Scully has broadcast sports, primarily baseball, since 1950: private, literate, "sitting on a mound," he said, "as a gigantic parade goes by." I was born too late to hear Vin's parade in New York—then raised too Eastern to hear it daily in Los Angeles. For a long time I absorbed Scully from a distance: a World Series here, an All-Star Game there. Necessity can become a virtue.

Like most of America, I truly met Vin in the 1970s: first on CBS Radio; next, NBC Television; today, Sirius XM Satellite Radio, ending exposure by fit and start. Distance can breed perspective. It also spurs mystique. This book explores the man behind it: connecting tissue between the public and its game.

Any book weighs past vs. present. Four conclusions color *Pull Up a Chair*. Film's *A League of Their Own* was released in 1992. Increasingly, Vin's league is of *his* own. The *Los Angeles Times* columnist T. J. Simers wrote: "It's not easy to get a handle on greatness, especially when . . . those who have achieved it subscribe only to hard work." Scully's handle segues from work via education to elegance. ("It was so hot today," he said once, "the *moon* got sunburned.")

The reason is conclusion two. Like Jesus, Maimonides, and Homer, among others, Vin grasps language's nub: storytelling. Anecdote studded Lincoln's narrative. Franklin Roosevelt invented a piano teacher to illustrate a point. Scully would have hated politics (too intrusive), yet been a fine politician (making the inanimate, animate). Baseball's last practitioner of One Booth, One Announcer, still addresses the listener; not happy talk with a peer.

Conclusion three is personal. To quote sociologist David Riesman, Vin is an inner-directed man. Speaking in 2000 at his alma mater, Fordham University, he cited William Penn's "No pain, no palm; no thorns, no throne; no gall, no glory; no cross, no crown," asking not only why "bad things happen to good people, but good things happen to bad people"? Scully is a family man, touting "self-discipline and responsibility," grounded and self-aware.

Fourth. In his book *Ronald Reagan*, Dinesh D'Souza notes how many still miss the Gipper. "He isn't returning," the author says. "The truth is, we don't need another Reagan"—rather, to ask what Reagan would *do*. Disliking it, Vin will one day retire: "It'd almost be like shutting off the motor. I'd be shutting off myself." Fast forward to 2020. Learning, not parodying, an announcer asks, "What would Scully *say*?" ESPN's Jon Miller insists, "There's not one thing he does I wouldn't recommend." Most Voices descend to meet an audience. Vin asks *his* to rise.

In 1993 I helped write Scully's *Reader's Digest* tribute to mentor Red Barber. Vin spoke to me for such prior books as *Voices of The Game*, *The Storytellers*, and *What Baseball Means to Me*. I wish to thank him and other announcers, some now deceased: Mel Allen, Red Barber, Bud Blattner, Jack Buck, Joe Castiglione, Jerry Coleman, Bob Costas, Jerry Doggett, Dick Enberg, Lanny Frattare, Joe Garagiola, Earl Gillespie, Curt Gowdy, Hank Greenwald, Milo Hamilton, Merle Harmon, Ernie Harwell, Pat Hughes, Jaime Jarrin, Harry Kalas, Peter King, Jon Miller, Lindsey Nelson, Ross Porter, Ed Randall, Pee Wee Reese, Ray Scott, Charley Steiner, Chuck Thompson, and Bob Wolff.

I am indebted to Southern California journalists for reporting Scully so long and well: J. A. Adande, Steve Bisheff, Mike Downey, Frank Finch, Tom Hoffarth, Gary Kaufman, Doug Krikorian, Jim Murray, Bob Oates, Paul Oberjuerge, Mike Penner, Bill Plaschke, Diane Pucin, T. J. Simers, and Larry Stewart. Other writers helped in print and/or person: Maury Allen, David Barron, Brad Buchholz, Jack Craig, Gary Deeb, Phil Elderkin, Doug Gamble, Richard Hoffer, Stan Isaacs, Leonard Koppett, Phil Mushnick, Eric Neel, Ben Platt, Rick Reilly, Rob Rains, Bob Raissman, Harold Rosenthal,

Richard Sandomir, Leonard Shapiro, Dave Sheinin, George Vecsey, and Jon Weisman.

I want to thank Thomas Oliphant, the *Boston Globe* columnist and author of the book *Praying for Gil Hodges,* for reading the manuscript and making suggestions. Baseball, radio, and television officials include Dick Brescia, Scotty Connal, Harry Coyle, Carl Lindemann, Bill MacPhail, Tom Merritt, Joe Reichler, Al Schwartz, Lou Schwartz, and Bruce DuMont, president, Museum of Broadcast Communications and National Radio Hall of Fame, of which Scully is a member. Fordham Library's Archives and Special Collections was also very helpful.

The National Baseball Hall of Fame and Museum staff was, as always, Ruthian, especially Jeff Arnett, former director of education; Bill Francis, senior researcher; and Pat Kelly, director, Photograph Collection. Andrew Blauner helped conceive the project. I wish to also thank Potomac Books's John Church, Claire Noble, Jennifer Waldrop, and Vicki Chamlee, and Kevin Cuddihy, Phil Hochberg, John Miley, and Ken Samelson. My wife, Sarah, endured a twin bill of research and writing. Our children Olivia, 9, and Travis, 8, now know how Vin was never wasted on the young.

Pull Up a Chair is Scully's invocation. Researching, I did 75 interviews; heard hundreds of broadcast hours; and visited, among other sites, the Hall, Fordham, Library of Congress, the *Sporting News*, and the *Los Angeles Times*. I also wrote where I am privileged to teach: the University of Rochester in New York. Four years ago the noted educator Joel Seligman became its president. Aptly, the Angeleno grew up "a passionate Dodger fan"—above all, on Vin. "I never heard an announcer in any sport," he said, "who had a greater sense of poetry, dignity, and respect for the sport that he was describing."

The sixth-century Greek Heraclitus said, "A man's character is his fate." Broadcasting's fate has profited from this Artful Dodger's character.

PROLOGUE

OCTOBER 26, 1991, is still as clear as my boyhood hula hoop. All day I worked on a speech for then-president George H. W. Bush. At 10 P.M. I left the White House, found my car on the Ellipse, and turned to Columbia Broadcasting System's radio coverage of the 88th World Series.

Already Atlanta and Minnesota had forged a classic Fall Classic. Three of the first five games were decided by a run. In Game 6, a Twins runner reached second base. At this point announcer Mel Allen blurts, "How about that!"; Jack Brickhouse, "Hey-Hey!"; Bob Costas, wit via Casey Stengel by way of David Letterman.

Instead, CBS's Voice cited Broadway's *Death of a Salesman*'s "tiny ship" (runner) seeking "safe harbor" (home plate). Listening, I almost drove off Pennsylvania Avenue. Only Vin Scully could fuse baseball and Arthur Miller—indeed, has since "Tokyo Rose" went to prison, William Faulkner won a Nobel Prize for Literature, and *South Pacific* cried gotcha to the soul.

At 81, Scully's lingua franca ties depth and verve, declining to deviance or dumb down. "The best ever," Ernie Harwell mused in early 2009, Scully's 60th straight major-league year. "A unique part of baseball history," noted former Commissioner Fay Vincent. The un-twenty-first-century, Dick Enberg added: "against the flow, deep and authentic." Baseball's gold standard remains its half currency and half command.

Sportscasting can be Shakespeare's "much ado about nothing." Football or basketball carries the announcer. The announcer carries baseball. A three-hour game may put the ball in play 10 minutes. The Voice navigates a sea of dead air, using persona as a paddle. Bob Prince aired hockey, even jai alai. Who recalls? "Only baseball's pace reveals your personality," said

Al Michaels. Costas has done late-night TV, *Dateline,* and eight Olympics. "Despite that, I'm linked to baseball. Filling time, you bare your core."

In 1950 Scully, 22, joined Red Barber at Ebbets Field. In late 1957 the Dodgers left the Borough of Churches for the City of the Angels. "[Each] April," Rick Reilly wrote, his "mellifluous musings . . . drifted up from every [Los Angeles] traffic jam and outdoor café, every limousine and ice cream truck." Jerry Coleman deems Vin "the only broadcaster I know who's bigger than the players. He's the Babe Ruth of the broadcasting business," scaling a hill of syntax and vocabulary, a peak of phrase and mood.

At one time or another, Scully has aired NBC Television's *Game of the Week,* 12 All-Star Games, nonpareil 25 World Series and 18 no-hitters, and CBS football, golf, and tennis; made every major radio and TV Hall of Fame; got an Emmy Lifetime Achievement Award and Star, Hollywood Walk of Fame; and been named "most memorable [L.A. Dodgers] franchise personality," four-time National Sportscaster of the Year, and "Top Sportscaster of All-Time" by more than 500 national members of the American Sportscasters Association.

"He may live long. He may do much," British prime minister Edmund Burke etched a colleague. "But here lies the summit. He can never exceed what he does this day." To Vin, *this* day became *each* day, playing English like Jascha Heifetz played the violin.

EDDIE GOMEZ, who played bass with pianist Bill Evans, termed the jazz-man's aim "to make music that balanced passion and intellect." Dizzy Dean's bred idiom. Joe Buck's reflects our hipper, edgier time. Scully's changes tune within a batter's count. One pitch recalls a Brooklyn stopper. The next eludes a catcher, evoking the Ancient Mariner: "And he stoppeth one of three." A dribbler turns infield hit, Vin quoting Eugene O'Neill: "a humble thing, but thine own." Of pornography, Supreme Court Justice Potter Stewart said that it was hard to define, but "I know it when I see it." Defining Scully can mime throwing darts in the fog. We know him when we hear him.

Churchill called rhetoric "words that become bullets—ammunition to use." Vin's parry and pirouette, ricochet and chime. He can speak, thus, educate. Listening, we learn. Barber gave the score like clockwork. Dean made it, to paraphrase Ring Lardner, a side dish he never ordered. Vin added realism, lyricism, intimacy, love of history, grasp of workaday joy and fear, and a voice less Pavarotti than Perry Como. Bill Stern turned heads. Scully woos them.

Graham McNamee was radio's 1920 Cortez. "He took a medium of expression," wrote Heywood Broun, "and [gave] it a sense of movement and of feeling. Of such is the kingdom of art." The layman draws dots. The artist connects them. Some Voices denote a team: Detroit's Harwell, the Yankees' Phil Rizzuto. Some conjure place: Keith Jackson, rural Georgia; Sean McDonough, Boston; Jimmy Dudley, Virginia's pine and brush. Others stir existential pleasure: the Falstaffian Harry Caray, "Holy Cow!"ing cable television. Scully means the game.

"He might not be the Voice of God—not deep enough, someone might quibble, not scary enough—but surely it is the Voice of Heaven," wrote the *Washington Post*'s Dave Sheinin in 2005. "Surely, Vin Scully's is the voice you hear, elegant and neighborly, as you lower yourself into the Great Easy Chair in the Sky and reach for the dial. 'Hi, everybody,' the voice would say, 'and a very pleasant good afternoon wherever you might be. It's a beautiful day here in heaven. . . .'"

To Sheinin, earthlings "have it nearly as good. The Voice of Heaven is still as alive as a triple in the gap, and more accessible to more people than ever before"—satellite radio, joining local wireless and TV. "As some baseball fans have [long] known and others are just learning, heaven on earth is a good car and an open road, or a soft chair and a cold beer, and Vin Scully calling the action, painting word-pictures, soothing souls. You cannot watch Babe Ruth play the game anymore, but thanks to marvels of technology, anyone can hear Vin Scully call one." Church or angel, the sanctuary was the field.

Circa 1958: Bums become Angelenos. In Beverly Hills, Cooperstown Class of '90 pitcher Jim Palmer, 13, fell asleep to Vin. In Santa Monica, future Dodger Rick Monday, 12, already knew him. "Vin traveled with us and beside us"—vacation, pool party, trek to the store. "A friend of our family years before we met." In Milwaukee, a recent University of Wisconsin graduate joined his dad's auto firm. "The Braves' great rival was the Dodgers, so I hated Scully," said Bud Selig. A half century later, phoning Dodger Stadium, baseball's commissioner asked to be put on hold. "I just want to hear him for a few minutes. I don't know how to say it, really, but hearing Scully's voice just makes me feel better." Like home plate, Vin had become safe harbor.

"The Fordham Thrush with a .400 larynx," observed the *Los Angeles Times*'s columnist Jim Murray. This book fathoms why, from baseball, Scully seldom lets us wander far away.

1

BEGINNINGS (1927–1938)

IRONY, MEET GEOGRAPHY. On November 29, 1927, the future Voice of the Brooklyn Dodgers was born in the Bronx to Vincent Aloysius Scully, a traveling silk salesman, and wife Bridget Freehill. "She was Irish, red-haired, and excitable," said son Vincent Edward. "What kind of mother would I have?"

The Scullys had left County Cavan, 70 miles northwest of Dublin, for northern Manhattan, near the Harlem River. Founded in 1841, nearby private Jesuit-based Fordham University flanked the Bronx Zoo, New York Botanical Garden, and tenements, shops, and diners. The émigrés often walked Vin in a baby carriage across Fordham's Rose Hill campus. Later, Bridget would say, "Vincent, I dream that you will study here." Her hope directly seemed as distant as putting on the Ritz.

By 1932, the number of New York breadlines matched bars soon reopened after the repeal of Prohibition. Bank failures spiraled. Unemployment roiled one in four Americans. The cityscape brooked soup kitchens, "a nickel, mister" apples, and billboards reading "I Will Share." One Depression couple was found sleeping in a Central Park cave. "We are at the end of our string," said President Herbert Hoover. A rusted car-turned-tent became a "Hoover hovel"; jack rabbit, "Hoover dog"; park bench newspaper, "Hoover blanket." The Republic seemed alone and in the dock.

Writer Rud Rennie left Florida training camp to travel north with the New York Yankees: "We passed through southern cities which looked as if they had been ravaged by an invisible enemy. People seemed to be in hiding. They even would not come out to see Babe Ruth and Lou Gehrig." Radio was a decade old. Hoover's Democratic rival used it to pledge "bold, persistent experimentation . . . a New Deal for the American people." Franklin Roosevelt would try anything. If it didn't fly, he tried something else.

"Government," he said, "has a final responsibility for the well-being of the citizenship." Scully didn't take a chance, learning early not to pass the buck. A ballad says, "Being Irish means laughing at life knowing that life will break your heart." In 1932, Aloysius died of pneumonia, his son barely knowing him. Vin and Bridget crossed the Atlantic—James Joyce's "bowl of bitter tears"—to mend in Ireland. "My mother told me later," Scully said, "that when we came back I had a brogue you could cut with a knife." Cutting also meant make-do, or do without. "You stretched things," feeling responsibility for *en famille*.

"We weren't poverty-stricken, just poor," Vin recalled, self-reliant and contained. To cope, Bridget began renting two spare rooms, usually to merchant sailors. One, Allan Reeve, a British seaman, worked for Cunard Lines. In 1935, he and Bridget married, siring daughter Margaret Anne. "From his Irish forebears, Vin inherited a strong streak of poetry and romanticism," Jim Murray wrote. "From his English parent he accepted a strong strain of practicality and dependability." Such amalgams are hard to find.

The family soon leased a fifth-floor $40-a-month walk-up at 869 West 180th Street in Washington Heights. On one hand, unlike, say, Mel Allen's in rural Alabama, their flat had indoor plumbing and electricity. On the other, to later quote Mike Huckabee, Reeve did not think that *summer* was a verb. He became a doorman at a Central Park West apartment building. Residents gave Vin patchwork clothes. The Brit-turned-Yank gave him love. "He'd spent his life at sea, now he was going to live on land and it was difficult," Scully told the *Los Angeles Times*. "I learned from this lovely, quiet, pipe-smoking man. I developed tremendous admiration in every way."

Life meant sweating rent, stretching a bill, a fondness for the familiar, and reverence for everything American. Dad—"To me, that's what he was"—and son mistrusted gloating, bragging, and thinking you had it made. Not born on third base, they never fantasized having hit a triple. Duty mattered: also, grace, bonhomie, and faith. "You know, I could be a Catholic," Richard Nixon once told an aide. "It's beautiful to think about, that there is something . . . really meaningful, something you can really grab a hold of." Scully did.

Knowing death, Vin could be fatalistic, liking an old Czech proverb: "Plan for next year and make a devil laugh." His sanctuary was religion—and trust in work's nobility/mobility. Robert Lowell wrote, "The mausoleum [is] in her heart." Ambition was in Scully's.

TENNESSEE WILLIAMS called the 1930s "that quaint period when the huge middle class of America was matriculating from a school for the blind." At eight, Vin enrolled in a school for the ear. "It is written that in every childhood a door will open," he once said, "and there's a quick glimpse of the future." Scully's future stood on four legs in the family living room: "one of those radio monsters with a wooden crosspiece under it for support that sat high off the ground."

At 1 P.M. each Saturday, Vin opened a box of crackers, poured a glass of milk, and literally crawled under the radio, "actually sat *underneath* it," putting a pillow on the crosspiece. "I'd stay there all afternoon. The teams were secondary. I mean, Alabama-Tennessee should have meant nothing to a kid in Washington Heights in New York. But I would listen and the crowd noise would come down like water out of a showerhead," pouring over him. "I hadn't seen a crowd, but I had heard one. I loved its roar—I'd get goose bumps long before I saw them on my skinny arms. I used to think, 'Oh, my gosh; that must be great.'" In 2007, still enamored, he mused how "to me, no sounds . . . can possibly sum up a situation better."

In 1895 Guglielmo Marconi sent and received his first radio signal in Italy. 1909: Explorer Robert Peary messaged, "I have [found] the pole." 1912: The RMS *Olympic* telegraphed a wireless operator: "RMS *Titanic* ran into iceberg. Sinking fast." For three days and nights David Sarnoff sent "updates to reporters and friends," later founding the National Broadcasting Company. August 5, 1921: KDKA Pittsburgh's Harold W. Arlin, 26, bought a ballpark seat, used a telephone as a microphone, and began baseball's first play-by-play. What did the Westinghouse Company foreman say? No one lives to testify. "We didn't know if we talked into a vacuum," he noted. "Everything was so primitive."

By 1923, 10 percent of Americans owned a radio. Sixty-three percent did by 1933. In 1924 you could hear the 103-ballot Democratic National Convention; 1925, Calvin Coolidge address Congress; 1927, Charles Lindbergh leave Paris for New York. In 1928 Lucky Lindy backed Hoover for President.

"Now you all remember Hoover, back in the war," a wireless ditty went.

"He saved us from the Kaiser, now he'll give us something more.

He'll serve as the President of the land of the free.

If he's good enough for Lindy, he's good enough for me."

Hoover, as it happened, wasn't. Radio's first leading man was. "How do you do, ladies and gentleman of the radio audience?" began each broadcast. Each closed like a séance: "This is Graham McNamee speaking. Good night, all." For a long time, his career lit the dawn.

Debuting in 1923, the former opera student covered foreign visits; coronations; 10 sports including boxing, track, and marbles; and NBC's first Rose Bowl. Ring Lardner typed: "I don't know which game to write about, the one I saw or [the one I] heard Graham McNamee announce." A reporter pierced the air: "McNamee, will you pipe down?" Such bile revealed fear: Why pay to read if you heard for free? Braving rain, Graham one afternoon removed his coat, covered the box seat microphone, and avoided a potential short. Wrote Heywood Broun: "He made me feel the temperature and the tension."

In 1934 McNamee aired his 12th straight World Series, "opened by the umpire who will howl 'play ball.'" The grandstand housed "wild-eyed rabid fans." Any "hint of rain has been dispelled." Next year, Commissioner Kenesaw Mountain Landis dispelled Graham from the Series. Vin still heard him, since each weekend baseball's future Olivier followed another kind of ball.

TV HAD NOT YET profoundly changed our Sunday and Monday: same time, same channel, pro football *live*. "The National Football League," said Scully, "was nothing but a bunch of pot-bellied longshoremen."

Football meant those college guys, not small-time Sabbath ministry. Beating its drum, McNamee helped interest beat the band. Ted Husing had a basso voice, fine diction, and *Roget's* vocabulary. The average "guy talked about the 'secondary,'" said Scully. "Ted talked about 'tertiary.' Blood was a 'sanguinary flow.'" Bill Stern could be inaccurate, yet drew you in, "the most electric quality to his voice I ever heard, so dramatic and colorful." Once, shelling peas in the kitchen, Vin heard a Navy-Georgia Tech game; whereupon a pass pivoted the second half. At that point Scully threw the bowl in the air. "It wasn't the game: I couldn't have cared less. It was what Stern could do with it."

From his window, Scully re-created Stern for pals in a courtyard. In the street, Vin hit fungoes, played games of pepper, and fueled stickball fantasy. A sawed-off broom handle became his bat; tennis ball, Spalding horsehide; sneakers, baseball spikes; and white manhole covers, bases. Looking on, apartment dwellers heard the trouper's play-by-play. "It's a base hit to right field!" Vin raced to the first base lamppost. "Scully rounds first and heads for second as the ball bounces sharply off the curb and lands in Mrs. O'Brien's ash can for a ground-rule double!"

Each day Vin's 175th Street parish grammar class was taught by "a wonderful group of women" known as the Sisters of Charity. Sister Virginia Maria wore glasses, had blue eyes and a black habit, and carried a pail of water and sponge to clean the blackboard. One morning she asked her group of 50 students to write a report on what they hoped to be. "The girls wanted to be nurses and ballet dancers," said Scully. "The boys wanted to be cops and firemen. I was hooked. This new thing [radio] had hooked me. I wanted to be a sports announcer." Sister Virginia Maria asked him to read aloud daily to the class.

Wright Morris wrote of Norman Rockwell, "His special triumph is in the conviction his countrymen share that the mythical world he evokes actually exists." Radio's triumph convinced Scully. After school, he climbed to the family flat. The spiral was a way up. The wireless might be a way out.

EVEN NOW SOMETHING REMAINS, if but a faint recollection, of the 1930s. Radio carried the Kentucky Derby, Drake Relays, Vanderbilt Cup Auto Race, boxing, golf, and tennis; also George Burns and Gracie Allen, Jack Benny and Bob Hope, Glenn Miller and Harry James, Guy Lombardo at Manhattan's Roosevelt Hotel, and Benny Goodman in the Manhattan Room of the Hotel Pennsylvania.

Film blared Tom Mix and Shirley Temple and Lionel Barrymore and Claudette Colbert. Print meant newspapers (the Big Apple had 13

English-language dailies), periodicals (*Vogue, Vanity Fair,* the *Saturday Evening Post,* and the *Sporting News,* baseball's "Bible"), and guides, yearbooks, and annuals—baseball's *our* game, bub, and don't you forget it. "All sports had been on paper," said McNamee. "Now, increasingly it came through a box."

For a time, network radio covered only the World Series, then the All-Star Games. Gradually, teams added a local home schedule. Away games were too expensive, which set some to studying. Q: How to air the road without *being* there? A: Wireless telegraphy "[fueled] play-by-play," wrote the *Sporting News,* "within three seconds of the time it occurs." A park operator sent Morse code to the station. *B1L* meant ball one, low; *S2C,* strike two, called. Eureka! A studio announcer could "re-create." By Roosevelt's first inaugural, the re-creation was a rite like gloves left on the field between innings. A pencil tapping wood simulated bat hitting ball. The soundtrack starred background murmur. Infielder: "Come *on.*" Skipper: "Don't give *in!*" Fan: "You couldn't hit my *house!*" Vin would eagerly have listened, had there been local baseball to hear.

In 1934 the Apple's three major-league teams signed a five-year radio ban. By 1938, Scully mused, "you could get local major-league coverage everywhere but there." To the man who defines *hearing* baseball, the sport then meant reading or seeing it. More irony: Vin's first object of big-league zeal. On October 2, 1936, the 8-year-old passed a Chinese laundry posting the World Series' line score: Yankees, 18 runs, 17 hits, 0 muffs; Giants, 4-6-1. "This little red-haired kid on the way home from school stopped to read it. I had only a vague idea of what was going on, but I instinctively felt terrible for the losing team, and from that moment loved the Giants."

In 1997 Florida scored 7 Series runs vs. Cleveland in an inning. For Scully, it evoked 1936. "I believe I became a Giants fan, honest to Pete," he told his CBS Radio audience. Later, Vin described a castle of "pure white Carrara marble" in Washington Heights where he and the Indians' Manny Ramirez lived in the 1930s and '80s, respectively. Let Manny be Manny. Scully was being Scully.

A VISITOR TOOK CAB (FDR Drive), private car (Eighth Avenue), or subway (Independent Line D train to 155th Street Station) to the Giants' Polo Grounds. Vin found it by walking about 25 blocks from home, or

20 from school, to the two-tiered horseshoe in a hollow 115 feet below Coogan's Bluff. Polo was never played there—after 1890, baseball was. Foul turf formed a vast semicircle behind the plate to each line. Roofed bullpen shacks anchored left-center and right-center field. An upper-deck overhang made left field's 279-foot foul line 21 feet closer. Right's 257 continued the oval shape. Center's 483 feet—"binocular territory," *Sports Illustrated* wrote—completed it. At 460, stairs reached each team's club-house. The rear wall read 505.

Playing roller hockey, Vin saw one Rangers game a year. "We'd hol-ler," said the tyro, "not knowing what we were hollering about. Base-ball I knew," seen from bleacher seats "courtesy of the Catholic Youth Organization and the Police Athletic League. Lifelong visions of blue cigarette smoke hanging like a gauze curtain over the infield, verdant green grass and sparkling uniforms." Sitting where no one had hit a ball, he pondered a puzzlement. "I would see the batter hit the ball. I would see the ball in the air. I would see the ball leave the infield. Then it's on the way to the outfield. Then I hear the crack of the bat." One day, curious, Scully asked a Coogan's neighbor to explain. "He gave me a lesson in elementary physics, that light travels at a speed considerably faster than sound. It's nothing, but to me it was a big thrill. I was charmed."

His team was more Ulysses than Sisyphus. 1932: Mel Ott had a league-best 38 dingers. 1933: New York won the Series on his homer off Washington's Fred Schulte's glove. 1934: Carl Hubbell K'd five American League All-Stars in a row. 1936: King Carl took 16 straight games; the Giants, a pennant. 1937: For Hubbell, another eight straight; his club, another flag. In 1938, prepotency ended with a third-place thud. "As a play," wrote the *New York Times*, "the Jints would be cancelled."

Sixty years later Cubs mikeman Pat Hughes heard a Scully tape. "Until then, I hadn't known that he liked the Giants—or once saw Ott homer thrice at the Polo Grounds." At 15, Mel's first dinger went inside the park. His next/last 510 went out. "I see him now," recalled Scully, "not enormously big [5-foot-9 and 170 pounds], right leg lifted as he swung. Yeah, Mel was my favorite player." Ben Platt became the Dodgers' 1990s computer whiz. "Something about his decency appealed to Vinny. When he told a Giants story, it always reverted back to Ott."

In 1938 Mel led the National League in three categories. That January it asked Cincinnati Reds President Larry MacPhail to help the Dodgers avoid going under: title, executive vice president; control, "full and complete." MacPhail was severe and tart and brilliant. In further irony, he augured a man Vin didn't know, airing a team he didn't like, in a borough a world away.

2

WHO'S A BUM? (1939–1949)

BY 1939, RADIO ferried baseball from far-flung sites: Sportsman's Park's playful furnace; Briggs Stadium's fort at Michigan and Trumbull; Forbes Field's acreage grown heavy with base hits. "Millions come to the park each year," said Ernie Harwell. "Others can't or don't." Broadcasters became a listener's eyes and ears. In New York, green with envy, Larry MacPhail turned the Jints and Yankees blue.

Arriving from Cincinnati, the new Dodgers don disclosed that Brooklyn would use the wireless. His Reds mikeman followed, a distant relative of writer Sidney Lanier. Like MacPhail, Walter Lanier "Red" Barber grasped how radio "made a game played by two teams [into] a contest involving personalities who had families, troubles, blue or brown eyes." Like Scully, he seemed born to chat around a stove.

In 1918, Barber, 10, left Columbus, Mississippi, for Sanford, Florida, later hitchhiking to the university at Gainesville, where he worked his way through school. One job was cleaning a busy professor's boarding house; another, reading his paper on WRUF campus radio. Red had wanted to teach English. "By the time I finished the paper, I wanted to drop out of school."

Barber became the station's $50-a-week announcer and director. "When school ended, I'd look for broadcast jobs." In 1933 the Reds went broke. A bank hired MacPhail, who sold Powel Crosley a majority percent.

Halving Red's salary, Crosley hired him for then–500,000-watt WLW. "I want a chance," Red told his father. Said MacPhail, "Barber didn't know how to score a game. On the other hand, especially re-creating, it was like nothing they'd ever heard."

Many Voices used crowd noise to feign being at a park. Baseball's Diogenes placed the mike by the telegraph. "No con. Never in a million years. You heard the dot-dash," noted Scully. "The first time I heard Barber I could sense his justness. I knew before ever meeting him that this man could not be bought." One taxi driver groused, "That Barber, he's too fair."

In 1935, Red marked two firsts: a major-league night game and Mutual Radio's World Series. Landis collared him before its opener. "Suppose a player . . . spits in my face. Report each step he makes. Report how much spit hits me. Report my reaction. Don't worry about the Commissioner. That will be my job. Yours is to report the event." Barber did: to Vin, a palatine kibitzing with the listener.

"Red didn't talk to analysts, like we do today," Scully said six decades later, "nor did he hector, like guys did then." What was not to like? "His gentle voice informed raucous fans. He couldn't be compromised. He was radio's first poet, the beloved voice of the Dodgers for 15 years, and a baseball announcer for 33"; save Bridget Scully, "the most influential person in my life." That, as they say, was in another country. In 1939 Vin was merely glad for baseball on the air.

"MACPHAIL BELIEVED in [radio's] promotional power," said Barber. "He became sold on it." Over WOR, 710 AM on your dial, Red sold the game— live, at home; away, by wire. In turn, WABC inked the 1939 Yanks' and Giants' home schedule. "It did each home game, then re-created away wherever it had space," Red sniffed. "No way could they give Brooklyn a monopoly." General Mills paid $400,000 for rights, hiring the "Rembrandt of the Re-creation." Since 1934, the Senators' Arch McDonald had bayed "right down Broadway" (strike), "ducks on the pond" (runners), and "There she goes, Mrs. Murphy" (home run).

"McDonald was not at all New York," wrote columnist Morris Siegel. General Mills didn't care. The Arkansan knew baseball and could peddle Wheaties: In theory, he would please. Instead, after one year Arch rejoined the Senators. Successor Mel Allen referenced *the* Yankee Stadium, easy to see why. Steel girded the 71,699-seat basilica one-quarter mile from Coogan's Bluff. Bleachers trimmed the fence. The grandstand wrapped home plate beyond the bases. "Both New York teams staggered their schedule," explained then-WABC's Allen, "so that they weren't home at the same time. With the Giants away, I did the Yankees live."

Roads led from New Haven, Rye, and Valley Stream. The No. 4 subway train, on elevated tracks, eyed an overhang screening flys, Roman facade atop the third tier, and numbers that would change when one plus one equaled three: 301 feet (left-field pole); 402 (left side, left-center bullpen gate); 457 (left-center); 407 (right-center); 344 (right side, right-center bullpen gate); and 296 (right). Center field was 461. At one point its duce led the American League in runs, homers, total bases, and slugging.

"A close friend loved Joe DiMaggio," Vin recalled, "so we'd walk almost to the Polo Grounds, take a bridge," and cross the Harlem River. "That's how it was: almost no Dodger fans around. In our area it was Yankees and Giants." In 1942, Ott, ditching Bill Terry, became player-manager. The Polo Grounds housed that year's All-Star Game. One day the Jints and Phillies stranded a record 30 runners. Fourteen years older, Allen prepped Scully unaware: "Imagine," said Harwell, "without either knowing it: baseball's future *greatest* Voice hearing its future most *famous* Voice."

On a clear night, a New Yorker caught Philadelphia's Byrum Saam. "Would you please talk a little louder?" a woman wrote Saam from New Jersey. "My radio battery is getting weaker." Inevitably, Scully returned to the announcer who became "like a father to me in every way."

In 1938 Nazi Germany crushed the neutral state of Czechoslovakia. Next year it gutted Poland, lighting a horror house that convulsed the globe, introduced the Bomb, and killed 55 million people. America would never double back before World War II. In Brooklyn, Barber crossed a line that baseball would not retrace, too. "The players were clearly distinguishable," wrote the *Sporting News*'s Harold Parrott of August 26, 1939's Dodgers-Reds bigs TV baptism, "but it was not possible to pick out the ball." You *could* pick out Barber, in Ebbets Field's second deck, as familial as your Uncle Fred, hawking Ivory Soap, Mobil Gas, and General Mills. "Yes-suh," he drawled of Wheaties, "that's a Breakfast of Champions": making history and flying blind.

"No monitor, only two [W2XBS] cameras. One was by me, the other behind the plate, and I had to guess from which light was on where it pointed." The Scullys lacked a TV until the early 1950s. "You didn't need one," reasoned Barber. "The age's leather was radio," airing nine of his 13 Series and 5 All-Star Games; NFL title and Army-Navy Games; Rose, Orange, and Sugar Bowls; and *College Football Roundup*. "Due to him," wrote David Halberstam, "and radio's importance then, we remember the messenger as distinctly as the message." To Vin, Barber exteriorized a borough. "People thought Manhattan looked down on them. Then along he came," mixing "walkin' in tall cotton" and "FOB—Full of Brooklyns" with Carlyle and Thoreau.

"Red's appeal soared," said Bob Costas, "because people sensitive about the image as Dees and dems—'I'll meet ya at Toydy-toyd and Second Avenue'—liked how this erudite man represented"—and respected—"them." The mound became a "pulpit." From the "catbird seat" Red described a "rhubarb." The pitcher "tied the hitter up—turned him every way but loose." Said Barber: "The sky is a beautiful robin-egg blue with, as the boys say, very few angels in the form of clouds." Robert Creamer wrote that you could walk down the street, 100 windows open, and not miss a pitch. "To care, to root," Red said, "are not the rights of the professional": rather, of the independent city incorporated into New York in 1898.

In 1845 baseball's first organized team began at 26th Street and Madison Avenue, later moving to Hoboken, New Jersey's Elysian Fields. Elysian means paradise in Greek. In 1852 it meant Brooklyn's first club. Scully, an unofficial historian, later chronicled the amateur Eckfords' and Atlantics' 1861–65 and 1870 national title and baseball's first enclosed field, in the Williamsburg section. Outfield distances were 500 feet. The exception: a one-story building, 350 feet from home plate, in play inside the right-field fence. Already baseball was Flatbush's link to the outside.

In 1884, Brooklyn joined the American Association, playing as the Atlantics, Grays, and Bridegrooms; 1890, made the National League as the renamed Trolley Dodgers; 1898, built Washington Park, near factories and the Gowanus Canal. Breezes from Jamaica Bay made pop flys a riddle. The right-field scoreboard stood on supporting legs. Between them, fielders retrieved balls by crawling in the mud. "It's like Red said," Vin laughed. "'Yes-suh, anything can happen at Ebbets Field.'" Anything included birth.

In 1902 the Dodgers nearly left for Baltimore. Instead, they built a "narrow cockpit of iron and concrete," wrote author Roger Kahn, "along a steep cobblestone slope." The 4½-acre Crown Heights site linked Bedford Avenue, Sullivan Place, Franklin Avenue (later, Cedar/McKeever Place), and Montgomery Street near the Brooklyn Rapid Transit Company. It had been a garbage dump, "Pigtown." Owner Charles Ebbets hoped for pearls, not swine.

Ground broke March 14, 1912.

Reporter: "What are you gonna call your park?"

Ebbets: "I hadn't even thought about it."

"Why don't you call it Ebbets Field?"

Ebbets nodded, then sold half interest to businessmen Steve and Ed McKeever.

Opening April 5, 1913, the park blared things to come.

THE SUPERINTENDENT lost his key. Designers had forgot to build a press box: "the boys" or "scribes" typed in the lower deck. First-day pols and players trudged to the center-field flagpole. Ebbets turned to an aide. "The flag, please," he said. The aide reddened. "Sorry, Charlie. We forgot it."

Later, Brooklyn built a fun house of raucous peals. "A lot of people think of William Bendix," Barber said of TV's 1950s Chester A. Riley. "He was in so many [World War II] films, always playing a Brooklynite, that he came to mean the park," not intended to become a laughing matter. Ticket windows were gilded. A brick facade studded Roman arches. Italian marble with baseball stitches tiled the main rotunda floor. The 1916 Dodgers even won a pennant.

George Cutshaw once benignly grounded to right. The ball hit a nine-foot-high concave wall, bounced up, landed on a shelf, and stayed there for a homer. In 1918 Brooklyn dealt Casey Stengel for Burleigh Grimes. By and by Charlie Grimm lay down in the batter's box.

"What are you doing?" said umpire Bill Klem.

"Grimes is going to throw at me anyway," said Grimm, "so I thought I'd duck early."

Next year Casey returned to Flatbush as a Pirate. The crowd rose. Bowing, Stengel doffed his cap. A sparrow flew away. "Brooklyn's funny," said 1914–31 manager Wilbert Robinson. "They get a silver lining, and keep looking for the cloud." In 1920, Uncle Robbie tied and lost twice in 26, 13, and 19 innings, respectively. "It has to get better," he said, and briefly did. The Dodgers won another pennant, took a 2-1 game Series lead, then hit into an unassisted triple play. Cleveland won the then-best-of-nine. A cry began: "Wait Till Next Year." Next year waited till 1955.

"Baseball here didn't set out to be daffy," said Scully. "It just evolved." In 1926, Floyd Caves "Babe" Herman batted with Hank DeBerry, Dazzy Vance, and Chick Fewster on base. Herman lined off the right-field screen, DeBerry scoring. Nearing third, Vance turned the bag. The outfielder threw home. Retreating, Vance met Fewster, sliding into third, who met Babe, head down. Three Dodgers now shared a base. Leaving, Fewster and Herman were tagged out.

Line: "The Dodgers have three on base."

Punchline: "Yeah, which base?"

Cartoonist Willard Mullin later spawned the Brooklyn Bum. "Where else but Brooklyn," wondered Robinson, "could you double into a double play?" Memory grew like vines around a trellis. 1932: Lefty O'Doul (.368) won the batting title. 1938: Babe Ruth (briefly) became a Dodgers coach. The second (Johnny Vander Meer's straight no-hitter) shall be first (Ebbets's night inaugural). 1931–38: If losing was an art form, the Bums were Cezanne (seventh twice; sixth, thrice).

"Anything can happen" was Red's cliché, except it was no cliché. Brooklyn's real star was the field.

It MAY SEEM ODD for a structural steel, reinforced concrete park to become the personality of baseball in the flesh. At Ebbets Field, it seemed natural. The park became Green Acres, the urban place to be.

Red stirred the pot. Baseball was daily: Said Vin, "A city can rally around a team." Brooklyn was needy: second-guessable and insecure. Above all, Ebbets was participant, not spectator. A U.S. football field is 100 yards long and 53⅓ yards wide. A diamond merely decrees 90 feet between bases and 60 feet, 6 inches from home plate to the mound. Amazingly, Scully never saw Brooklyn's until "the [1950] day I went to work." Mom and Pop didn't own a car, never learning how to drive. Train, bus, and trolley seemed impractical: "Brooklyn was so far away. We just never went," missing its high and low walls, long and short distances, history and hyperbole. It *mattered* where you played.

A long out to Yankee Stadium's left-center field — "Death Valley" — was a homer here. A 20-foot barrier tied left to center field, whose wall began at 15 feet, became 19, and shrunk at 13 at a screen. Protruding five feet at a 45-degree angle, the concave wall linked center and the right-field line. Its "lower 19 [bottom 9 sloped; top 10, rising vertically] were concrete," wrote the *New York Daily News*'s Dick Young. "Above was another 19 feet of wire screen." The scoreboard and wall had 29 different angles: Only Carl Furillo truly mastered them. The park was a calliope. Pinball was the effect.

Scant acreage compounded it: ultimately, left field, 343 feet from the plate; left-center, 351; deep left-center at a bend of the wall, 395; center, 393; right side of the right-field grandstand, 376; right-center, 403; right-center scoreboard, 344 and 318 (left and right side); right, 297. Brooklyn's largest bar had 35,000 stools. Most had a good view—if you weren't behind a post. Vin followed Brooklyn to see what it was up to. As seen by a Jints junkie, usually no good.

"This was a sports rivalry unlike any that ever was or probably ever will be," Steve Jacobson wrote of Brooklyn-New York. "The fans rode the subway from their homes to the turf of the other team and cheered their raving hearts out. Each meeting was an angry collision. And sometimes it was close to hatred." In September 1940 the Bums taunted plate umpire George Magerkurth. "It was bad," said second-year player/manager Leo Durocher, "even by baseball standards." On the final out a parole violator attacked Magerkurth before he could leave the field. "Just rushed from his seat," said the ump. "Before I know it he's beating me."

The archetypal fanatic screams, "Kill the ump!" Fearing injury, umpire Bill Stewart tackled the jaybird, freed Magerkurth, and let police haul the con away. National League head Ford Frick then fined and suspended Durocher for "inciting a riot." Just another day in Flatbush.

In April 1941, Barber was honored with a day at Ebbets Field, then read a script for the New York Philharmonic's *Symphony in D for the Dodgers*. In the Bronx, Vin ended his freshman year at Fordham University's Preparatory School at Webster Avenue and Southern (now Kazimiroff) Boulevard.

Schoolmate Bill O'Donnell was later a *Navy News* editor, Syracuse University basketball and football Voice, and 1966–82 Orioles announcer.

Bronx-born Larry Miggins was a "tall rangy kid," said Scully, "our best athlete," and already pining for the bigs.

In 2000 Vin told Fordham University's commencement how they had spoken in a less mock-suspense than will-o'-the-wisp way. "I want to be a major-league baseball player," Miggins whispered in a Prep assembly. "I wonder what the odds of *that* would be."

"I want to be a major-league broadcaster," Scully countered in the back row of the auditorium. "Whoa, I wonder what the odds against *that* would be."

Vin mused "about the odds if we both make it." Then: "I wonder what the odds would be if *I* were *broadcasting* a game in which *you played*."

Making the 1948 Cardinals, Miggins resurfaced in 1952. That May 13, he batted in the fourth inning at Brooklyn: "one of the two [usually third and seventh] I did each game," said Scully. Suddenly, "I'm sitting there, overwhelmed, that this is happening."

Preacher Roe threw a fastball: "a cantaloupe," said Miggins, clearing the wall. Stunned, Vin called his pal's first of two big-league homers: "as close to breaking down doing a baseball game or any other sports event I have ever experienced"—still towering, like the time.

In Prep school, Scully studied Latin, English, and history; made the student council and council of discipline; joined the *Ramkin* newspaper and *Rampart* yearbook; was named "most popular" and "wittiest" senior; played center field on the baseball team; and acted in such plays as *Brother Orchid*, based on a 1940 Edward G. Robinson film. The principal steered him to drama, debate, and elocution; held inspection; and maintained proper dress. Vin represented Fordham in an American Legion oratorical contest. Problem: He had a navy blue suit but only brown, not black, shoes. Solution: The principal borrowed 13 pairs of black shoes, which came from every other priest. "Try them on," he told Scully, pointing, "till you find a pair that fits."

A class picture shows Vin, 13, dressed neatly in shirt, narrow tie, pants, and double-breasted jacket, hands tucked behind. The freshman looks ahead, scrubbed and tubbed, an urban Opie Taylor. "Give me a child until he is seven," said Francis Xavier, "and you may have him afterward." Put one way, we rarely stray from DNA. Put another, as Al Gore malapropped, "A zebra doesn't change its spots." Scully wouldn't.

The photo brandishes a sharp chin, high forehead, rail-thin face, thatch of red in a pompadour, and blue, luminous, piercing eyes. It also augurs Vin's "just refus[ing] to let my emotions show [1985, to Rick Reilly]," modesty and privacy neither bogus nor offensive. John F. Kennedy's ancestors left New Ross, near Dunganstown, 60 miles from County Cavan. William Manchester termed children Caroline and John "friendly but reserved with strangers, alert, bright, possessed of immense curiosity, and fired by awesome energy." He could have been describing Scully.

Vin's rookie year ended as FDR and Winston Churchill forged the Atlantic Charter, Nazi U-boats stalked the U.S. destroyer *Greer*, and sailors readied daily 8 A.M. Pearl Harbor flag raising. At the Polo Grounds, Scully "stared at the old battered, horseshoe-shaped press box behind home plate." In Brooklyn, Dolph Camilli led the league in homers (34) and RBIs (120). Shortstop Harold "Pee Wee" Reese supplied the glove and glue. "He came here a boy," Barber liked to say, "and wound up a man." The Dodgers drew a record 1,214,910. September 25, 1941, made the getting that was good even better: Flatbush clinched its first title since Woodrow Wilson's last full year as President.

Another first followed: a Bums-Stripes Subway Series. Behind, 2 games to 1, the Dodgers led, 4-3, in a two-out ninth. "Welcome," said Mutual's Allen of reliever Hugh Casey, "to the most infamous curve in history." Yankee Tommy Henrich swung—and missed. "Strike three!" boomed umpire Larry Goetz—before catcher Mickey Owen's passed ball settled near the screen. Next day, winning, 7-4, New York took its ninth Fall Classic. To Red, "This was the real start of the Dodgers' agony and ecstasy," a team seemingly unable to bump into luck.

The '42ers won 104 games, but lost a huge August lead. Next year Germany began to irrevocably lose the war. At Casablanca, Roosevelt and Churchill demanded "unconditional surrender." Cairo plotted Pacific Theater stratagem. Tehran named date and commander for the Normandy invasion. America bought war bonds, grew "victory gardens," rearmed, and mobilized. Total war meant full employment. Each day Scully's stepfather left at 4:30 A.M., took buses and subways to the Brooklyn Navy Yard, and began a 14-hour shift. Returning home, he found Vin asleep. Allan Reeve meant to pay the rent: also, do more than run in place.

One day he was offered a job on a ship bound for Europe: more pay—but in a combat zone. A ritzier flat might cost his life. Vin recalled his natural dad, a mother's hurt, a family's pain. "I was afraid he might be put in harm's way," he told the *L.A. Times*. "I didn't want him to risk the family to make a few more dollars." He wrote a note, left on Reeve's breakfast plate, asking him to reject the job. The father did. Reciprocating, the son delivered beer, milk, and mail; rolled racks in New York's Garment District; and "ripped wire copy" as a *New York Times* telegraph office boy in 1944.

That year a friend asked if Scully would like to work in "the Silver Room" of the Hotel Pennsylvania. Nodding, Vin imagined pouring cream for dining room grandees. In fact, the Silver Room was a basement hovel "through which every piece of silver in the hotel would come down a chute into a room not much bigger than a closet." Scully had to catch and "scald each piece and polish it." His partner, a Moro Indian used to humidity, reveled. The ruddy Irishman recoiled.

In the ballroom, partiers were so remote from what Scully knew that they might have sprung from another planet altogether. Some fainted from heat or gin. Vin fainted from silver's stench. "To this day," Jim Murray wrote in 1961, "he breaks out in a sweat" hearing of a silver anniversary. "The smell's still in my nostrils," Scully said of 1944. "I'll take it to the grave." That spring Brooklyn took training north: "war restrictions," said Durocher. "We had 15 players." Describing them was a man who might have been Vin Scully. The Victorians called cloudless spells "Queen's Weather." A dreambox voice lit Connie Desmond's.

Connie cracked radio with the '30s Toledo Mud Hens. "One year we were mathematically eliminated in July," he told Scully. "Next month they condemned the park. We had to finish on the road." In 1942 the now-Columbus Triple-A Voice got a call. "Help me do the Giants and Yankees," Allen urged Desmond. Before long, Barber hired Connie to do the Bums. He was Eddie Fisher, losing Elizabeth Taylor; Bill Clinton, blowing greatness; or ESPN founder Bill Rasmussen, selling pre-*SportsCenter* gold.

"I never thought of succeeding Barber," said Desmond. "Who thought he'd *ever* leave?" Ultimately, Red did. Replacing him, Connie flushed a knockout future down the flask. In 1942 Brooklyn's flagship became WHN 1050 AM. Scully listened when he could, soon trading one Fordham for another.

"NOW, THIS IS NOT THE END," Churchill said of Britain's victory that year at El Alamein. "It is not even the beginning of the end. But it is perhaps the end of the beginning." In September 1944, Vin entered the University his mom had praised while pushing her infant's carriage. More than six decades later, the end of Scully's beginning seems ordained.

A partial scholarship helped. Allan and Bridget toiled doggedly for their boy. George Will wrote the best-selling book *Men at Work: The Craft of Baseball*. In 2006, Vin said, "The mere thought of it [retirement] is frightening. A man really determines himself by what he does." Determined to finish college, Scully spent a year at Rose Hill, joined the Navy, was stationed in San Francisco, and returned to Fordham in 1946. Off campus touted double features and weekly newsreels, comics like *Alley Oop* and *Major Hoople,* writers from Edgar Wallace to P. G. Woodhouse, and Broadway's golden age, begun with 1943's *Oklahoma*, tying Mayberry and Dodge City. The young man in a hurry did not overly obsess.

Instead, Scully anchored the barbershop quartet the Shaving Mugs; wrote *The Ram* newspaper column *Looking Them Over*, inherited from later Pulitzer Prize–winning Arthur Daley and *Information Please* radio host John Kieran; and covered Fordham pigskin as a *Times* stringer. More Notre Dame than Slippery Rock, Rams football meant the '30s Seven Blocks of Granite; guard-turned-assistant coach Vince Lombardi; and Saturday afternoon at the Polo Grounds, Vin scribbling four miles from home. Soon Fordham's nascent radio station, WFUV, carried him beyond.

One photo shows Arthur Godfrey, emceeing its dedication. In another, Scully—hair slicked down, later dried; skin and bones, later rounder; in tie and checkered sweater, later suit and wingtops: sturdy, not flashy, less nervous than intense—leans toward a microphone: "WFUV sports staff," said the *Maroon* yearbook, "broadcasts play-by-play of Rams games." The voice was chipper and musical, less bewitching than welcoming, neither Stradivarius nor Gatling gun.

A staff picture bares Scully, smile out ahead of him, like a day right behind the rain. "You see it, and think of millions of ordinary people you've known at the office like him," said Brooklyn-born author and *Boston Globe* columnist Thomas Oliphant. "Yet hearing him, we found that he was like nothing we'd ever known: conversational, but erudite. Seemed like a bar pal, but with Einstein's wisdom. Funny, but encyclopedic": an anecdotalist, above all.

"My ambition had been to have a literary career," Vin said, tellingly. "I got cured by radio." Each week WFUV aired a *Saturday Shakespeare* series. By contrast, "we had a Saturday night disc jockey show. It was funny"— pause—"we thought it was funny, anyway. We had the Queen Mary docked at Fordham Road"—U.S. Route 1, the main college drag—"just a great training ground." Eventually, its new Communication Arts Department major became an "ultimate, even unattainable, measuring stick," said *New York Times* critic Richard Sandomir, "for succeeding generations of student sportscasters."

Michael Kay graduated in 1982. "There was almost a mystical aura about him when I was there. You spoke in reverential terms." Kay now televises the Yankees. Mike Breen '83 airs the basketball Knicks. "It was hard to imagine that Scully was actually a student once." Alumni include ESPN's Sal Marchiano, football Giants' Bob Papa, Washington Nationals' Charlie Slowes, and WFAN and TV's *Talking Baseball's* Ed Randall. "A common man's touch with a regal grasp of English," said Randall, growing up near Yankee Stadium.

Like most students at one time or another, Vin could seem more commoner than royalty, conceding to "often starting to laugh and talking in class." Once, sentenced to "jug—a mindless punishment"—Scully was forced to walk up and down Dealy Hall. "[Another] night I'm with a few characters who suggested, Let's sing. Soon we're bellowing 'Someone's in the Kitchen With Dinah.'" Interrupting, a dean raised the kitchen's temperature.

"Who *started* this?" he bellowed.

"I did," Vin raised his hand.

The dean evicted everyone but a red-faced redhead. "You stay, and sing at the top of your lungs." Complying, Vin added good-sing to great-field, no-hit.

Fordham archives read: "Vincent Edward Scully, 1947–48 varsity baseball." Trainer Johnny Dziegiel termed Vin "The Phantom." Added teammate Nick Baldino: "Fast, terrific in [like Prep] center field, a left-handed Terry Moore-type. We'd tell Vin the swing was OK, but you have to *hit* the ball." One day he singled thrice vs. New York University. Pleased: Coach Jack Coffey, like Frank Frisch '19, the Fordham Flash, a then-rare bigs college man. The 1909 and 1918 Boston and Detroit catcher drilled like a shogun, was a crack fungo hitter, relived Cobb and Mathewson, and spoke French and Latin fluently. In 1947 Scully traveled to New Haven to play a man who termed English "my *second* language."

Batting eighth—to him, "second cleanup"—George H. W. Bush reminisced in a '90s video. "Hey, Vin, this is your old friend. Remember a few years back in our baseball-playing days when you were roaming the outfield for Fordham University and I was that heavy-hitting, smooth-fielding first baseman for Yale." The 41st President smiled his lopsided, unflim-flam grin. "If I remember correctly, when we played each other, we each went 0-for-3," Yale winning, 2-1. "Well, I think it was right after that I realized I'd never make it in the bigs, and I needed to find work—and I'm still trying," offsetting privilege by seeming a regular fellow. "What about you? You still playing in the outfield? . . . You're as good as it gets. Congratulations, old friend."

Each friend prized normalcy, a stiff upper lip, and "Yankee trait of competing hard," said the *Globe*'s Robert Healy, "then picking your opponent up off the floor." Playing, Vin broadcast sotto voce, etching players isolated in his attention, "repeating the score and the outs and the men on base. The funny thing is that it kept me alert." The Phantom's "closed circuit hookup [was] interrupted," Bob Verdi wrote, "only when the ball went his way," each game staffed by Vin's *Bronx Home News*. "My great dream!" said Scully. "Homer and get my picture in the paper. However, Fordham's field was like a parade grounds. The fences were so far away from home plate that no college kid could reach them." Going deep meant inside the park.

Vin lined the sole dinger of his career over a City College of New York outfielder. "*The Home News* shot a picture of me crossing home!" Next morning he saw a fuzzy photo and caption feting "Jim Tully." Ultimately, Scully decided he needed a different kind of résumé: "I couldn't play and broadcast at the same time, so I gave up varsity my senior year." Downside: "I missed the game," said Vin. Up: More time to speak and learn.

A classmate recalls him "everywhere, recording himself, carrying this huge contraption, probably thirty pounds." Later Scully famously put forth irony, a fluent phrase, and graceful front when under pressure. By 20, already skilled at social intercourse, he wed beguiling word and boyish gesture. Broadcasting's fuel is likability. At Fordham, Vin's ran on charm.

In 1947 Scully heard Brooklyn air its first entire live radio schedule. 1948: Tyro WCBS Channel 2 telecast each game at Ebbets Field. By then, an event far surpassing each had transformed Vin's game, and age.

IN 1945, Branch Rickey—to Tom Meany, "Mahatma," recalling John Gunther re Gandhi: "a combination of God, your own father, and Tammany Hall"—and Walter O'Malley and John Smith bought 50 percent of the Ebbets' estate. Brooklyn's future raged around the corner: a lion at the plate and tiger in the field, with "wounds," said Branch, "you could not feel or share."

On October 23 Rickey broke the color line by inking Jackie Robinson. Soon the bigs's first black player reported to Montreal's Triple-A affiliate. Barber was "one of the first Rickey told. I was the Voice, and from the South." Red considered quitting. Later, Jackie hailed his healing. The '46ers lost a best-of-three playoff to St. Louis. Next year almost spoiled the borough on the game. On April 9, 1947, Commissioner Happy Chandler suspended Durocher, replaced by Burt Shotton, for the year for "conduct detrimental to baseball." Six days later Robinson, at first base, debuted in Brooklyn. Vin recalls Red never saying, "or had to, that Jackie was the big leagues' first black."

By May, the Cardinals debated boycotting him. Even mates petitioned his return to Montreal. What would the Captain do? "Growing up [in Kentucky]," Pee Wee said, "I didn't come into contact with black people. I was taught that Negroes were to ride in the back of streetcars." Reese refused to sign. In Atlanta, a writer vowed to shoot Robinson if he played. Pee Wee sidled over in warm-up, laughing, "Don't stand so damn close to me. Move away, will you?" Jackie moved, never stopping. "Perpetual motion," said Vin, who saw it on the radio. In person, he saw a man sensitive, bright, and brave.

"The one thing that has stood out to me," Scully noted, "is how Jackie was able to produce so well on the field with so much pressure on him. He had to know, more than anyone else, that if he failed, it may have set back the cause for years, maybe forever." Unlike Reese, Camilli, a Pete Reiser, Jackie couldn't *afford* a slump. "If he were benched or sent back to the minors, who knows what would have happened? But with all that on his shoulders, he went out and produced."

Could Brooklyn? "We'll beat 'em," growled Pee Wee of another Striped Series. "[Flatbush had] three million people," Red said, "and if every person there wasn't rooting for the Dodgers, everyone seemed to be." They began, losing, 5-3 and 10-3, then won a 185-minute 9-8 parody. Next day froze time. "I respected the tradition of not reporting [Bill Bevens's possible] no-hitter," said Mel Allen, calling Mutual's first 4½ innings. "What I did or didn't say wouldn't influence what happened. But players on the bench think you jinx it by talking. The superstition is part of the romance—one of the great things that separates baseball from other sports." Passed the baton, Barber leaked Brooklyn's line score. Mel gasped, Red said, like he had a mouth full of chinaberry seeds.

"For a while," Vin later said, "I went back and forth about ignoring a no-hitter." In 1955, noting Bob Purkey's near no-no, he asked the audience to vote. "The mail strongly indicated it was with me. That means we got two postcards in favor and one opposed." By contrast, Scully lent "romance" to Don Larsen's 1956 perfect game. Again Allen did NBC TV's first 4½ innings, treating no hits like leprosy. Succeeding him, Vin prolonged the indirection—"Mr. Larsen has retired 24 straight batters"—then permanently U-turned. "Today I would have started in the seventh inning, 'Hey, call your friends, this guy's pitching a perfect game,'" he said in 2009. "But in those days it was not done. I'd do it differently now." Stripes skipper Bucky Harris would redo 1947's ninth inning.

Behind, 2-1, Brooklyn's Al Gionfriddo stole second base. Reiser worked Bevens to a two-out, 3-1 count, then was ordered walked: the potential winning run. "The pitch [to pinch-hitter Cookie Lavagetto]," said Red. "Swung on, there's a drive hit out toward the right-field corner! Henrich is going back! He can't get it! It's off the wall for a base hit! Here comes the tying run and here comes the winning run!"—on Brooklyn's only hit. Seconds later: "Well, I'll be a suck-egg mule!"

Game 5 laid an egg: New York, 2-1. Next day laid a golden egg: largest Series crowd (74,065), longest nine-inning game (3:19), and Al Gionfriddo's catch (vs. the Great DiMag). Brooklyn led, 8-5, in the sixth: two out and on. "Joe leans in. He has one for three today, six hits so far in the Series," Barber said. "Outfield deep, around toward left, the infield overshifted." Then: "Swung on. Belted! It's a long one! Deep into left-center [toward Yankee Stadium's 415 sign]! Back goes Gionfriddo! Back,

back, back, back, back, back! He makes a one-handed catch against the bullpen! Oh, Doctor!"

DiMaggio kicked dirt near second base: a rare fit of fury. The Stripes knit the final, 5-2. Fordham's would-be Faulkner shook his head. Brooklyn's last chapter still needed work.

THEN AND NOW, THE BOROUGH intrigued even a Jintsophile. Reese wore No. 1 on his 1941–42 and 1946–58 uniform. "You joked with people on a first-name basis," he said. "It was like entering a bar and saying, 'Hi ya, Ben?' or 'How you doing, Joe?'" Ernie Harwell broadcast there in 1948–49: "the only place I've known where people made a vocation of being a fan." A visitor heard players jabber, saw faces harden, felt pressure creep.

Flatbush took baseball straight. Gladys Goodding—"one more 'd' than God"—played the organ, serenading umpires with "Three Blind Mice." Housewife Hilda Chester had "a very good warm heart, a very loud deep voice," said Vin, and rang a cowbell in the stands. Behind first base, straw-hatted Jake the Butcher roared "Late again!" of a pickoff. The Dodger Sym-Phony, a vaguely musical group, used a trumpet, trombone, snare and base drums, and cymbals to snare a visitor. "Their specialty," said Steve Jacobson, "was piping a strikeout victim back to his bench with a tune 'The Army Duff.' [Because] the last beat was timed for the moment the player's butt touched," he might tardily sit down. "The Sym-Phony still had that last beat ready."

On 1947's Schaefer Beer scoreboard, one ad fixed the borough: "Watch for Danny Kaye in *The Secret Life of Walter Mitty*." Another hailed clothier and New York City Council president Abe Stark: "Hit Sign, Win Suit." Con: Only 700 parking spots. Most used the subway: BMT to Prospect Park, or IRT to Franklin Avenue. Pro: Of center field, a writer said: "You'll feel like you're playing shortstop." In 1948 catcher Roy Campanella arrived from the Nicetown part of Philadelphia, calling a fastball *The Express* and curve *Public Enemy No. 1*. On July 16 Durocher replaced the fired Ott, like Douglas supplanting Lincoln. Ten days later Leo returned to Brooklyn for a game: Play-by-play barely pierced the din. When Red nearly died of a hemorrhaged ulcer, Rickey sought Harwell's release from Atlanta's independent Triple-A working club. The Crackers agreed—if

Branch would swap Dodgers catcher Cliff Dapper. A Voice for a player: Only in Brooklyn USA.

At 30, Ernie swelled New York's Dixie colony of Barber, Allen, and then-Yanks' Russ Hodges. "I'm asked why so many guys were Southern. I say we were too lazy to work!" yelped the Georgian. "Actually, it's where we grew up," fusing oral density and a lulling, siren past. "On the porch you'd hear about the local banker and beauty parlor operator and who married whom." Their rhythm became radio baseball's, mythy and sweetly rural.

Picture a Dodger hitting to left-center field. "Mentally, you saw it all at once," said Harwell, "base runners, fielder chasing, shortstop with the relay, the catcher bracing." Radio was a sonata, falling lightly on the ear. TV was still life, deadened by statistic. Barber was "the first to study players, take you behind the scene," yet was a worrywart. "You'd say something, and Red'd off-air glower, 'Why in the world would you say that?' A tough taskmaster, not the warm guy we heard on radio, entirely different people": a gulf widened by the borough's plasm.

"Red was the boss, and all he cared about was the betterment of the broadcast": tension high, Ernie said, "since Dodger fans were fanatically loyal." One day wife Lulu sat down in front of a fat fan in a T-shirt. Reese led off the first. Standing up, the man shouted, "C'mon, you bum. Get a hit."

Irked, Mrs. Harwell tapped the man on his shoulder. "I beg your pardon," she said. "Do you know Mr. Reese?" The man replied, "No, lady, why?" She said, "If you did, I'm sure you'd find him a very nice gentleman." The man replied, "OK, lady, I'll lay off him if he's a friend of yours."

Billy Cox batted next. Flushed, the man stood: "*Do* somethin', Cox! You're a bum." Again Lulu tapped him. "Lady," he swiveled, "is this bum a friend of yours, too?"

Mrs. Harwell nodded. "What about the other bums on this team?" asked the man. "I know almost all the players," she said. Muttering, he walked away.

"Lady, I'm moving. I came here to root my bums to a win, and I ain't gonna let you sit here behind me and spoil my whole afternoon."

BASEBALL ENGLISH is often incidental to profanity. The late '40s Bums dressed off-color, wearing satin unies on "selected nights." Vin first saw them at the Polo Grounds. "The visiting satins were blue. At night, they *shimmered*." In 1949, new sponsor F & M Schaefer Beer joined General Foods and General Division on WMGM née WHN. Robinson led the league in batting (.342) and steals (37). The Brooks and Yanks waved a last-day flag. "Going way back, back, that's the ball game, a home run for Tommy Henrich!" Barber crowned Mutual's 1-0 World Series opener. "Look at him grin! Big as a slice of watermelon." Next day Flatbush won by the identical score. "Poi-fect! We got 'em!" a fan outside Yankee Stadium told Brooklyn's Cox. The Stripes took the next three at Ebbets Field.

Too busy to fixate about the hero of every dog that was under, Fordham's soon-to-be graduate began to worry about a job. In 1945, signing Japan's treaty of surrender, Douglas MacArthur said, "We have had our chance. If we do not devise some greater and more equitable system, Armageddon will be at our door." Decision now stood at Vin's.

"Marguerite Clark, a girl in our station, volunteered to type letters," said Scully, "so we go through a guide, picking out small stations, where I'd have a better chance." An exception was WTOP Washington.

"Never mind that one," Vin told her.

"Why?" said Marguerite.

"It's too big—fifty thousand watts."

"Send it. You don't have anything to lose but a stamp." Scully mailed about 125 letters. WTOP's was his one response.

The CBS affiliate made Vin the summer news, weather, music, and, replacing Arch McDonald, sports substitute. Problem: Set to replace Charles Collingwood, Eddie Gallagher, and Allan Jackson, "I'd been so preoccupied, I hadn't done all my exams." Solution: Enlisting, *they* replaced the rookie. "Finally, I graduate but owe everybody so much time that for most of the summer I was opening the station at 5:30 A.M. and closing it at 1 next morning." Vin lived "with some guys in an old place in Georgetown. You talk about *Animal House*, I had it." He slept under a storm coat in the basement.

One night Scully met a woman leaving D.C. for the summer. Could the novice house-sit? "The house," wrote Jack Mann, "was a modest three-story thing at 29th and O Streets, across the street from Dean Acheson," President Truman's then-secretary of state. Vin announced a "party, now that he had a place to throw one," to thank Collingwood & Co. Accepting, guests expected Tobacco Road. "They tried to keep a straight face," said the house sitter, "but thought I lived in a loft over a candy store." More showman than con man, Scully liked what worked. The in-house maid and butler agreed to serve for $10 each. Arriving, each guest had a car parked. "'This *can't* be the place,'" Vin recalls them thinking. "It was a success, if only as my first victory in gamesmanship against the world."

That summer a schoolmate heard Scully on WTOP. "I was amazed, being on a 250-watt station in Pittsfield [Massachusetts]," said Mack McGarry. "I called him, asking *how* about his rise": so far, so fast, even Vin did not believe it. Professor William Coleman had written six letters of introduction, explained The Phantom. "Try it. They open doors." (McGarry later opened NBC's.) In July 1949, meeting CBS Radio news director Ted Church in New York, Scully was introduced to its post-1945 sports director, Red.

Vin said, "He didn't have much time to talk," with wife Lylah waiting in the car. At the elevator, Barber said, "Leave your name, address, and number." Vin left thinking he would never again see CBS. That Saturday Scully tuned to *College Football Roundup*, simultaneously airing four games. "It bounced from game to game for an update on what had happened and, if there was time," he mused, "the announcer'd do a minute of play-by-play."

The Southerner likes a twice-baked potato. Vin liked twice succeeding Harwell. That fall a spot opened on *Roundup's* Boston University-Maryland. "I got bumped up to a bigger game, Notre Dame-North Carolina," said Ernie. "It was at Yankee Stadium, North Carolina had All-American Charlie Justice, and my partner was another big name, sportswriter Warren Brown."

B.U.-Maryland loomed: Who to replace Harwell? Red evoked his future Telemachus—the stick figure with the shock of hair.

IN ANY GOOD SCRIPT, the hero surmounts a hurdle. Vin's was how Barber forgot his name. "Who's that young man you brought around?" he asked Church. "You know, that red-haired fellow."

"I didn't take down his name," Ted said.

"Call [Jack] Coffey," Red told an aide. "Great memory. He'll know it."

Barber phoned WTOP for references, then Scully's home. "He got my mother," Vin said. That night Bridget waited at the door.

"Vinny, you'll never guess who called you. It's such a great thing that he called here, such a busy man. It's so exciting. He wants you to call him."

"Who was it?" said Scully.

"Red Skelton," mama said.

On Friday Vin proceeded to Boston's Kenmore Hotel. Next day, assuming a glassed-in booth, the rookie shed coat, gloves, hat, and scarf. "I made a dumb kid's move, because what I really cared about was that night's alumni dance [Fordham, playing Boston College]. It was a beautiful day. Plus, I was 21 years old." To Scully's chagrin, he found no booth at Fenway Park: only a roof site between home plate and right field. "My engineer was great, finding an old card table strong enough to hold my equipment. I also had a cord letting me walk the full length of the field." B.U.'s star was Harry Agganis, "the 'Golden Greek.' Every time he threw a pass, I'd run down the roof to see what happened."

Depending on the game, *Roundup*'s Voice called a play, drive, or quarter. "They'd phone first, then tell you how much time you had." Vin had a watch, microphone, 50 yards of cable, 60-watt bulb for light, and lineup card. By the third quarter, the "wind [was] up, sun down, I'm fighting frostbite." Meanwhile, Red warmed in studio: "Scully's game was close [Maryland won, 14-13], so in the second half we shifted there." Vin aired *Roundup* through 1955. "By the time the game ended I was sure I'd blown the greatest opportunity I'd ever had in my life."

Down, he found Barber up. "Several days later Red got a letter from the authorities at Fenway apologizing for not having a broadcast booth. I guess that impressed him." Scully's intuitions were in tune. Already the stickler for preparation felt a gentle protectiveness for "the son I never had." Two days later, he called Vin's residence. "You'll have a booth next week—Harvard-Yale."

Barber often quoted an old prayer for travelers: "Amid the changes and chances of this mortal life." By chance, he said, "a lot of little things [soon] had to happen for Scully to get his break."

In November 1949, Harwell left Brooklyn for Coogan's Bluff. The vacancy led Red to again conjure Vin. "I'd always had the idea in the back of my mind that it would be interesting to take a promising young man and train him," he said, selling Rickey.

"Fine," the Mahatma said, "that is, if you find the right man."

Barber phoned Scully, turning 22. "How would you like to broadcast for the Dodgers?" Vin's eyes, he said, "got as big as teacups."

Scully called Rickey, who, in turn, phoned Red. "I don't want to trespass upon your territory, Walter, but you have found your man" — as Barber said, "my legacy." The context was more complex.

3

YOUNGER THAN SPRINGTIME
(1950–1953)

In 2007, Harwell relived 1949's sally to the Polo Grounds. "Vinny took my place, which I consider my greatest contribution to baseball." His gift was not then fully grasped.

At mid-century, Allen and Barber formed sportscasting's John Gielgud and Ralph Richardson. Mel's voice was deep, full, and Southern, fusing Billy Graham and James Earl Jones. The five-star mouthpiece once hailed a cab. "Sheraton, please," said Allen, simply. The cabbie's head turned like a swivel. Mel aired the Rose Bowl, a record 24 All-Star Games, Little League World Series, and Fox newsreels: "This is your Movietone reporter." The real Series dwarfed them. Doing 20, Allen became its postwar badge.

Meanwhile, Ernie felt, Brooklyn's ambassador without portfolio became more detached, interior. "Even in 1948, Branch Rickey thought Red'd lost enthusiasm. He had an ulcer; lost half his stomach. The voice was a little weaker," still dwarfing Russ Hodges: "in New York, a distant third." Harwell left because "surely Red'd be there forever. If something happened, Connie would take over—great voice and expression." Intoxicating, Desmond might have become Coronado. Intoxicated, he brooked Churchill's "Terrible Ifs."

Barber hymned baseball from Maine to Malibu. Hodges pounded piano at a roadhouse. "Wouldn't talk as much," said Harwell, "no gimmicks, but authenticity."

Once, Red called the first quarter of a football game. "Now for the second quarter," he began, whimsically or not—who could tell?—"here is Russ Hughes." "Thank you, Red Baker," said Hodges. Barber was not amused. He was intent, however, on hiring Vin.

In 1950 Brooklyn's new television outlet, WOR Channel 9, added WHNC Channel 6 New Haven. "We had a lot going on," said Red, even as the tightfisted Rickey reconsidered signing Scully. "For a while Branch thought Connie and I could handle everything for the year," finally softening at Vin's price. "For $5,000," wrote the *Christian Science Monitor*'s Phil Elderkin, "a star was born."

The club offered a one-month option at its Vero Beach, Florida, spring training site: Dodgertown, an abandoned World War II 2,000-acre naval air base with barracks for nearly 1,000 people. "At the end of the month," mused Scully, "they might have left me in the Everglades." He roomed in a two-cot bedroom off the Western Union operator's office, also reserved for soused writers from out of town. "The Dodgers would put him in the cot next to me. I didn't do too much sleeping that first year with all the snoring going on."

Meeting Reese and Robinson, Vin "called them by their first names, but I was totally overwhelmed." Don Newcombe recalled "a youngster, who was green, really afraid of where he is, afraid of the whole thing." Carl Erskine saw "the red hair"—to the *Sporting News*, "more tawny-haired than Barber"—and said, "'This is a pup out of Red!' Prophetic."

Duke Snider met "this little kid, thinner than he'd be, cheeks sunken." "I'm Vince Scully," he said, later trimming to a less formal Vin.

"Who?" Snider said. "Where do you work? The clubhouse?" The "kid" told Duke that he had played college ball. "We sort of chuckled, but he fit right in, knew the game, knew the right things to ask."

Vin's first exhibition foretold a franchise more Byzantine than most: "If you can believe it, a triple play by the A's at West Palm Beach. An augury, if there ever was one." In April, the club yearbook introduced the "third and youngest member of the Dodgers airlanes trio. Vince Scully, 23 [sic], single," began radio/TV baseball's longest same-team skein, bridging two O'Malleys, eight bigs Commissioners, 12 U.S. Presidents, Korea, Dallas, Viet Nam, Watergate, first Gulf War, 9/11, and Iraq.

For the rookie, humility, not history, hovered. "Red'd rag him," said Ernie, "especially about his lack of minor-league experience." Vin concedes to "on-the-job training. I'd bring the lineup and Barber'd say, 'This man batted seventh yesterday. Why is he fifth today?'" He never taught "me how to broadcast. He *did* teach an attitude. Get there early and do your homework. Bear down. Use the crowd. And probably the two words I would use if we were playing word association: Red Barber, 'he cared.'"

Next year Willie Mays became a rookie. "Maybe the best player I've ever seen," Scully told the audience. Barber warned, "You're just starting out. No one really cares about what you think." Red scolded Vin on air—"He didn't like it much at times. The audience, of course, loved it"—teaching Scully to shun players socially ("you lose objectivity"), use dead air ("it's not how much, but what, you say"), and spurn hearing other Voices ("Don't copy. You will water your own wine."). To Barber, "only then," said Vin, "could I bring to the booth a precious ingredient no one else could—me, and whatever personal qualities made me a human being."

They surfaced slowly. "'Vin busy,' as I put it," Red said, "'toting our briefcases if necessary,'" doing an "inning here or there" on upstate New York network outlets in Albany, Binghamton, Cortland, Hornell, Jamestown, Niagara Falls, and Syracuse. Angst stoked art. "When I was allowed to [broadcast], it felt like I was all alone in an empty room," Scully mused. "Everybody left": Red, to video; Connie, to "get coffee. Holy mackerel, how do I fill the time? So I began amassing anecdotes." Barber introduced him on TV: nirvana, except that Vin's clan didn't own a set. "The only way they could see him," wrote Elderkin, "was to reserve a booth at a neighborhood bar and grill and, with friends, watch the owner's video set." Work was even less upscale than the saloon.

Harwell had Miss Lulu. In 1950, Vin was a bachelor. "He had a quiet confidence, but was getting pummeled and had no one to defend him," said Ernie. "Red even delayed saying Scully had joined the team" till Rickey cried *no mas*. Persevering, Vin trooped to Harwell's Larchmont, New York, home. "Lulu'd fix a nice dinner. 'How do I handle this?' Vin'd say. 'Am I doing this right?' Baptism under fire. Fortunately, he had the right stuff"—and site.

At Ebbets Field, Scully could almost reach out and touch the field. The booth—"small, jammed, but it's what we knew"—hung suspended above boxes behind the plate. "It was open. No wire protected us" until a foul almost struck Barber's face. "Balls came right back. We were so close, and also very aware of individuals."

Once Dodger *über*fan Hilda Chester bayed, "Vin Scully, I *love* you!" The crowd cackled. Flushed, Vin hung his head. "*Look* at me," she ordered, "when I'm *talking* to you!" Even the P.A. announcer wrote shorthand chic. Promoter Tex Rickard sat near the home dugout, wore a sweater, and spun Texisms: "A little boy has been found lost." Pitcher Preacher Roe left a game: "He don't feel good." Coats draped the left-field wall. Rickard asked: "Will the people along the railing in left field please remove their clothes?" No one could remove the Bums' postwar hybrid of victory and misery.

In 1914, British foreign secretary Sir Edward Grey eulogized World War I: "The lamps are going out all over Europe; we shall not see them lit again in our lifetime." To many, Brooklyn's lamps went out in 1957. "No other baseball team," wrote Leonard Koppett, "generated a richer collection of memories, more closely held by so many people." Campanella resembled a sumo wrestler. Snider shrunk the outfield. First baseman Gil Hodges had an altar boy's heart and ex-Marine's hands: "just massive," mused Vin. Pitchers had him squeeze the ball, actually raising its seams. Surnames were de trop: Oisk, Big Newk, No. 13, and Preach, not Erskine, Newcombe, Ralph Branca, and Roe—each an extended family member.

In 1949 Brooklyn finished 16 games ahead of Philadelphia. Next year it wrote the league's second straight last-day denouement. Growing up in suburban Philly, future Red Sox announcer Ned Martin liked its other team. "My dad took me to my A's first game at Shibe Park in '32," he said. "No matter. Nineteen fifty's special." Hodges hit four homers on August 31. Snider led the league in hits (199) and total bases (343). With ten days left, the Quakers held a seven-game lead. Casual fans became addicts. "Imagine their panic," said Red, "when the team began to lose." The Phils' last pennant had been 35 years earlier. Closing day brought them to Flatbush. A Dodgers win meant a playoff.

The Whiz Kids—average lineup age, 26—scored first. Reese's sixth-inning inside-the-parker stuck on the right-field wall ledge. Three innings later Richie Ashburn threw out Brooklyn's potential winning run. The score stayed 1-1: Dinners grew cold and were warmed again. In the 10th, Philly's Dick Sisler clubbed a three-run flag-waving poke. In New

York, many watched on store window televisions. More heard by radio, passing pitch-by-pitch like a chain letter on the street. "With games in the afternoon, the city stopped," Vin said. "Everybody was drained, but still, what a rookie year."

How to top the topper? Bobby Thomson had a thought.

In June 1950, President Truman announced a United Nations "police action" against communist North Korea. That fall, Scully, a Naval Reserve man, took a walk around Ebbets Field. "I'm thinking, 'My gosh, I might never come back here.' And that was a heartbreaking thought after getting a golden opportunity." Vin was never called. The Dodgers, though, were sold, Rickey peddling his share for $1,050,000. On October 26, Walter O'Malley—team lawyer, University of Pennsylvania engineering major, and "man," said Branch in an extempore pronouncement, "of youth, courage, and desire"—became new club president.

"Here I was, the team's No. 3 announcer now living with my parents in [Bogota] New Jersey," said Scully. "I was very unsure of the future." One day he answered the phone to find O'Malley—"he himself, not a vice president, not a director in charge of marketing, not a secretary"—on the line: "'Vin, I'm sure you're uneasy about the change in management, but I just wanted to take time out to assure that we want you back in 1951.'" Scully cradled the phone, wowed "that with all the things he had on his mind, that he would call this kid." Earlier, Executive Vice President and General Manager Emil J. "Buzzie" Bavasi urged O'Malley to "sign him. You took a chance on another kid [Bavasi, hired as g.m. at 1948 Montreal]. If we can't do it, we'll go down together."

Up: Hodges hit 40 homers, Robinson .338, Campy .325. Roe went 22-3, Newcombe 20-9. Down: a grisly end. In April, Douglas MacArthur invaded Flatbush. "I have been told," said the general, recently axed by Truman, "that one hasn't really lived until he has been to Ebbets Field." He became a regular, seeing Brooklyn go 0-13. That July it swept a series from the Giants. "We knocked 'em out," said new skipper Charlie Dressen. "They'll never bother us again." On August 11, the Dodgers led by 13½ games. What happened next wrote wonderwork. "Keep in mind the rivalry," Vin cautioned. Its 22 games a year coursed through the city. "In Brooklyn, fans'd pelt the Giants with beer, coins, umbrella parts, whatever they could find. I'd go to the ballpark just hoping that no would get hurt."

The Jints caught Brooklyn Friday, September 28. Each won Saturday. Next afternoon New York beat Boston, 3-2. In Philadelphia—the Dodgers had this thing about the final day—Robinson made "a diving 12th-inning catch," Scully mused, "then homered to win [9-8] in the fourteenth." The Giants closed 37-7. "People wrongly think the Dodgers blew the pennant. They finished well enough [24-20], but it's the playoff you recall." Its best-of-three began in once-Pigtown, Jim Hearn over Branca, 3-1. Next day changed place and score: Bums, 10-0, behind Clem Labine. A schoolboy knows the day-later plot. Brooklyn led, 4-2, in the ninth. "Too bad Game 3 wasn't at Ebbets," Rickard said. "I'd have introduced Thomson against Branca." Instead, Bobby introduced himself.

At 3:58 P.M., the "Flying Scotsman" transported a one-out, two-on, one-two pitch. "Branca throws. There's a long drive!" Russ Hodges bayed on Giants' radio flagship WMCA. "It's going to be, I believe! The Giants win the pennant! The Giants win the pennant! The Giants win the pennant! The Giants win the pennant! Bobby Thomson hits into the lower deck of the left-field stands! The Giants win the pennant! And they're going crazy! They are going crazy! Oh-oh!" Delirium draped The Shot Heard Round the World.

Confetti swirled. Eddie Stanky wrestled Leo Durocher to the ground. Brooklyn staggered to its clubhouse. A picture by 1937–57 team photographer Barney Stein showed Branca, on his stool, alone and desolate. "Everybody remembers it now," said Thomson. "But you have to understand the feeling between those teams. I didn't think of the pennant—only that we beat the Dodgers." Hodges ate noise thick enough to chew. "I don't believe it!" he bayed. "I do not believe it! Bobby Thomson hit a line drive into the lower deck of the left-field stands, and the whole place is going crazy! The Giants—[owner] Horace Stoneham is now a winner—the Giants won it by a score of 5 to 4, and they're picking Bobby Thomson up and carrying him off the field!"

Before videotape, a film camera had to tape a TV screen or monitor to record—a process called kinescope. "It was fuzzy, and kinescopes were bulky," said Harwell, "so folks threw 'em out. Even tape recorders were hard to carry around, so the average guy didn't have one." Brooklyn restaurant waiter Lawrence Goldberg, who did, taped the ninth. "Ahead, he thought he'd enjoy Russ cry. But he didn't take it personally, sending

Russ the tape." Pause. "Russ sent him $10." Television rules our orb. Radio ruled 1951's. Ernie aired the game for CBS TV: "the first sports event televised nationally." On contact, he said, "It's gone!" of Thomson's drive, then stopped. Brooklyn's Andy Pafko seemed glued to the left-field wall.

"Uh, oh," Harwell thought, "suppose he catches it." Andy didn't. At home, Ernie remained dazed. "I've seen that look in your face twice in my life," said wife Lulu. "When our first child was born and the day we got married." We trust her, since 1951 TV neither replayed nor kept the call. "What did I get? *Anonymity.* What did Russ get from his radio call? *Immortality!*" Ernie joked. "To this day only Mrs. Harwell and I know that I did maybe the most famous call of all time."

EVERYONE OF a certain age knows where they were when FDR died, Truman upset Tom Dewey, and Thomson swung. "Say 'Russ,' you think that day," said 1957 aide Jim Woods. ESPN's Jon Miller terms it "the most famous sports moment of all time. Hodges made it last," frozen in amber, as whiz-bang as he was not. "While Barber gave his listeners corn-fed philosophy and humor," penned Wells Twombly, "and Allen told you more about baseball than you cared to know, Hodges of the Giants told it the way it was."

In late 1951, Giants' sponsor Chesterfield cigarettes released a record of "the most exciting moment in baseball history." To some, it seemed revisionist. Russ was said to have screamed for 15 minutes. "For two minutes," wrote one, "he stood on his chair to chant, 'The Giants win the pennant!'" Barber dubbed Hodges "unprofessional." Russ lived on The Shot till his death in 1971, at 61. Scully recalls, even now.

"When they were going to the bottom of the ninth inning, and the Dodgers were leading," Vin mused, " I saw a man walking in the lower deck of the Polo Grounds carrying this great big horseshoe of flowers that you might see at a funeral home." A banner cloaked the horseshoe: "GIANTS, REST IN PEACE."

Scully "always wondered, after the home run, what did that guy do with those flowers? You can't hide that. You can't just suddenly put that under your coat." He was glad Red called the homer on WMGM. "Then [23] it would have been too much for me." Another flashback: "The clubhouses [were] located side-by-side, back of center field, and while we could hear the Giants whooping it up at their victory celebration, in ours it was like a morgue." In shock, Reese and Robinson lay on the rubbing table.

Finally, Pee Wee raised his head. "You know what I really don't understand?"

"What?" said Jackie.

"How after all these years playing baseball I haven't gone insane."

"JUST KEEP 'EM CLOSE," Dressen told his team. "I'll think of something." In 1952 "something" was a pennant. Barber aired his 13th World Series. Rookie of the Year Joe Black won the opener, 4-2. The Yanks then beat Erskine, 7-1. Crossing the East River, the teams split Sets 3-4. Each Voice uses pet turns of phrase. To Scully, a two-ball/two-strike count on a two-out batter meant "the deuces" were "wild." If so, Game 5 was flush: On October 5, his fifth wedding anniversary, Oisk yielded five fifth-inning runs. "Believe me," said Vin, a spectator, "I was soon watching for any other fives." By the 11th, New York had five hits. As Yogi Berra fanned, ending a taut 6-5 pastiche, Scully spied The Stadium clock. "It read 5:05. Weird." Going home, the up-3 games-to-2 Bums got the Bums' rush, 3-2 and 4-2. In the final, Duke found Bedford Avenue. "Boom," said the Redhead. "Look out. Look out." Noise crested. Finally: "You needn't look anymore." All season you *heard* on another Dodgers network.

The prior year O'Malley had Bavasi fuse a Voice (like Red, antebellum) and plan (Brooklyn Dodgers Radio Network). More than 200 announcers now call major-league radio and free/cable TV. Less than 40 did then. "It was exclusive," Scully nodded. "Getting a job, you stayed." The upshot was inertia. "The Yanks couldn't air games into Boston," said Harwell. "A gentleman's agreement thrived." Irked, O'Malley wished to broadcast where he liked. "Much of the East wasn't served by baseball," Bavasi added. "Walter saw an opening," driving Nat Allbright through.

In 1951 the Virginian re-created the South Atlantic League. Next year, forging the Dodgers' network, he knit a bigs-high 117 outlets from Cleveland to Miami. "People didn't know we re-created," Allbright said. Mail addressed to "Nat Allbright, Brooklyn Dodgers, Ebbets Field" was forwarded to his Arlington, Virginia, home. The listener imagined Nat and Scully, cozying.

One day Vin interviewed Big Newk, "not only calling pitches, as do all radio broadcasters," wrote the *Journal-American*'s Mike Gaven, "but young and energetic enough to get in the clubhouses and dugouts and find what the pitcher throws."

Scully: "Now tell our listeners about that slider of yours."

Newcombe: "I don't throw a slider. That just happens to be my best curve."

Nat fancied Don's spin from a Washington, D.C., studio. "I'd say, 'There's Newcombe, perspiration dripping down his face.'" Like Vin, he was personal. "Cincinnati crowds stunk, so I'd cut noise. For Milwaukee, we'd tape polka music." Even the Anthem cleaved. Burghers sang it in Wisconsin. Live bands played Forbes Field. Gladys Goodding played Ebbets's organ. Allbright prerecorded each.

By 1953 Dodgers' ratings walloped the Bucs' and Senators' in western Pennsylvania and D.C., respectively. Nat got 50,000 letters a year. His Eden on Bedford Avenue crashed in a place comic Fred Allen called "great, if you're an orange." Cause of death: "the [1957] move to California," Allbright said. "Home games would end at 1:30 in the morning." Like the Bums, "their audience was gone."

Nat's first game was Bobby Thomson's: "Walter's dress rehearsal for '52." His last was the 1962 Jints' playoff. That fall the network pulled the plug. Forty years later Allbright still missed radio's once seeming as in the saddle as the team.

THE 1953 DODGERS shucked their regular radio network, said the *Sporting News*, "in line with their announced policy of helping the minor leagues." Affiliates missed Brooklyn's 105-49 record, near-National League record 955 runs, and league-best in eight other categories. Five regulars hit more than .300. Furillo's .344 led the league. Snider had 42 homers. Campy yoked a catching record and league-high 142 RBIs. Erskine was 20-6. "Looking back, a team in flower," said Scully. Barber's was about to wilt.

By this point, Allen domineered the Apple. "The Yankees kept making the Series each fall," he said, "so I broadcast almost yearly." Since 1939, its exclusive radio/TV sponsor, Gillette Company, "had been growing an empire," huffed Red, "but announcers only got a demeaning $200 a game." Most took it, including Mel in 1953. Galled, Barber demanded "the right to negotiate my fee." Gillette told him to get lost. Instead, Red phoned a man who felt him a pain in the patootie.

Two months earlier O'Malley and Yankees owner Dan Topping had got gassed at Toots Shor's saloon. Yanks rookie Voice Jim Woods stared from a nearby stool. "I hate the son of a bitch," Walter raged of Barber.

"I'll go you one better," said Dan. "I can't stand Mel."

"Tell you what," O'Malley continued. "I'll trade you the son of a bitch."

Topping flushed. "Good. I'll give you Allen." Sober, next day they reneged.

O'Malley was cosmically unlikely to back Red's right to negotiate. "That is your problem," he told him. "I'll nominate Scully [earning a reported $18,000 vs. Barber's $60,000] to take your [Series] place." Later, Red wrote: "I said to myself, 'Walter, the Dodgers are now *your* problem.'" Resigning, he joined Allen in a cycle of irony.

Next day O'Malley phoned a Shor's regular. "Desmond had been with the Dodgers so much longer," said New York *Herald Tribune* reporter Harold Rosenthal. "By all rights Connie should have done the Series, but he was terribly unreliable." Walter likely called as a courtesy: To his relief, Desmond passed.

O'Malley then phoned Vin, who, heartsick, called Red and Connie "to see if it was OK. I said I could wait, that I wasn't going to do it without their blessing." Each gave it, Desmond barbing, "If you don't do it, somebody else will." Scully was not yet "perhaps the most outstanding and influential broadcaster in the game's history," wrote the *Scribner Encyclopedia of American Lives*.

Born "a rifle shot from Yankee Stadium," said Rosenthal, Vin reached 6 in 10 Americans (75 million viewers) over baseball's largest network (119 NBC outlets, in 113 cities). "I tried to play it pretty cool," he laughed. "Before the first game I sat down with my mother and father and sister at home for breakfast as if it was just another day. Then I went upstairs and threw up, just [lost] my entire breakfast." Would his team lose again?

CASEY STENGEL had juggled his team to a fifth straight pennant. Only Whitey Ford pitched more than 200 innings. Did platooning pique the Bombers? "When you're walking to the bank with that World Series check every November," Hank Bauer groused, "you don't want to leave. There were no Yankees saying play me or trade me." October serialized the fifth chapter of the Bums-Stripes novel. A best-selling button read: "MOIDER

DEM YANKS." Vin saw a cup half full. "With the team we had, you wondered how we could lose." Quickly, as it occurred.

The Dodgers lost twice at The Stadium. Next day, in chilly sunshine, before the largest Classic crowd (35,270) to elbow into Ebbets Field, Oisk, winning, 3-2, K'd 14 to top Howard Ehmke's 1929 record. The foils split Games 4-5. Back home, New York led, 3-1, till Furillo's tying ninth-inning homer. Billy Martin's single scored Bauer with the Series-ending run. Once Vin rued, "Good is not good when better is expected." Already he was tired of the script.

Growing up in Texas, Lyndon Johnson heard train whistles redolent of "child's dreams," John Connally said in a 1973 eulogy, "that could be as wide as the sky and as green as winter oats, because this, after all, was America." At 25, Scully's rise deserved "at least one line in the *Sporting News* 'One for the Book,'" wrote Rosenthal. Four years from Fordham, he embodied boundlessness: happy, with his home people, doing what he loved.

"Not as big as Barber, who remained very popular, and not as huge as he'd later get in L.A.," Harold said. "Not the attention given Allen. But Vin got better, with the fortune to cover a wonderful team." Future *New York Times* columnist George Vecsey felt him a continuum. "He'd been raw, but good. We heard Red fuss over and teach him, give his imprimatur. Barber to Vin was seamless." Scully fessed to "having been on the defensive, so to speak, in the early years. As a young broadcaster, I think my main concern was really not to mess up. And it was all on the run."

One night fog delayed a game. "For a full hour I desperately stalled—I showed how to keep score, read statistics out of the yearbook, did everything but tell bedtime stories." Coach Jake Pitler liked to showboat. When Snider walked to force in a run, Vin asked for a TV close-up, which showed "Jake just standing there and scratching himself." Scully had debuted on WTOP by saying "thummer sunderstorms." Later, he coined "'EYETH'—a combination of 'eighth' and 'ninth.'" Once, "Pittsburgh tied the Pirates, 6 to 6!" Ford tried to score on a Series fly. "'[He's] left third too soon!'" Vin said, recalling, "He was out, but what if he had scored? Millions of television fans would have protested that I said the tally was illegal." Lesson: "Keep my big mouth shut."

Red's exit pained him. It also freed him. "As the years went by, slowly whatever there was of me and in me came out." Initially, Scully struck a worldly pose. "A defense," said Rosenthal, "armor against insecurity." In *The Boys of Summer*, Roger Kahn etched Harold, himself, and Dick Young hearing Vin, "[with] a long-chinned, rather handsome face," discuss a friend who worked in Europe. "This guy travels to Florence, Paris, London. Well, we travel, too. *Pittsburgh, Cincinnati, St. Louis.*"

Anywhere, Scully turned toward a bookstore like a heliotrope did the sun. "I didn't know much about books," Snider said, "so I'd say, 'Vin, tell me what to read.' We'd go to a bookstore, he'd pick out a book, and sign it with a note: 'Whatever city, 1953, with Vin Scully.'"

In New York, Scully might have become a broadcast Ulysses. Ultimately, he did, if not in the way he expected, or hoped.

4

HEAVEN AND THE LOWER ROOM
(1954–1957)

In January 1954 surgery caused permanent deafness in Barber's left ear. "I'm going into a new league," Red said. "I don't know the players, my head's like a sea." Stengel could be hard on young players. By contrast, one old gentleman might save another. "Casey knew without my mentioning it that something was wrong. He'd brief me, take all the time in the world." Photos show the Yankees' skipper standing next to his new broadcaster's good ear.

NBC Television sports head Tom Gallery thought the Episcopalian lay preacher "a sanctimonious, Psalm-singing son of a bitch." Prim and distant, Barber hated flaws and fools. Increasingly, his core turned public in the Bronx. "In 1940s Brooklyn, Red may have been the best ever," said Costas, "but by the late '50s he'd turned dry, bitter, nowhere as good as Mel." Perhaps he simply missed being boss.

At first, some refused to believe him gone. A magazine pictured a Yankees fan watching 1954 Dodgers television. "Looka that flametop!" he yapped of Scully. "Who said the Redhead was in Yankee Stadium?" Brooklyn's radio/TV boss depended on whom you asked. The *Sporting News*'s preview issue termed Desmond top dog. "Connie's seniority officially made him number one," said Harwell. "Realistically, Vinny was," his team almost owning 1949–53.

"Think about it," Dick Young urged. "A stray hit or out and [like the Yanks] it's five flags in a row." The Jints owned 1954. Mays cooked a top-this 41 homers, 119 runs, and .345 average. Don Mueller hit .342. Inadequate: Reese's career-high .309, Hodges's 42 homers, and the Duke at peak: .341, 130 RBIs, and National League–best 120 runs. Douglass Wallop wrote 1954's *The Year the Yankees Lost the Pennant*, which they did, despite a Stengel-best 103-51 record. "For the Dodgers and Yankees," said Desmond, "a sabbatical from what they'd done and would do."

The last day Berra and Mickey Mantle played third base and shortstop, respectively. "Welcome," Casey said, "to my power lineup." Flatbush found 1954 less welcoming. Comic Phil Foster dubbed Thomson's Shot "D-Day—Dat Day." Mays now forged Dat Catch, over the shoulder, against Cleveland in the Series opener. Pinch-dinger Dusty Rhodes won Games 1-2. Each bred "Bye-bye-baby!"—Russ's riposte to "pull up a chair."

The Jints and Dodgers then resumed musical chairs. Said Vin of his former team, "That's how it was. If Giants fans were happy, ours weren't."

"I DIDN'T THINK OF IT AS A TRADEMARK," Scully said of first using *chair*. "People may have thought it conversational, like radio. My style is no style. I'm really nothing. I'm what I am." Another phrase changed in 1955: *Next* year became *this* year.

On February 7 Vin addressed 300 Boys Club alumni. "Scully Traces Bums' Tough Luck in Conn. Address," read the *Sporting News* of years that rang like chimes: 1916, 1920, 1941, 1946–47, and 1949–53. "Yes, everything has happened to Brooklyn," he said, its Diaspora bathed in fate. The '55ers opened 10-0, their clubhouse blackboard scrawling in Brooklynese: "The Bums Dood It 10 Straight!" In July, Reese, 37, was feted at Ebbets, Vin emceeing. Daughter Barbara, picking keys in a fishbowl, chose a new Chevrolet from among seven cars. Suddenly, lights dimming, a crowd of 33,003 struck matches and sang "Happy Birthday" to the Captain.

The team photo had Newk in the middle; Scully, in a dark suit, second row, far right; and Campy and Jackie below and above him, respectively— in all, six future Hall of Famers. Again the Dodgers, then Yankees, clinched. On September 16, 320,000 cheered players parading to Borough Hall. "Habit is a great deadener," wrote Samuel Beckett. Brooklyn lived to break *its* habit: seven straight losing Series. Unlike King Canute, could it reverse the tide?

"Each autumn comes a day in this great land of ours when the wheels of industry turn a little slower . . . when the white-collar worker takes a little more time [at] lunch . . . when classes pause in the Three R's . . . when almost everyone is stricken with WORLD SERIES fever," said its highlight film, "dedicated to the countless millions who follow the pulsating drama of baseball . . . everywhere the game is played." Game 3 was played in Flatbush, the Yanks holding a 2-0 set lead. Turning 23, Johnny Podres triumphed, 8-3. Brooklyn then won, 8-5 and 5-3; Ford, 5-1. The Faithful braced for another final. On TV's *What's My Line?* Ebbets Field's hand-operated scoreboard's numbers man was asked about Series strain. "Actually, it's a cinch for a single game," said Raymond Fadden. The pauper was 0-for-5 vs. baseball's prince. "Don't worry, Pee Wee," said Podres, taunting history, "I'll shut 'em out tomorrow."

In a family flat no more posh than Scully's, Tom Oliphant, 9, exhaled as Allen began Game 7. To the future *Boston Glober*, "This meant Vin Scully could be with us on the television set starting in the last half of the fifth inning." Director John Ford won an Oscar for 1952's *The Quiet Man*. That fall, 0-for-21 Hodges brooked a Series leather-lung: "Here comes the quiet man!" On October 4, 1955, Vin, to Oliphant "already a familiar and welcome figure," replaced Mel in the first Classic aired "in living color": Brooklyn ahead, 2-0, on Gil's two RBIs. Said Scully: "'The Quiet Man' finally made some noise."

In the sixth inning, Martin and Gil McDougald led off by reaching safely. Watching, even the unsuperstitious caved. With Brooklyn up, Oliphant separated his legs. Ankles crossed when the Yankees batted. Ten feet away, dad Homer smoked when, say, Snider faced Tommy Byrne. Arms folded as Berra now arced down the left-field line. Defensive substitute Sandy Amoros raced madly toward the spot. "If he'd been right-handed the ball probably would have dropped to tie the score," said Reese. "Berra'd have been on second with no outs." Instead—Bob Uecker found his front row; Heidi Fleiss became a nun—"Sandy stuck out his glove hand," said McDougald, "and found that Easter egg." Out of the corner of his eye, Vin saw Gil, turning second, stumble trying to U-turn. Amoros threw to Reese, who fired to Hodges. Double play! Said Podres: "Yogi hit that ball, and he made the greatest catch in the world."

Inning by inning angst fed on history. "Anguish," laughed Oliphant. "It simply felt better to have a friendly voice guiding me through the excitement, just as it felt better to look across and see my father." In New Jersey, Scully's mother, listening at home, started walking the family dog.

"Named Blackie," Vin said. "She began in the sixth. In the seventh, same thing, more pressure, she's anxious, she walked Blackie. Then, in the ninth, the Dodgers are three outs away from winning their only world's championship, she feels the pressure, she gets the leash, but she can't find Blackie! The dog's hiding."

Bill Skowron bounced to Podres. A borough held its breath. Bob Cerv flew to Amoros. You waited for the other shoe to drop. "Feeling spent, almost exhausted," Oliphant said, he saw Podres throw a change-up. Elston Howard slapped to Reese, who threw to Hodges: Captain to Quiet Man. Time stopped on The Stadium clock: 3:45 P.M. Homer stood, tearing. Tom leaped into his arms—into joy. Dad held him, "for the longest time, a minute, maybe more." Trying not to cry, he instantly memorized Vin's capper: "Ladies and gentlemen, the Brooklyn Dodgers are the champions of the world." If a picture is worth 1,000 words, The Stadium's roar seemed a glossary.

Today, Scully's words top a giant photo at the entrance to Dodgers offices in Los Angeles "of the joyful chaos on the field," Tom said, "that was unfolding while he spoke them." In 1955, numbed, Vin rose to leave the booth. "Hey," Allen said, "aren't you even going to say good-bye?" All winter, people asked how Scully remained so calm. "That was the happiest point of my career, because it meant everything. They had lost so many times. And then finally to win against the Yankees." Pause. "That's why I shut up when Pee Wee threw to Hodges. The truth is that it was an overwhelming emotional experience. If I'd said another word at that very instant, I'd have broken down and cried."

Erskine entered the Dodgers' clubhouse he first visited in 1949. "We'd lost ever since," he said. "Now there was a quietness when we first walked in, almost a spiritual feeling. Then someone opened champagne, and the lid blew off." Later the team bus entered the Brooklyn-Battery Tunnel. On one side, Manhattan scent of "winter and football," Vin recollected. The other bared a springtime of possibility. "Dancing in the streets, block parties, celebrating everywhere. No violence of any kind. I'll never forget the dichotomy. In Brooklyn it was V-E Day and V-J Day combined."

Next morning Willard Mullin's gap-toothed "Brooklyn Bum" filled the *Daily News*'s front page. "We dood it! We beat 'em!" he began. "We beat them Yankees. We spot 'em th' first two games . . . an' we beat 'em! That Podres! Woil Cham-peens! Me!" Another tabloid headlined: "DODGERS

CHAMPS!" Above it, the page one *New York Post* promo teased an inside portrait of Norman Vincent Peale's book *The Power of Positive Thinking*. The *Times*'s John Drebinger wrote: "Far into the night rang shouts of revelry in Flatbush. Brooklyn at long last has won the World Series and now let someone suggest moving the Dodgers elsewhere." In two years, someone did.

Podres went deer hunting alone near his Witherbee, New York, home. Tardily, the impact reared. "Hey, Podres," he bellowed, "you beat the Yankees in the World Series! Where do you go from here?" A place Vin did not suspect.

"ACCORDING TO [THE] consensus of listeners," Young claimed, "the best announcing job in the World Series was turned in by Vin Scully." Sacked in May 1955, his senior partner missed Brooklyn's Millennium in the Morn. "Connie will miss the balance of the season," a club release said, "on the advice of his personal physician." Like smoking, getting tanked in Ike's America was more kosher than today. In 1956, O'Malley gave Desmond a final chance, knowing that he might go a drink too far.

Vin's photo lit the *Sporting News*'s preview issue: hair, full and neat; face, razor thin. Brooklyn added 25 TV road games to 77 home-game coverage. The Jints's radio network knit six stations; Yanks, 36; and Dodgers, 19, in Connecticut (Hartford, New London, Putnam, and Waterbury), Massachusetts (Holyoke and Pittsfield), Pennsylvania (Pottsville and Scranton), and New York (Albany, Binghamton, Cortland, Glens Falls, Massena, Norwich, Plattsburgh, Syracuse, Ticonderoga, Utica, and Watertown). "A lot to cover," said Young, "even when you're sober."

In film's *My Favorite Year*, Peter O'Toole plays boozy actor Alan Swann. "With Swannie," an admirer says, "you forgive a lot, you know?" For a long time O'Malley forgave. "Desmond couldn't handle it," mused Barber. "There were times he'd stop showing up." His last show was in August, rookie Jerry Doggett replacing him. A once/again Bums Voice helped, too. "Al Helfer drank triples without any apparent effect," wrote Ron Bergman, "and sometimes wore a cashmere cardigan that cost the lives of a herd of goats."

In 1935 the 6-foot-5 and 275-pound Washington and Jefferson alumnus had joined Barber in Cincinnati. "Five bucks a week, and I was worth every cent!" They reunited in 1939: "Al, let's get together again [in Brooklyn]," said Red, "and give 'em hell!" Helfer later spent 3½ years in the Navy, launched Sicily's Allied invasion, and was played by actor Alfred Drake in radio's *Cavalcade of America*. At war's end, he jilted Flatbush for the Jints and Stripes. "Connie was now Number 2, and I didn't want him hurt."

In 1950 Al began Mutual Radio's *Game of the Day*, each day but Sunday, boarding a plane, even two. "Different game, different city," he said, repairing late Saturday to home outside New York. "The Ghost of Hartsdale" got fresh laundry "and left before the door swung shut. My daughter was growing up. I loved, but didn't know, her." By 1954 Helfer had traveled "4 million miles" for Mutual. "Finally, the doctor told me to resign." That April Gallic gadfly Andre Baruch became a Dodgers analyst, joined next year by Al.

"Great pipes, but hard to work with," said Doggett. "If Al'd been less temperamental, he might have gone West with Vin. [Instead, Jerry did]. After that, who knows?"

Helfer at least knew Jersey City. If not Sicily, in 1956 it was still the bigs.

THAT YEAR BROOKLYN played seven home games at 24,000-seat single-deck Roosevelt Stadium. "Part of our effort to spread Dodger baseball," said O'Malley, trying to make Flatbush build a retractable-roof 50,000-seat park. Jersey City had been a Giants farm. Many now booed the Bums. The series lured 148,371. The season wed Newk's 27-7, Snider's team-record 43 taters, and Sal Maglie no-noing his ex-Jints: "the only guy," Al observed, "to pitch for all three pre-Met New York teams." Only Helfer aired them.

On August 19 Hodges's wife entered a Brooklyn hospital. The doctor delivered a girl, resedated mom Joan, and tuned to WMGM. At 1:30 P.M., Mrs. Hodges woke to Vin's "And that home run was for Cynthia Eleanor Hodges, born at 12 noon today." Learning of the baby, she went back to sleep. The aging Dodgers clinched a last-weekend pennant. Ahead: the last pre-2000 Subway Series.

Like 1955, the home nine took Sets 1-4. Personae fuse: President Eisenhower, entering Ebbets at the opener; Brooklyn, next day bashing Don Larsen; Mantle, driving 12 rows above The Stadium's 407 sign. "It wouldn't have gone through the [Brooklyn] fence," mused Campanella. "Might have gone through it, though."

On October 8 the Big Ballpark housed Game 5. In the fourth inning, Mick whacked Maglie's 2-2 pitch. "There's one if it stays fair!" Allen boomed. "It is going, going, gone! Mickey Mantle achieves his third home run of the Series, his eighth in World Series play, two behind Snider and Gehrig and seven behind Babe Ruth!" Berra then drove to left-center. "There's a drive! . . . The Duke on the run! He dives! He's got it!"

In Tennessee, Bill Millsaps, later a Richmond columnist, was the schoolmaster's son. At about 2:45 Dad appeared at the teenager's class-room and led him to the hallway.

"Come with me," said the father.

Bill panicked, wondering what he had done. Finally they neared dad's office.

"What is it? What's wrong?"

"Close the door, Billy, and turn on the TV. You won't believe what Don Larsen is doing to the Dodgers."

Reese was the sole Dodger to work a 3-2 count. Only three neared a hit: Robinson, lining to McDougald; Hodges, robbed by Mick in Death Valley; Amoros, barely hooking foul. Gil would have cleared Ebbets's 351-foot sign. "In those days," wrote Stan Isaacs, "there was hardly a street corner analysis that wasn't replete with speculation of how the day's particular battle might have gone had it been played in the other ballpark. A drive to [right-] center in Yankee Stadium would have been a home run in Brooklyn; a home run down the short right field in the Stadium would have hit the high fence at Ebbets Field. It made a difference."

For Scully, the real difference lit the line score: Brooklyn 0-0-0.

VIN, 28, GRASPED history and enormity: Yanks vs. Dodgers; eighth post-1940 Subway Series; mid-century America's divertissement. No one had thrown a Grand Event no-hitter. The bigs's last perfect game was Charlie Robertson's in 1922. "Overwhelming," Scully termed the pressure. "You remember Larsen's no-windup delivery. The skim of smoke across the field. Noise starting to build." Able, trusting himself, Vin turned within. "Try to blot out everything. Be literal. Be focused. Concentrate on the field." In 1947–65, Gillette, NBC, and baseball chose TV mikemen: "each team's guy doing half of each game." Vin succeeded Mel in the fifth, likely tempted to *quaff* a fifth.

"Don Larsen is spinning quite a web today. He's retired 16 men in a row," Scully said. New York added a 2-0 run. Vin's "heart was in my mouth," silverware easier to abide. Allen sat, transfixed, breaking a blood vessel in his throat. Haze and sunlight wrestled. A no-hitter's code of silence held. Scully "was younger and thoroughly intimidated, just a kid, really, and I followed Mel's example." The *New York World-Telegram & Sun*'s Bill Roeder quirked, "We will admit that Scully had us worried. He is young and red-headed and has a stubborn inclination to state the facts. We were in constant dread that he would blurt out the full truth."

Salutation began the eighth: "Mister Don Larsen, through seven innings, has retired 21 men in a row." Roeder "said to ourselves admiringly, 'Mr. Scully . . . you're getting darned cute.'" In 1991 a kinescope surfaced of Larsen's web. "A film dealer shot it at home," said Doak Ewing, founder, Rare Sports Films Inc. "His reels lacked the first inning, but were too priceless not to buy. It's ancient, precious history." In January 2009, Scully saw a rebroadcast on the MLB Network's debut.

Vin was struck by the minimalism: "'ball one, strike one.' We were always told to be quiet. We were somewhat intimidated by talk." NBC used just four cameras: two behind the plate and one on each line. Missing: instant replay, glitzy graphic, center-field and fan-reaction coverage— "how primitive TV baseball was!"—and often Allen, "heartbroken that he didn't do the entire game." Pleasing: commercial breaks 60 seconds long. Glaring: game time, two hours, six minutes. Scully hawked Gillette's vest-pocket *The Encyclopedia of Baseball*, "free when you buy a razor."

Video preserves Vin's terminus. "Well, all right," he began. "Let's all take a deep breath, as we go to the most dramatic ninth inning in the history of baseball. I'm going to sit back, light up, and hope I don't chew the cigarette to pieces." Palms dripped. Throats dried. Ribbons fell from the right-field stands. Furillo lofted to right fielder Bauer. Campy grounded out, Martin to Joe Collins. Pinch-hitter Dale Mitchell worked a 1-2 count.

Strike three called—umpire Babe Pinelli, pointing skyward; Berra, in Larsen's arms—has been more replayed than Hitler's D-Day nap. "Got him! The greatest game ever pitched in baseball history by Don Larsen!" Scully yelped, his suit a greenhouse.

"I don't think you or I shall ever see such a thing again," said Allen, postgame.

"I think we can both just go now," said Vin, later allowing to "feeling baked, wilted like a rose."

The Yanks and Dodgers played six times between 1947 and 1956: "So often, it seemed safe to assume that everything possible had happened. What more could happen?" Isaacs wrote. "Larsen had an answer. He strolled to the mound and retired twenty-seven straight Dodgers. That effort must have destroyed the scriptmaker. There was nothing else to say. So the Yankees and . . . Brooklyn never played another World Series after 1956, at least for the price of a subway ride."

William Manchester wrote of mid-1950s' America: "To those who cherished it [the age] has come to be remembered as an uncomplicated, golden time, mourned as lost childhoods are mourned, and remembered, in nostalgia, as cloudless." Game 6 was Brooklyn's last baseball moment in the sun: Vin airing every pitch, Mel shelved by laryngitis. Inning after inning Clem Labine and Bob Turley matched zeroes. In the 10th, Jim Gilliam reached second base. Soon-to-retire Robinson singled: 1-0, Dodgers—on No. 42's final hit, Brooklyn's final Classic run.

Like Larsen, Newcombe had flunked Game 2. Ultimately, he went 149-90, hit .271, stole home once, played first base in Japan, and beat booze, but not the Yanks. "I want to beat them more than anything else in my life," Don said before the final. "I won't rest until I do." Instead, Berra clubbed two two-run blasts onto Bedford Avenue. Fans taunted Newk's 21.21 ERA: "a sad way," said Scully, "for him to bow out." Bowing regularly, the 1947–60 Washington Senators resembled the Atlantis of the American League.

To DISTRACT, SENATORS announcer Bob Wolff founded the local Knothole Gang, "fan in the stand interview," and celebrity in the booth. Vin had little use for language to condense trouble. "Our team was different," said Wolff. "Tuning in, people knew who was winning. I just gave the score." At 35, he chafed at network anonymity. "I kept bugging Gillette for the chance to broadcast network. Finally, it gave me Washington's '56 All-Star Game," adding that fall's Series.

In 2006 George W. Bush disclosed reading "three Shakespeares." Bob's Don Larsen script is still more often heard than *King Lear*. "I'll guarantee that nobody—but nobody—has left this ballpark," Wolff blared on Mutual. "And if somebody did manage to leave early—man, he's missing the greatest! Two strikes and a ball! . . . Mitchell waiting, stands deep, feet close together. Larsen is ready, gets the sign. Two strikes, ball one. Here comes the pitch. Strike three! A no-hitter! A perfect game for Don Larsen!" Next day Robinson worked overtime. "Slaughter's after it, he leaps! It's over his head against the wall! . . . Jackie Robinson is being pummeled!"

Duke Phi Beta Kappa '42 may not immediately suggest parallel with Fordham '49. Yet connecting threads exist. Bob and Vin were born November 29, got a college baseball scholarship, and joined the Navy. (Wolff wrote its World War II supply procedure manual.) Each was precise, felt obscenity a crutch, and made Cooperstown (Bob '95). Scully and Wolff became radio's and television's longest-running sportscasters, respectively. "If someone said, 'Be nasty to succeed,' I'd say no," added Bob. "A guy who professes to tell it like it is actually tells it like a clod." Scully couldn't have said it better, trying in their next joint gig: 1962's Jints-Dodgers playoff. Wolff moored NBC. Vin braved déjà vu.

Game 2 took a then-nine-inning record 4 hours and 18 minutes, "each half-hour NBC saying, 'This program will not be seen tonight because of baseball,'" Wolff said. "Thirty minutes later they'd axe another." He aired its 1962–65 Series pregame show, "Vin twice doing play-by-play, always alone and talking to you at home." Already Voices had begun to converse. "Vin's now extinct," a mastodon or corset zipper. "Except for him, nobody does it solo. Like any great soloist, why would he share?"

Allen's bass register "made it easy to go up in pitch with excitement. A high voice has a tougher time, but Vin does it." The writer italicizes a word. "It's the best he can do, because he works in cold type." Scully *sang*, Bob said, "so nuanced that you don't even notice that he emphasizes." Best ever? "That is a judgmental thing. Certainly Vin's the most important," his pretty game still a melody.

DRIFTLESS ARE MANY baseball radio/TV men. "It's hard to rouse yourself for the same event year after year," said Wolff. "I don't see how Vin does something that long and still keeps his passion." To dent boredom, Harwell visited pals in every city. Allen spent days doing ads. Bob made a list of household names he wished to meet—then, say, in Kansas City, near Independence, phoned Harry S. Truman out of the blue. For a time, travels with Scully seemed to pique the principal.

A chartered bus snakes through downtown Boston. Suddenly a rotten egg thrown through an open window hits sitting-in-front-of-Vin Cal Abrams in the head. In Cincinnati, hotel electricity shorts. Scully walks down 27 floors of stairs to breakfast. Chicago: A reservation glitch diverts the Dodgers to a dive. Vin sees a blond in the lobby upchuck into a potted plant. Milwaukee: At a National Junior Chamber of Commerce convention, a hotel courtyard loudspeaker plays "Goober Peas" for 36 straight hours, making Scully insomniac. "You miss so much because of your job," he said. "Mother's Day, Father's Day, birthdays, anniversaries, birthdays, games, conversation, you name it." Eventually the road paled.

By 1956, "after Connie and I trained him," Barber wrote, "loved him, teased him, and rejoiced in his remarkable development," Scully sailed a sloop less beached than at high tide. One day he taped a 16-millimeter Babe Ruth League World Series film; another, "sipped pure lemonade [at a team party]," wrote Young, "because he has given up the basic ingredient for Lent"; later, narrated a 33⅓ r.p.m. "high fidelity 12-inch long-playing record [text read]" of "Look! Listen! And Learn! Taught By the Stars [Campy, Oisk, Hodges, Labine, Jackie, and Duke] of the Brooklyn Dodgers!"

O'Malley liked him: "an outgoing kind of guy," Rosenthal said, "a friend of bartenders, the clubhouse guy," easy to think of, like Barber did, as a son. Most felt Vin as dependable as a metronome. Labine was once fined for missing curfew. Alarmed, wife Barbara phoned. "But honey," said the pitcher, "I was with *Vin Scully*," drinking coffee at a café. To Murray, he was as "valid an alibi as a letter from the chaplain."

In Chicago, the Dodgers played in the afternoon. "Then Vin'd go to a movie," said Rosenthal. "Didn't matter what it was, he'd be there, and ask me to go along."

Once the 20-something said, "You know why I go to so many movies at night?"

Rosenthal said no.

"It keeps me out of trouble."

Harold laughed. "Women, I guess."

At Ebbets, Vin, clad in tie, jacket, starched shirt, and loafers, arrived four to five hours before a game, stopping at the front office, field, clubhouse, then booth, where a man eerily ahead of the curve opened "a briefcase similar to Mary Poppins's bag." In 1969 the bigs's first game in a foreign nation filled Montreal's Jarry Park. The crowd wore Gallic garb, ate corned beef and pastrami, and sang "The Happy Wanderer" in French. The P.A. announcer was bilingual, seats largely backless, and binoculars a must: Women were the most gorgeous in the league. Modern banks flanked old churches and shops and inns. Even to native Allan Roth, the Continental effect was dizzying: "sort of like," said Jerry Doggett, "his impact on the game."

At 3, Roth amazed relatives by counting backward from 100—in twos. Later, the teenager became obsessed by baseball numbers. "Keep in mind, this was unheard of," noted Tom Oliphant. "Baseball men went by their gut, not head." Dizzy Dean called statistics *statics*. Roth found them active. Montreal was Brooklyn's 1939–60 conveyer belt. "He kept writing Rickey about his results," Tom said, "using different statistical situations." Branch was intrigued, then wowed.

"Close, low-scoring games follow a definite pattern," Allan wrote. "Eleven men usually get on base in the nite pattern. Eleven men usually get on base in the first eight innings on hits, walks, and errors. Going into the ninth inning 24 men have been retired, making a total of 35 who have gone to bat. The first man up in the ninth, therefore, completes the fourth complete swing through the batting order and then come the top two men. In tight games, hitters below the second slot seldom get five chances to hit."

Pining to be baseball's first full-time statistician, Roth, an epileptic, had to first cross the U.S. border. Admitted in 1947, he began by recording data from bunts to RBIs in context, not isolation. "He was the guy who began it all," said guru Bill James. "He took statisticians into a brave new world"—to Roth, terra firma. "Basically, baseball is a percentage game," Allan mused. "I thought that everything in the game should be tabulated and developed a number of theories which Rickey went for."

In 1951 Rickey went out the door, Roth tumbling to the booth: a most fortuitous turn. David Halberstam described "the perfect combination" as "Joe DiMaggio doing deeds, and Mel Allen calling them." The Dodgers' duo became Roth feeding statistics, and Vin digesting them. Allan "jigger[ed] Scully's tools," wrote the *Times*: score book, lineup, latest press release, batting averages, and commercial text. "Sometimes," said Vin, "the problem is to find the right paper at the right time." To Oliphant, "Data is only numbers reported and analyzed in an understandable fashion. Allan had these incredible numbers, and Vin meshed them into poetry."

Other stat men glimpsed the forest. The Dodgers' Roth and Scully saw the trees. "All of a sudden, a righty striking out twice against a lefty in the day nightcap of a doubleheader wasn't an accident," Tom laughed. "Roth found *trend*," helping Scully compare day and night, road and away, dry and wet, vegetable and mineral.

Not everyone rejoiced. In 1984 a *Sporting News* reader, Artemus Marshall of Huntsville, Alabama, fancied Vin saying, "[Pedro] Guerrero is the only Dodger to hit a homer right-handed off Braves pitching with two out and two on in the bottom of the third with the moon full since 1958." Most, however, did. If the devil's in the details, Scully found Roth's divine.

AFTER 1956 BOB WOLFF confessed to seeking "new worlds to conquer: TV, radio, books." Scully seemed glad to follow Red, never split an infinitive, and build his clientele. "I never thought of leaving," he said. "Why would I? The glamour was all here. It was Willie, Mickey, and the Duke. Everything I cherished was in New York."

Debate still roils O'Malley's apostasy. His white Jewish and Catholic base was moving to suburbia. Ebbets was primitive; said Vin, "Tiny seats, few amenities." Worse, pinched by a city grid, "Walter couldn't expand. The infrastructure was too weak to build up. There was no way to build out." O'Malley and New York City Parks commissioner Robert Moses prized real estate at Flatbush and Atlantic Avenues, hard by three subway systems, near the Long Island Railroad. Cynically, Moses proposed a Dodgers stadium at two other sites. "One was next to the Battery Tunnel," said Walter. "The other was [on a 78-acre tract] in Flushing Meadows": the New York Mets' future yard. O'Malley declined. They would not be, he said, the Brooklyn Dodgers in Queens.

"Walter felt the discord was Brooklyn's doing," Scully told the *Daily News*'s Bob Raissman. "Had the city followed his thinking, you would have had a new stadium, which would've revitalized the borough. Had Walter got what he wanted, the team would've never left. For him, it came down to either he got a place in Brooklyn where he could draw to compete"—or move. New York University president John Sexton termed O'Malley "in the seventh ring of Dante's Hell on the list of the most vile people of the Twentieth Century." Vin differed, having viewed him unplugged. "To know a person, see him when he's happiest. You would find Walter in the early morning at Vero Beach," in khaki shirt and pants, digging. "He loved the earth. He was an orchid grower, if you will"—a "businessman," not lout.

The businessman craves profit. In 1957 O'Malley's $750,000 TV revenue led the league. His rub was attendance: Televising its home schedule, Brooklyn drew 779,268 fewer than a decade earlier. Even so, "[he did] doggone well during the past few years," Walter conceded in 1958, "with the *best earnings record in baseball*." If O'Malley "worried about the gate," wrote the *New York Post*'s Phil Mushnick, "all he had to do was stop giving away his product." As it was, seeing Reese, Oisk, and Campy on Channel 9 didn't cost a dime.

It is true that O'Malley tried to get Brooklyn to build a new park as early as 1951. It is also true that 1990s Cincinnati, Detroit, Milwaukee, Philadelphia, Pittsburgh, San Diego, and San Francisco, among others, successfully tried longer. Safeco Field's 1999 debut tied ferries, cargo ships, and Seattle sunsets from Albert Bierstadt. Next year Houston's then-named Enron Field opened "with more nooks and crannies," wrote *Sports Illustrated*, "than an English muffin." The Mets baptized Citi Field in 2009. "It's been a long wait," said owner Fred Wilpon, "but worth it."

Many of these teams were said to be losing money. O'Malley wanted to make more than a team 900 miles away.

On March 18, 1953, Milwaukee acquired the Braves of Boston since 1876. "It was a holiday when we heard they were coming," said Bud Selig, 18, his town fixing to kill its new team with love. A parade reached downtown's Schroeder Hotel. "People put up a Christmas tree!" said pitcher Ernie Johnson. "Since we'd missed Christmas they said let's celebrate it now," presaging hysteria akin to Brooklyn's. The seventh-place 1952 Braves played to 281,278. The second-place '53ers drew a league-record 1,826,397. In 1955 Milwaukee hosted the All-Star Game. 1956: "rush for tickets," wrote *Sports Illustrated*, "rivaled only by *My Fair Lady*."

Through 1959, Milwaukee won two pennants, barely missed two more, and approximated an All-Star team. Del Crandall caught. Henry Aaron, Bill Bruton, and Wes Covington outfielded. The infield vaunted Joe

Adcock, Red Schoendienst, Johnny Logan, and Eddie Mathews. Burghers gave players free beer, milk, and cars. "We'd go into Forbes Field—Pittsburgh was lousy—and there'd be 30,000," said Voice Earl Gillespie. "Ebbets was jammed. Baseball's smallest town became its capital."

One night in 1953 O'Malley flew to Brewtown's Billy Mitchell Field. "Look at this," he said, pop-eyed, of County Stadium's full house. "They're outdrawing us a million. We can't afford this—not even a couple years." Vin vocalized a borough. Allen meant the Big Ballpark in the Bronx. Harry Caray packed the Church of Cardinals Baseball. "None had what we did," said Gillespie, Milwaukee topping the bigs in 1953–58 attendance.

Earl's was the first franchise to change sites in half a century. The river of hand clapping running through the Upper Midwest ensured it would not be the last. The Los Angeles Dodgers likely would not exist had there not been the Milwaukee Braves.

By 1957 JET TRAVEL cut the New York–Los Angeles flight time from 9 to 4½ hours, enfranchising California. Earlier O'Malley had bought a 44-passenger twin-engine airplane for $775,000. "We'll be the first club to have a plane," he told reporters. Young wrote: "You could see he was gone." Pols and papers sermonized: Ebbets is good enough; expand the unexpandable; call O'Malley's bluff. On May 28 the National League refused.

"It said the Dodgers could move if we eased scheduling by getting another team to go to California [by October 1]," Doggett said. The *Daily News* screamed: "GIANT-DODGER MOVE OKd. Mayor, [Borough President John] Cashmore Aim to Keep Them." America's Venus kicked out the first ball at a Flatbush U.S.-Israeli soccer game. A player named whom he would like to meet: "As athletes . . . the Brooklyn Dodgers. As men, Marilyn Monroe." By quirk, Bob Costas, 5, saw his first game that May. "Baseball'd been radio or gray TV images," he said of black and white. "I walk into Ebbets Field at night and see this vision—like *The Wizard of Oz* when they land in Oz and change to Technicolor." Blind, Brooklyn did not see.

Like two people in a house awaiting divorce, the Dodgers kept up appearances. Scully hosted between-game twin bill guests in a basement TV studio. In the booth, he kept vending, "one lazy and humid day" placing a warm beer bottle behind him, which exploded, scattering suds and broken glass. A 300-pound ex-radio, TV, and band man hosted *Happy Felton's Knothole Gang* and postgame's *Talk to the Stars*. Clown Emmett Kelly, parodying Willard Mullin's Bum, was hired "to relieve tension at Ebbets Field." Vin helped June 4. Don Zimmer fouled high and right. "And somebody makes a great catch by the name of Barney Stein! Barney, who takes great sports photos for the *New York Post*. And that thing kangarooed"—14-karat Scully—"from the dugout roof right up into the camera booth! And there was Barney to grab it," dropping a $9,000 camera. "Naw, not really."

Reality grabbed Vin's boyhood team. In 1948, buying Triple-A Minneapolis, Horace Stoneham hailed "the finest minor-league park in the country." Vexed, O'Malley warned, "If you're there, and we stay in Brooklyn, our rivalry'd be dead." In 1954 San Francisco touted a $4 million park bond issue "contingent on the city getting a big-league team." Manhattan's borough head countered with a 110,000-seat site! Contractor Charles Harney offered part of Candlestick Point, above San Francisco Bay, of rock and trees that rose like candlesticks. Stoneham yielded in August 1957. "We're sorry to disappoint the kids of New York, but we didn't see many of their parents out there at the Polo Grounds in recent years [since 1947, attendance down a million to 653,923]." The page one *New York World-Telegram & Sun* mourned: "IT'S OFFICIAL: GIANTS TO FRISCO."

O'Malley had first eyed Los Angeles in the early 1950s. By 1956 Damascus Road led to Chavez Ravine, two miles from center city, a steep-ridged site peopled by dogs, goats, squatters, "possums, skunks, jackrabbits, gophers, rusty tin cans, rotting tires, moribund mattresses, and broken beer bottles," the *Los Angeles Times*'s Frank Finch added. "Beverly Hills it wasn't." Available, it was. In a helicopter, O'Malley nudged Buzzie Bavasi: Nearby, several freeways merged. "Walter liked everything—the access, the vicinity, potential, above all," said his aide. "Even then he was ready to make a deal."

In 1921 Cubs owner William Wrigley Jr. bought the Pacific Coast League Angels, then built a $1.1 million small-scale version of Wrigley Field. On February 1, 1957, Chicago dealt Southern California big-league rights—the PCL park and team—for the Bums' Texas League franchise. "Walter was looking ahead," Scully said, "in case he couldn't get what he needed to stay": insurance, should Brooklyn's go unredeemed.

On March 6, an eight-man group, including Los Angeles mayor Norris Poulson, City Council head John Gibson, and L.A. County supervisor Kenneth Hahn met O'Malley at Vero Beach. "The rumors really began," said Snider, "when they came to spend the day." By evening, Poulson yelped, "We've got the Dodgers!" He was prescient, if premature.

WHILE O'MALLEY SALLIED, the Apple dallied. In 1957, Jack Paar said, "I kid you not," on TV's *The Tonight Show*. Abe Stark charged the West Coast with "organized piracy . . . an unsportsmanlike attack." Hoping to become governor, Nelson Rockefeller belatedly offered financial aid. Incumbent Averell Harriman showed why Rocky would swamp him in 1958. "The Dodgers won't move," he fantasized. I kid you not: "Los Angeles smog won't let them play at night." Brooklyn didn't believe O'Malley would go — until he had.

On March 19, Duke, homering at West Palm Beach, also broadcast an inning. "Your voice is excellent," wrote a reader, "like velvet — nice and smooth." Scully kept his day job. On September 8, Brooklyn and New York played a final time. Their El Escurial: the Jints' quilt of girders, puny lines, and canyon of an outfield. Gilliam and Hank Sauer traded early homers. Mays scored on Ray Jablonski's jumbo triple. Periodically Vin left TV to introduce still-tyro Doggett: "Mr. Drysdale, meet Mr. Mays. Here's Jerry." In the fifth, inheriting radio, he began to sum up and say good-bye.

"I don't know how you feel about it at the other end of these microphones, whether you're sitting at home or driving a car or on the beach or anywhere but, I know, sitting here, watching the Giants and Dodgers apparently playing for the last time at the Polo Grounds, you want 'em to *take their time*," said Scully, elongating each syllable. "You just feel like saying, now, don't run off the field so fast, fellahs, let's take it easy, we're going to take one long lingering look at both of you."

The look lingered for the next 4½ innings, still wistful to rehear. The players wanted "one parting shot at each other. . . . Already a bit of bitterness has started to pop up." Curt Barclay dusted Don Drysdale and Gilliam. Big D hit Barclay, "stared down the barrel," and "lowered the boom." Sparta and Athens "are at it again," Vin said, gliding to identification: "This is the Brooklyn Dodgers' radio network." Returning, he "sensed the feeling that [the crowd is] ready to let out a holler at just about anything." Scully wished not to holler but to mourn.

"Boy, it's funny, being a kid raised in New York," he resumed, "you sit here watching this ballgame and looking at the Polo Grounds and your memories go wild." Had you "ever seen a Fordham-St.Mary's football game years before the war? That's something you'd remember." Below, Snider was "on his horse," unhorsing a double play; Gilliam "went flying through the air like a rag doll"; pinch-runner Don Zimmer "tripped and fell down." New York led, 3-2. Again Vin segued. "It's kind of a funny feeling. Memories. Memories."

Remember "Walter Brown with the Giants? Musta' weighed close to three hundred pounds. As a kid sitting in the bleachers, I looked in the [center-field] dressing room" to see him, reading a paper in T-shirt and shorts, near a lighted cigarette left on a chair near the window. Vin was "too scared to even holler" as the fat man sat down. "Ever see an angry 300-pound man?" Ed Roebuck relieved Drysdale. Outfielder Sauer was replaced by—Bobby Thomson. Another history chapter hit in Brooklyn's ninth. "If time's gonna slam the door on this great rivalry, then Sandy Amoros has . . . his foot in the door, trying to keep it open." It closed, on a 4-3 grounder.

The Jints finished sixth. Milwaukee eliminated Brooklyn September 20. Three days later the Braves hosted second-place St. Louis, Henry Aaron batting in the 11th. "A swing and a drive back into center field!" bayed Gillespie. "Going back towards the wall! It's back at the fence . . . and is it gone or not? It's a home run! The Braves are the champions of the National League!" Next night the Cathedral of the Underdog held a final Mass for 6,702 parishioners. "It was dark," said Duke, allegorically. "The lights didn't seem to be on as bright." The clubhouse doorframe wore a good luck horseshoe. The Quiet Man had the last RBI: Bums 2, Bucs 0.

Forty years later the Dodgers, California's sole bigs team with an organ, led Vin to ask, "Who is the only person to play for the Dodgers, the Rangers, and the Knicks?" Answer: Gladys Goodding, organist at Madison Square Garden and Ebbets Field, feting each Dodger with a song. Pafko's was "On Wisconsin"; Furillo, "O Solo Mio"; O'Malley, "When Irish Eyes Are Smiling"; Vin, "classical music," she said, like *La Bohème*. Ebbets's farewell played none of the above.

"That last game was very sad, as you can imagine, and Gladys was known to take a drink," said Scully. "Well, she showed up with a brown paper bag and went into her little booth with the organ and 'locked' the door." Her first song was "My Buddy." The repertoire sank from there. "Drinking, Gladys became more sullen; her songs, more funereal." Irate, O'Malley "sent word over with an usher: 'Hey. C'mon. Pep it up! Pep it up!'"

He couldn't threaten her, Vin laughed. "She had the door locked. He couldn't fire her. After all, they were leaving!" She continued to play "very, very sentimental sad songs, sadder and more sentimental each time she took a visit to the brown paper bag. It was something that just stayed with you—besides the game itself."

ABC TELEVISION's *World Series Special* showed Vin interviewing Robinson and Mays. By Game 7, Gladys was likely *in* the bag. In the ninth, Milwaukee led, 5-0, at The Stadium. "Hank Aaron is pulled around in left-center field," said Gillespie. "Burdette's [bases-loaded] pitch. Swung on, lined, grabbed by Mathews who steps on third—and the World Series is over and the Milwaukee Braves are the new world champions of baseball!"—the first non–New York titleist since 1948. Only 61,207 saw the final. "You could feel it," said Rosenthal. "There was a bitterness in the air."

In 2007 Bavasi revealed a "vote among the top eight people in the [1957 Dodgers'] front office" to the *New York Times's* Dave Anderson. "It was 8 to 1 to stay. The one vote was Walter's." On October 7, L.A.'s City Council voted, 10-4, to accept Wrigley Field, let O'Malley buy 300 acres of the Ravine, and spend $2 million on infrastructure. Next day Walter confirmed the elephant in the room. "In view of [this] action . . . the stockholders and directors of the Brooklyn Baseball Club have met and unanimously agreed that the necessary steps be taken to draft the Los Angeles territory." Mayor Poulson cooed, "Well, that's the news I've been waiting to hear. Now Los Angeles is major-league in every sense of the word." Brooklyn had been major league since 1891. Did it not adore the team: to writer Joe King, "unsurpassed on the public interest scale"? Had *Sports Illustrated* not read, "No baseball park is more fun . . . a continuing riot of noise"? Had O'Malley not said, "My roots are in Brooklyn"? They withered, like the club.

L.A. deserved a franchise. It did not deserve Brooklyn's. "The league should have made O'Malley and Stoneham sell [to potential buyers Sinclair Robinson and Louis Wolfson, among others]," said Rosenthal.

"Then give Walter and Horace '58 West Coast expansion clubs." Instead, expanding in 1962, it bore the Mets. Vin looked on, torn. "I was a very young broadcaster when Walter said he was taking the team out of Brooklyn. My first feeling was of tremendous relief when he told me I was in his plans," ignoring advice to hire West Coasters. "There wasn't any real decision involved because I was in my love with my job. But I was saddened because of being a New Yorker." He felt like a wife whose husband had been transferred. "She might not want to go, but she goes."

In dark fedora, suit, and tie, O'Malley deplaned October 23 at Los Angeles International Airport. His Convair, repainted *Los Angeles Dodgers*, carted Scully and 28 other passengers. Mixing metaphors, an *L.A. Times*man wrote: "The dawn of a new era began last night." Crowed the *Sporting News*: "L.A. Flips Lid in Greeting to 'Its' Dodgers." Signs hailed the landing. "Welcome Los Angeles Dodgers!" A man held a large plastic bat: "Welcome O'Malley And Lads To a Big Town!" City Councilwoman Rosalind Wyman wore an L.A. Dodgers hat: "As one member I am thoroughly convinced that this is a good proposition for the City. It means much business. It means jobs in the fact that Mr. O'Malley will build a $10 to $15 million stadium": the Ravine's Dodger Stadium.

"A Tory?" Walter once said. "But a Tory I am." Locking one door, he unlocked another. "I just hope for all of you an early World Series championship team," he told the crowd. "And I just don't know when we can do it, but we're going to give an awfully good try. So thanks to everybody for being so nice to us," not noting a process server-turned-skunk at the cotillion.

"From the citizens of Los Angeles, we're glad to have you here," he said, approaching O'Malley near the plane. "Here's a summons from the [soon-to-be-evicted] people of Chavez Ravine."

As Roger Kahn wrote, "Afterwords on the life of kings." On January 26, 1958, Campanella, 36, left his Harlem liquor store on a cold, clear night. Driving home, he crashed and overturned the car on an icy Glen Cove, Long Island, road. The three-time Most Valuable Player never walked again.

In January 1960 Mullin drew the Bum aloft with wings: "A Phantom Flies in Brooklyn." Fordham's Phantom could read the *Daily News*: "Ebbets Field will be the largest haunted house in the world. The ghosts are all there waiting—to move in." Dick Young would shortly visit. "Care to join us? Just send along a memory or two."

Next month a demolition crew in Dodgers blue and white began wrecking the basilica. Lucy Monroe had sung at many Series: Her Anthem now mimed a dirge. The first blow broke the visiting dugout roof. "I just got sick," said Erskine, with Branca leading 200 pallbearers. "I left. I didn't want to see any more," missing the clubhouse blackboard's final scrawl: "I was her [*sic*]. Why are you breaking Ebbets Field?"

An April 24 auction wiled the devoted and curious. Gold-plated bricks sold for $1; flower pots with infield soil, 25 cents; the cornerstone, $600, to league president Warren Giles, who let the Bums skip town. Eight light towers were moved to Downing Stadium on Randall's Island. The right-center-field clock now crowns a scoreboard at Asheville, North Carolina's McCormick Field.

By 1963 the Ebbets Field Apartments housing development rose where a child's game made grown men love, then weep. I.S. 320 Intermediate School lies across the road. The nearby Jackie Robinson (née Crown Heights Intermediate) School houses the Brooklyn Dodgers Hall of Fame.

"There'll never be another like Ebbets Field," said Pee Wee Reese, softly, gently. "No sir, no way." For Scully, Moving Day had truly come.

5

CALIFORNIA, HERE WE COME
(1958–1961)

RECALLING 1957, a Brooklynite ignores Sputnik, the Asian flu epidemic, and TV's *Leave It to Beaver*. Baseball's exodus still sears. Coney Island's Louis Gossett, Jr., was then 21. "Without the Dodgers, there was nothing for everybody to homogeneously identity with." The pastime suffered, too. "Who said the National League *has* to have a team in New York?" Warren Giles jawed that fall, misreading big-city TV, finance, and ad men. Baseball's decline as Big-Game America began with its split Apple.

In 1956 *Sports Illustrated* wrote: "To your average, balding, loose-bellied, sedentary [U.S.] male, baseball is something to read about, to talk about, to listen to on radio, to watch on television. Why? Baseball is a game of limitless dramatic possibility, an incredible melodrama, a constant theater of delight": as American as Betsy Ross, Betty Grable, or a Davy Crockett cap. Meanwhile, the National Football League's anonymity even smote the New York Giants. Their game rivaled wrestling—except that wrestling had a niche.

"When we won the [1956] title, the town was still baseball, always baseball," mused football Giants TV Voice Chris Schenkel. Its sudden exit changed Madison Avenue's DNA. "New York dominated the media," Harold Rosenthal observed, "and what dominated New York grabbed the networks." Soon football Giants bit players and glamour boys filled baseball's void at Toots Shor's and 21: new game, our team, on top.

"No one knows the exact effect of the Giants' and Dodgers' transfer," said Schenkel. "We do know what millions did." Many went underground. Others forswore baseball for an age, or life. If timing is all, the NFL's December 28, 1958, title game compounded everything: high-topped John Unitas, a lion's jaw of a Giants defense, Yankee Stadium, and Baltimore's 23-17 sudden-death victory: "the greatest game ever played." Fifty million viewers included Vin. "It was freezing cold in New York, and all the players were covered with mud, but outside my [L.A] window, the weather was warm," like Brooklyn's in July.

Pro football might have surged, in any case. Huddles spur anticipation. Each team can be entirely viewed on-screen. Analysis, replay, and stop-action help "make football a better TV sport," said Ernie Harwell. Many first saw it in late 1958. In a 1964 Lou Harris poll, America preferred baseball to football, 48–15 percent. By 2007, the NFL led, 33–14, and in every demographic, especially among 28–39-year-olds, homes earning $35,000–$75,000, and blacks—ironic, given Robinson.

"Ask not for whom the bell tolls, baseball fans," *Sports Illustrated* wrote that year. It first tolled when, needing something to talk about, New York's media saw pro football raise a hand.

"IF THE MOVE hurt nationally," said Jim Murray, "you could never tell it here." Frank Finch added: "The Dodgers made the greatest impact on Southern California's millions since the 1933 earthquake left them shimmying and shaking." Au courant signs scripted "Ball Game Today: Win Dodgers." Storefront windows vended team jackets and $300 suits. A welcoming parade jammed 300,000 downtown. O'Malley then addressed a civic luncheon. "The next time you will be asked to stand," he said, "is when your own Duke Snider hits a home run for your Dodgers here." *Vindication*? It seemed *absolution*.

"Twice this area had been close to big-league ball," Murray wrote of the 1941 and 1953 St. Louis Browns. "First, the Japanese bombed Pearl Harbor. The second time a commission told baseball to get lost." To much of Los Angeles, in turn, O'Malley appeared paradise found. Dodger Stadium was to open in 1962. A site at Avalon Boulevard, San Pedro Street, and 41st and 42nd Places might suffice till then. Wrigley Field had an ivied wall, in-play light tower, right-center pavilion, and trademark office tower.

The 1958 L.A.-moving-to Spokane Angels didn't care. The moving-to-L.A. Dodgers did.

Wrigley hosted TV's 1959–60 *Home Run Derby* with "its short lines [340 and 339] and alleys [345]," Walter said. "Originally, it's where we were going to play." A what-might-have-been sketch suggested the Polo Grounds—enclosed, two-tiered left to right, and center-field pavilion. "Then we found it would take a while to expand [a 22,000 capacity]." Ticket orders topped $1 million by December 4, 1957: "Almost all of it in cash—money on the barrel," said Buzzie Bavasi. "It wasn't that way in Brooklyn. There it was largely [a] down payment." The crush stunned O'Malley. "We knew then we couldn't expand Wrigley enough by Opening Day."

At sea, he eyed the Rose Bowl. "Architects told him 10 rows would have to be removed in right and left to deepen the lines to 300 feet, and center would stay 460," said Jerry Doggett. "The field would have been oval [home plate and center field in the end zones] and box seats put behind the plate [and along first and third]." Desperate, Walter spurned Pasadena—"too little time, too much to renovate"—for L.A.'s Exposition Boulevard, Merlo Avenue, Santa Barbara Avenue (now Martin Luther King, Jr., Drive) and South Figueroa Street. Its cabash made Ebbets Field look sane.

The Los Angeles Memorial Coliseum mimed the 50,000-seat Roman Colosseum, completed in A.D. 80. (Two stones from Rome and the Altis in Olympia, Greece, sat under a peristylum beyond right-center field.) Opened in 1923, the ex-travel pit armory, agricultural park, and museum swelled to 74,000 for the 1932 Summer Olympics. "Before that it housed saloons, livestock, and burlesque," noted Murray. As we shall see, baseball burlesque helped Scully.

"The problem is that the Coliseum was a football and track and field place [debuting with '20s University of Southern California]," said Vin. "And football and baseball demand different configurations." The Dodgers carved dugouts, a wire screen, and huge tunnel behind the plate. O'Malley spent $200,000 for three banks to light the infield. A 4-foot-high concrete wall circled most of the field, including right's 301-foot foul line. It waxed to 390's belly, met an 8-foot right-center fence (440), and waned to center (425). A Sahara divided the inner fence and last bleacher row 700 feet from the plate.

Left field's 251-foot line glued a visitor. Fearing dinger procreation, O'Malley built a 40-by-140 foot screen, a.k.a. the Great Wall of China, angling to the ground at the 348 mark (cables, towers, and wires were in play). Commissioner Ford Frick consoled those worried about Babe Ruth's 1927's home run record. "I do not think [it] is in particular danger. Foul lines are not especially important where home runs are concerned. The other distances in left-center and right determine the number of homers." Privately, Babe's ex-ghost fumed. "Frick had this absurd idea," said Murray, "to build a second screen 333 feet from the plate in the stands. Clear both screens, it's a homer; the first, a double." Quake and shake: the California Earthquake Law refused.

The first-base stands almost met the line. Third's lay off Catalina Island. "I'd run a mile," said infielder Gilliam, "and still not see a fan." The rim lay 110 feet from ground level; field, 33 feet below. Capacity was 94,600: "the only place," said a barb, "that can house almost a hundred thousand people and two outfielders." The Bums weren't the Coliseum's first baseball team. "USC practiced before we did," Reese laughed. "The least they could have done is told us what's in store." Baseball seemed so alien—back bleachers needed binoculars to spy the plate—that many brought radios to *hear* what they couldn't *see*.

"It was an uneasy time, not knowing whether we'd be accepted. For a while I had a suitcase over a closet," said Scully, halting, and then, "but California just took to us. People knew about Mays. They knew about Musial. But they didn't know the rank-and-file players. So the transistor radio became a necessary thing for the fan, to learn by hearing me. I always thought it was strange knowing that thousands of people are listening to you describe a play they are watching. Then it became a habit even after we left the Coliseum."

Radio engineers, wrote Rick Reilly, "often [had] to adjust for the noise of Vinny's voice cascading from the stands into the booth": actually, rows of seats reserved for TV, radio, and print inside the west tunnel football entryway, behind the backstop. "It was a wooden structure, fastened to the roof of the tunnel," reached by an iron staircase, added Scully. "The strange thing was that even though the Coliseum was so big and formidable, those press seats made everything feel so intimate and close."

Ultimately, Harwell would say in a slow, thoughtful way, "Vin became almost like the stadium P.A." To Snider, he "was the one thing that stands out about the Dodgers' acceptance." In 2004, he paused. "Still is."

BASEBALL AS PANTOMIME—"At the Coliseum, people were so far away, I gave them a goodly connection," said Scully—helped give Vin a goodly portion of the Coast. Yet his late 1950s perfect storm stemmed not from geography alone.

Technology helped. Imagine carting Scully's boyhood monster or finding an electrical outlet at the park. You can't. The portable radio was invented in 1948. "Before the mid-1950s," laughed the *L.A. Times's* Larry Stewart, "forget radios at a game. And without that, Vin's craze doesn't happen." Instead, "Scully's vivid descriptions of the action made him a cult figure," said the *2006 Scribner Encyclopedia*. Vin would "crack a joke," wrote the *Orange County Register's* Steve Bisheff, "and the whole ballpark would erupt in laughter, often startling players on the field." Getting a Dodger Dog, "You'd never miss a beat. Even at a concession stand, he was describing every pitch."

Chronology helped. Southern California's frame of reference became the DeSoto that mimed a Cadillac: "It could have been someone else, very easily," Vin said, "who arrived here around the same time under the same circumstances, and it would have been his good fortune instead of mine." Born there, the Pirates' Bob Prince knew the territory. "I wonder how the area'd have reacted to some Gunner's razz-ma-tazz," he said. "Vinny's baseball's poet laureate. It just helped to be the area's first [*sic* Dizzy Dean, below]." Chuckling, he seemed reflective. "Vin set the tone, and it's what people now expect." Prince later spurned San Diego radio: "You've got desert to the east, ocean to the west, Mexico to the south, and Scully to the north."

Baseball's predominance helped. "Think Ted Williams, Stan Musial, and Mickey Mantle," said 1956's *Sports Illustrated*. "Their names tower over other sports." The Southland lapped them up. "O'Malley knew there were probably more radios in this area than anywhere in the world," Scully said, "and that for every guy listening on the beach at Laguna, some would come to the Coliseum." The Portable Vinny, coined Reilly, "may be the single largest influence on transistor radio sales in Los Angeles." Vinny didn't "do the Dodgers. Vinny is the Dodgers."

Congestion helped. O'Malley's son Peter would one day succeed him. "L.A. may be the most important radio market in the country," he said, "because of people traveling in their cars." Most eastern and central time games began on the Coast at 5 or 6 p.m. — "all when people were stuck in traffic," Bob Costas mused. "So they're in traffic for an hour, two hours, and they're listening to Vin Scully. This is how they first came into contact with major league baseball."

Knowledge helped. The March 19, 1958, *Sporting News* had Vin planning to live in New Jersey. "For a while I'd go back to Philadelphia and if I had a day off, I would try to get up to New York," he later said. "After a year in Los Angeles, I started to feel at home." Either place, Vin was the sole Voice "using the same detailed scorebook the writers did," said Rosenthal. Bill Roeder wrote, "He never gives you the feeling, as so many broadcasters do, that he spent his entire life building model planes in a cellar and didn't discover baseball until he got paid to talk about it." Greeting Snider after a game, wife Beverly asked if he choked up on the bat. Yes, about three-eighths of an inch. Why? "Vin Scully told me." She had never noticed at the park.

Literacy helped. In an inning, Vin could turn from phrase ("a terrier [fielder] nipped at an elephant's heels") via simile (pitching "like a tailor: a little off here, a little off there and you're done") to resolution (crowd roars, voice recedes). "They say radio is like skywriting," said Reilly. "The words, once spoken, merely float away to the winds, lost forever. But only Scully can still the sky." A batter "was pumping the wood back and forth." A game-starting walk was "a sour note to begin any concert." His register sang subtlety, telling fact, attention to detail, and standing in the player's shoes.

Finally, courtesy and hospitality bespoke how "Vinny respects the fans," Rick continued. "Vinny does not scream at you. Vinny does not try to impress you. Flip on the car radio, and you can almost see him riding shotgun, swapping stories," evoking a time before elbow-in-the-rib scatology, when cool and base cleaved, and a wiseacre deserved bile, not praise.

It helped, too, that most televised baseball locally disappeared.

In 1953 Jay Hanna (Jerome) Dizzy Dean began ABC's *Game of the Week* — TV sports first network series — two years later entering the swanker household of CBS. Ol' Diz sang "The Wabash Cannonball," read telegrams to "good ol' boys," and assaulted English. Runners "slud." Fielders returned to "their respectable positions." A hitter stood "confidentially" at the plate. "In the hinterlands, small towns, and especially the Sun Belt," said CBS Sports head Bill MacPhail, "watching Dean was religion." Each weekend Pleasantville closed down.

Game aired Saturday through 1956, next year adding Sunday, each barred within 50 miles of any major-league park. "Protect local coverage!" mused ABC's Edgar Scherick. Since St. Louis was the bigs's nearest city, Southern California didn't care. "Not a single market in the state was blacked out," said MacPhail, Larry's son. "Every town saw Diz": to Ron Powers, "a mythologizing presence," not courtly, like Barber; or Eastern, like Bill Stern; or lyric, like Vin. Los Angeles loved the 300 pounds, string tie, and Stetson—the whole rustic goods.

The 1957 Southland was mostly suburban, middle-class, white, and Protestant—*Grapes of Wrath* émigrés from the Dust Bowl and beyond. Ma Joad lived in Pomona and Whittier. In Dean, she found an Okie from Muskogee (actually, Lucas, Arkansas): Fenimore Cooper, greet Tennessee Ernie Ford. Even Hollywood read the Ozark encyclopedist. Bud Blattner was his 1953–59 partner—to Diz, "pod-nuh." Clark Gable golfed each Saturday. "He'd play nine holes," said Bud, "watch us in the saloon, then play nine more." Mail from TV Land blitzed CBS: "Bananas! Actors. Actresses," one celeb hailing another.

In 1957 Dean made Gallup's 10 most-admired list. Among other markets, the bigs's next-year odyssey KO'd *Game* in the City of the Angels and by the Bay. "L.A. and Frisco loved having the Dodgers and Giants," said MacPhail, "but not necessarily at the cost of losing Diz." Many called and wrote affiliates. Some drove to hotels beyond the 50-mile blackout radius or bought roof antennas to catch the son of a migratory cotton picker. Stewart recalls a Saturday. "San Diego was far [122 miles] from Los Angeles, so the CBS affiliate carried Diz. Dad'd be up on the roof trying to clear the picture. Otherwise, no network ball."

A 1958 Californian found local-team TV axed, too. Brooklyn televised each home game. In L.A., O'Malley broadcast almost *none*. "To see the club," wrote Tommy Holmes, "the new Dodger fan had to advance cash in hand." The change gave Vin vast leverage. It upped attendance, hiking interest; made radio preeminent, of which Scully was a wiz; and illumined his command of language: twilight's "little footsteps of sun-shine"; "he fought it [an elusive grounder] to a draw"; "he catches the ball gingerly, like a baby chick falling from the tree." Vin once said, "There's something redundant about giving noisemakers to youngsters under 14 years of age."

One Saturday the Dodgers played the Cubs. "I'm *Game*'s WBBM Chicago stage manager," said Al Schwartz, later producer, Golden Globes and American Music Awards, now Senior V.P., Dick Clark Productions, "and sitting in the press room with people, including Diz." Visiting, Vin leaves. "Pod-nuh," Dean says, "there goes the best commentator in the game." Until 1958, baseball in Los Angeles meant the Pacific Coast League—and Diz. "Now the Dodgers had to sell," said Murray, "and Vinny did it," airing 190, including 36 exhibition, games.

"He was more than just their announcer when the Dodgers came west," Jim continued. "He was the link to the great Dodger past explaining the new family in the block." Baseball is "a game of lagging periods, and he distracts you, like a Celtic poet. He'll segue into a story about Duke Snider that happened years ago, and do it so smoothly you'd swear Duke was playing. It's almost impossible to overstate his worth to the team—somewhere between a twenty-game winner and 100-runs-batted-in hitter": to wit, how L.A. soon forgot Dean.

KMPC AM's 11-outlet network ferried Scully to Las Vegas and Cali-fornia's Bakersfield, Banning, Blythe, Brawley, Indio, Lancaster, Palm Springs, San Bernardino, Santa Barbara, and San Luis Obispo. "They'd never had baseball," Harwell was saying. "As Vin observed, you had a lot of factors helping there that didn't exist elsewhere. What made it click was Vinny, who beautifully narrates without gimmicks": a description of Ernie, too.

The Georgian smiled, 91 turning 21. "It was a great marriage given the team's history, their novelty, and Vin's ability to express." On February 15, 1958, Vin himself married not the actress but dark-haired model Joan Crawford in California. Three children followed: Michael, born in 1960; Kevin in 1963; and daughter Erin in 1971.

"L.A. WAS SO BIG [that] it was really a time of adjustment for everyone," Scully later told the *Los Angeles Daily News*'s Tom Hoffarth. His first adjustment—where to live—was affected by Vin's 1945 stay in San

Francisco. At the time, he had a friend in the Marines, based in Camp Pendleton, near Los Angeles. Scully took a free Navy transport flight, met his pal, and "we'd walk around looking for movie stars" on Hollywood Boulevard.

Once they saw Harold Peary, radio's *The Great Gildersleeve*. Another day the servicemen got dinner on a lark from a girl "driving by," said Hoffarth, "in a convertible." Eating at her home, Vin asked its location. A part of town named Brentwood, she replied. Thirteen years later the Dodgers roomed at downtown's Biltmore Hotel until meeting "the [team's] gentleman," Scully said, "in charge of helping get everyone settled. I asked, 'Where's Brentwood?'" A hopscotch (15 miles) from the Coliseum.

Renting a small apartment, Vin one day carted home an armful of groceries. Spotting him, a Good Samaritan opened the gate to the apartment complex courtyard. The neighbor introduced himself: John Wooden, starting his eleventh year as UCLA's basketball coach. On Tuesday, April 15, 1958, another sport took precedent: baseball's transplanted tag-team opener in San Francisco. Ruben Gomez retired L.A.'s first batter, Gino Cimoli — strikeout, looking.

Three days later, despite independent outlet KTTV Channel 11's telecast, a National League record 78,682 packed L.A.'s home debut: "curious fans," said Erskine, pitching. "We had to earn being heroes." Helping: "Good afternoon, everybody, this is Vin Scully speaking to you from the Los Angeles Coliseum as Opening Day has finally come to Southern California." The rivalry traveled well. "After [apparently] tying the game in the ninth," Vin later said, "[Jint] Jim Davenport was called out for failing to touch third [on Willie Kirkland's triple]": Dodgers, 6-5. Soon Scully began a fund. "Every time Jerry or I said 'Brooklyn' Dodgers, we'd put $1 toward a needy kid, say, trying to buy a glove."

The '58ers could have used a team. Newk was swapped. Snider slid to 15 homers. Gilliam led with just 145 hits; Furillo, 83 RBIs; Podres, 3.73 ERA. The ex-dynasty finished seventh. "Realizing that I was trying to be anecdotal," said Vin, "some players were coming to *me* with stories." Producer David Wolper built a Dodgers baseball museum, Scully and Babe Herman board members, on Wilshire Boulevard. The first three-game series drew 167,209; games 1–9, 377,601; July 3, 66,485, a twi-night doubleheader. Attendance (1,845,556) dwarfed '57's (1,028,258): "fantastic," Finch wrote, "considering the [team's] subterranean status." Supernatural was June 3's "Dodgers Referendum" to let O'Malley buy Ravine acreage. "If this bill fails," stormed Giles, "the Dodgers will leave." Its vote pivoted on O'Malley's five-hour June 1 KTTV "Dodger Telethon."

Joe E. Brown emceed. Jack Benny, George Burns, William Frawley, Jerry Lewis, and Debbie Reynolds, among others, pitched. O'Malley and Poulson pleaded. Nearly 2 million watched. More than 7,500 welcomed the team, in a DC-7, returning from Chicago. Scully, Finch wrote, introduced "the gang as it stepped down the landing ramp," helping the referendum pass. To Councilwoman Wyman, "It was a matter of argument, conviction, salesmanship." Chavez was choice real estate. Hearsay charged hidden oil and mineral rights. Trying to block the sale, "their [opponents'] stand was that it was a giveaway." The State Supreme Court twice ruled for O'Malley. On October 19, the U.S. Supreme Court ditched the Ravine's last appeal.

"It wasn't easy," said the Irish Tory. "The squatters and a goatherd had to be evicted." One family slugged a visiting U.S. Marshal. Ground broke September 17, 1959, Vin emceeing. Pols staged a "spading" contest. Players took up position on rock-strewn land. On signal, said the *Sporting News*, "seven huge tractors began gouging." Two days later, O'Malley began "the task of constructing what he terms the perfect baseball stadium."

Fused: 21,000 precast concrete units. Removed: more than 8 million cubic yards of earth. Bossed: by architect and engineer Captain Emil Praeger. Constructed: by more than 340 workers. "A ballpark built into the land," said Scully of "'Golden Gulch.' What a future." Six miles away, in as *im*perfect a stadium as baseball had seen, the present seemed sublime.

"KEY TO COPING," Vin said, much later, "is work." In late 1958 he launched a weekday 15-minute drive-time program. The poor boy never forgot his youth. One night he ordered cereal, sliced banana, and milk at a hotel. Cost: $2.75. "Sure, it was a *big* bowl of cereal, but whoever heard of paying 90 cents for a *banana*?" Above all, talk remained as essential as breath.

At dinner, Vin and Allan Roth—"He can't run, throw, or go to his left," wrote the *Times*'s Jeane Hoffman. "But he can write with his right and swing a pencil high and wide"—decided to order wine.

The waiter brought Chablis 1953, leading Scully to inspect the label. "Was this a good year, 1953?" he asked.

"*Was* it?" said Roth. "We won by 13 games."

Another night Vin played a guessing game in the clubhouse: given initials, identify the name.

"E.C.," Cimoli instructed in the orchestra/band leader category.

"Eddie Condon," Vin guessed.

"Earl Conroy," said Reese, wrong, too.

For five minutes Cimoli let them twist. Finally: "Exavier Cugat." Danny Kaye might have known.

That June, Vin and the Brooklyn-born actor ate at a restaurant in Philadelphia.

"I'll have a draft beer," Kaye told a waitress.

"Sorry," she rasped, "but we don't carry draft beer in a bottle."

Danny paused: "Is it all right to have a bottle and drink it out of the glass?"

"What are you?" she smiled. "A comedian?"

An Angeleno still smiles about 1959. Despite guides and annuals consigning the Dodgers near the basement, they never trailed by more than 5½ games. A preacher's son, Maurice Morning Wills, became Vin's "The Mouse That Roared." The Duke knighted 88 RBIs, Charlie Neal and Wally Moon had a league-high 11 triples, and Moon's wrong-field "Moon Shots" fell over the Bamboo Curtain. The trumpet "C-H-A-A-R-G-E!" evoked USC-UCLA. Deposits filled The O'Malley Banque. Used to Ebbets Field, a Sportsman's Park—"Everywhere [but the Polo Grounds] was relatively small," said Scully—"to suddenly come here and see 80,000 at one game—that was overwhelming."

Exempla gratia. On May 7 professional baseball's then-largest crowd, 93,103, feted Campanella before a Dodgers-Yankees exhibition. Four years earlier, Reese, moved by his birthday bash, asked Campy to steady him at the plate in Ebbets Field. Now, in turnabout, he wheeled Roy across the first-base line toward the mound. Beautifully, magically, Scully began to speak, like no announcer before or since: "The lights are going out in this final tribute to Roy Campanella, and everyone at the ballpark, 93,000 people, are asked in silent tribute [on signal] to light a match. . . . And we would like to think that as 93,000 people light a match, that would be 93,000 prayers for a great man."

Later, Campy said, wistfully: "my number backwards"—39.

Vin resumed: "The lights are now starting to come out, like thousands and thousands of fireflies, starting deep in center field, glittering around to left, and slowly the entire ballpark"—then, indelibly, "a sea of lights at the Coliseum. Let there be a prayer for every light, and wherever you are, maybe you in silent tribute to Roy Campanella can also say a prayer for his well-being." Finally: "Roy Campanella, for thousands of times, made the trip to the mound to help somebody out: a tired pitcher, a disgusted youngster, a boy perhaps who had his heart broken in the game of baseball. And tonight, on his last trip to the mound, the city of Los Angeles says hello."

At such a time, Vin seemed to splice a listener and his game.

ON JUNE 21, now-Red Don Newcombe reached first base for one of six times in the game. Ahead, 17-1, he told behemoth Frank Howard, "Next up, I'm throwing batting-practice speed. Let's see how far you hit it." Hondo hit it "578 feet, 14 rows from leaving the Coliseum." On July 29, 1958, the Dodgers had bottomed out: eighth in an eight-team league. A year later they took the National League's same-date lead. The Giants remained public enemy No. 1. Mays pulled a drive that umpire Dusty Boggess called fair. "Gil Hodges, right now, is jaw to jaw with Boggess . . . Drysdale appealing to the gods," said Vin, who appealed to prose. Don Zimmer "will be hoarse in two minutes," and gladly: Boggess reversed the call. The U-turn made Jints manager Bill Rigney "about ready to eat his glasses . . . mad as a traffic cop." L.A. skipper Walter Alston "walked away like a Philadelphia lawyer who has just won his case"—or had he? Ump Tom Gorman awarded a ground-rule double: "the loudest double ever heard."

On NBC, Scully found the Coliseum one-third empty for 1959's weekday second—his first—All-Star Game. The noise meter rose August 8: 90,751 (67,132 paid) watched the Bums and Braves. Three weeks later, 82,974 saw Koufax fan 15 Giants in the first eight frames. Eddie Bressoud commenced a 2-all ninth: "Cut on and missed!" Sandy then "got him [Danny O'Connell] looking!" to tie Dean's single-game 17-K league high. Bob Feller's bigs record was 18. "Koufax is shooting for all the marbles. . . . Fastball, got him [Jack Sanford] swinging!" Sanford began *his* ninth, relieved by Al Worthington, who pitched to Moon. "There's a high fly ball to deep left field! It is gone!" Forty seconds later: "This was the night!"

Eleven nights later the Dodgers hosted Pittsburgh. A "direct line to San Francisco" let Scully report Jints-Phils. "Well, we're doing two games, almost simultaneously. Boy, if someone turns in late, feeling good, they're really going to get confused." Philly led, 1-0, in the ninth. "The crowd here at the Coliseum, many of them with transistors, and the oohs and ahhs really whirling around the saucer." The saucer shook as Orlando Cepeda lofted—"and it is caught! Philadelphia won it!" On September 15, "[Milwaukee's] Joe Adcock cleared the screen but the ball struck a girder and lodged in the mesh," Vin recalled. "The umpires ruled it a double, then homer when fans shook the screen and the ball landed in seats behind, then reversed themselves." Adcock never scored, L.A. winning. "A homer, and the Braves take the pennant by two games." Instead, each finished 86-68.

The Dodgers took a 3-2 best-of-three playoff opener. Next day, behind, 5-2, they "came roaring back in the bottom of the ninth," cried Scully, "and 36,000 people are roaring with them." Four singles and a sacrifice fly tied the score. In the 12th inning, Hodges led off second. Furillo swung. "Big bouncer over the mound, over second base. Up with it is [Felix] Mantilla, throws low and wild! Hodges scores! [L.A., 6-5] *We go to Chicago!* . . . The Cinderella team in the National League . . . and it had to be the Dodgers!"

A photo shows Gil, arms raised, scoring. Umpire Al Barlick eyes the plate. On deck, Wills exhales. "A city honked its horns," Wyman smiled, "and banged its pots and pans in the living room." A *New Yorker* cartoon quoted Ernest Thayer's *Casey at the Bat* above a Brooklynite crying at Ebbets Field: "Somewhere the sun is shining, somewhere hearts are light." Somewhere now meant the Coliseum: also, Chicago's two-tiered, arch-windowed, white-cubed Comiskey Park.

By 1959 the Yankees had waved nine pennants in a decade. Pennant-less since 1919's Black Sox, the White Sox no longer worried about peaking too soon. Cy Younger Early Wynn went 22-10, Nellie Fox hit an MVP .306, and Luis Aparicio became the first great Latin shortstop. "We beat you, 2 to 1," said Sox WCFL Radio's Bob Elson. "No Murderers' Row"— rather, pitching, defense, and speed. On September 22, Chicago won the American League flag. Mayor Richard Daley then activated air raid sirens. "Prophetic," mused Bob, their wail preceding his.

Improbably, Elson and NBC Sports director Tom Gallery had grown up on the same Chicago block. "They'd rubbed each other wrong as kids," said the Peacocks' Lindsey Nelson. "Plus, Tom thought Bob was a lousy announcer, not nearly, say, in Mel Allen's league. I remember Gallery shouting, 'That bastard won't do our Series [TV]!'" Problem: NBC needed a Pale Hose Voice. "You know," Nelson said, finally, "Jack Brickhouse does their [WGN] television. You could name him with Scully," and did.

Allen and Byrum Saam did NBC Radio. Other Voices listened, glumly. Until May 26, no one had pitched a perfect or no-hit game for more than nine or 11 innings, respectively. Earl Gillespie described Pittsburgh's Harvey Haddix retire 36 straight Braves. In October, he went golfing. "Those damn Dodgers! With wins the last day of '56 and '59, I make four straight Series." In San Francisco, Russ Hodges cursed the calendar: The Jints had led September 19. Elson was still wintry near his 1976 death. "Not doing the Series was the biggest hurt of my career."

By contrast, NBC TV viewers topped a composite record 120 million, including Game 6's still-high 90 million: growing up in rural New York, my first baseball tickler. "NBC paid [a then-extraordinary sports high] $3 million for Series exclusivity," said Lindsey. "Leave it to Vin to make them feel they underpaid."

BROOKLYN WAITED 55 years for a happy Classic ending. Like Scully, California got one in Dodgers' Year Two. Coca-Cola later produced the 35-minute highlight film: Dick Borden, producer; Lou Fonseca, director; Martin Bovey, Jr., editor; voice-over, Scully. "It's World Series time," he said, "but what a change of scenery for baseball's great drama." The lens eyed Comiskey Park; then "Los Angeles, which never has had a Series"; then Willard Mullin's bric-a-brac: Ted Kluszewski, slugging; Norm Larker, swinging; Little Looie, eluding Wills's tag.

"Save some runs!" a fan pled of the Pale Hose Game 1 seven-run third inning/Kluszewski two home run/providence-exhausting rout. "Klu really whacks one! Deep to right field!" said Vin. "Larker goes away back! To the base of the wall! And this one is gone! In the lower deck! Home run, Kluszewski!" Chicago soon led, 8-0, except that eight was not enough.

Thrice hitting 40 or more homers, Kluszewski had become baseball's Christian Dior. "We had these heavy woolies. I'd feel cramped," Ted explained, cutting his sleeves at the shoulder. His bare-arm look made women throw propriety in the pit. In the fourth, Adonis hit again. "Klu belts another one!" cried Scully. "Deep to right field! It goes all the way upstairs for his second home run!"—final, 11-0. Next day, Senator John

F. Kennedy, readying to run for President, sat in Daley's box. The early precincts pleased.

"Landis scores to give the Sox a quick 2-0 lead," Vin said of Sherm Lollar's single. In the fifth, Charlie Neal drove to left. "It's Al Smith, and not [Hose pitcher Bob] Shaw, who takes the shower. Unintentionally, an eager fan knocks over his drink. And in front of 40,000, Al Smith takes a [beer] bath in left field." The photo won an Associated Press award. In the seventh, the home team lost its 2-1 lead. Chuck Essegian pinch-dinged. Neal then "rips into the ball again for a long drive to deep center," pitcher Billy Pierce snatching it in the White Sox bullpen.

Behind, 4-2, Chicago countered. "Smith gets ahold of one and drills it into deep left-center field!" Vin said. "Over goes Moon, but it's going to the wall for a double. Torgeson scores. Moon plays the rebound to Maury Wills. His relay to Roseboro cuts Lollar down at the plate by a big margin." Dodgers win, 4-3. "The World Series is all even!" moving to a place it had never been.

"Now, BY JET to Los Angeles," Scully mused, "and the first World Series west of the Rockies. This is Los Angeles, where a long-time dream of big-league baseball suddenly came true two years ago." Film showed visors and binoculars, sunglasses and escalators, hausfrau dresses and Hawaiian shirts. The California Republic flag flapped. TV's *Lassie* star Robert Bray chowed. O'Malley, "with his wife, Kay, happily surveying the scene."

Game 3's 92,394 record Series crowd rolled away, row after row. "[Pinch-hitter] Furillo rams one up the middle," Scully said in inning seven. "Aparicio comes over but the ball takes a bad hop and goes for a [two-run] base hit into center field": Los Angeles, 3-1. Next day was "a Monday, but you wouldn't know it at the Coliseum [another record 92,650]. It looks like a holiday!" Behind, 4-1, "Lollar connects. A long drive to deep left field! It's away out and gone! Fox, applauding happily, and Kluszewski tallying ahead of Lollar. The score is deadlocked!" Hodges then played Screeno. "There it goes! Al Smith goes away back to the base of the fence! But she is gone! Here comes Gil! And the Dodgers are back in front, 5 to 4!" —3-1, in games. A tear grew in Brooklyn.

"The fans are in a gay mood!" Scully prefaced Set 5. "The Dodgers need only one more victory [before a still-record 92,706] to give Los

Angeles its first baseball championship of the world!" Shaw and Sandy Koufax parlayed, warming up. Reliever Larry Sherry, twice saving victory, "has a reason to grin." L.A. trailed, 1-0, in the seventh: two on and two out. "Neal slams the ball deep into right-center! Landis speeds toward it—but now [Jim] Rivera comes across and makes an over-the-shoulder catch!" The Sox escaped expiration, not knowing for how long.

Wynn claimed he would deck his grandmother to win. In Game 6, crying uncle, he was dinged by Snider, "look[ing] like the slugger of old as he levels on Wynn's pitch." By the ninth, "only Aparicio stands between the Dodgers and victory!" Vin cried. "Little Looie flies out to Wally Moon! ... The Dodgers win, 9 to 3, and bring Los Angeles its first world baseball championship! The players swarm around Larry Sherry!" Chicago skipper Al Lopez blamed the righty's 12⅔ innings, 8 hits, and 0.71 ERA. Aparicio scored "the white shirts, noise, those crazy dimensions." Said Fox: "It was a great year." The Hose's 43 runners left on base made the Dodgers' season greater.

With handheld mike, Scully faced the post-final's camera. Alston, players, and coaches jammed the clubhouse floor. In 1938, Mel Allen, 25, had ad-libbed 52 minutes about boat races and tennis matches from a plane above Long Island as rain delayed the Vanderbilt Cup Auto Race. "He went up a kid from a [CBS Radio] turntable department," wrote Ron Powers. "He came down a star." Vin entered 1959 as a phenom. He left it as a phenomenon.

BARBER HAD TOLD Scully to be himself. That fall Vin began to wonder who he was. "Living on the West side," he later told *Variety* magazine, "all of a sudden there were placards on all the lampposts all through Westwood and Brentwood, and it was Vincent Scully lecturing at UCLA": the famed Yale architecture professor and historian. Baseball's Scully was approached all winter by proud pops, son in tow. "Their boy'd memorized the Mantilla call," Vin laughed. "Now Dad had him recite it."

At 32, Scully was still Joe College. The *Saturday Evening Post* quoted Frank Frisch saying, "They don't make ballplayers like they used to." Irked, Rose Hill '49 told him: "And another thing—they're even playing better ball now at Fordham!" In December, Vin won *Look* magazine's 1959 Broadcast Excellence Award for Series play-by-play. The Southland was unsurprised.

"L.A.'s a vast stretch between the coast and the desert," *ESPN The Magazine's* Eric Neel one day wrote, "a spread-wide place, with communities distant and often cut off from one another." Pulitzer Prize author Theodore H. White quoted a local politico on sprawl sans core: "Out here, people are lost. They have no one to talk to. And the doorbell-ringer has an importance far beyond his normal . . . quality." Scully became "Los Angeles's greatest living treasure," said *Daily News*er Paul Oberjuerge, "the one intellectual concept that a fractured, fractious region can agree upon" because he sounded like a doorbell-ringer, someone to trust and whom you'd want to know.

Shrewdly, O'Malley had telecast the '58ers last eight games from San Francisco, "leaving the door open for screening additional road games in the populous Southern California area," wrote Finch. Bavasi grasped why: "A ploy to pass the referendum, and it worked." Next year just two clubs only televised away: Athletics (10 games) and Angelenos (11 from Frisco). "[TV] is a public service," said Walter, sensing supply meets demand. "The Dodgers will derive no . . . revenue from telecasts" aired by American Tobacco Co. and Pabst Brewing's Eastside Old Tap Lager Beer. That changed by 1960: Video rights hit $600,000. Radio got a new flagship (KFI 640) and sponsor (Union 76 Oil). "KMPC cut night power," Doggett said. "KFI's [50,000-watt] clear channel blanketed the West."

In February, O'Malley "overpaid [$494,000 for the Ravine's $92,000-valued property]," Murray wrote, "while his team underplayed [fourth]." Of a National League–record 2,253,887, most drove from downtown (10 minutes in light traffic; 30, peak), parking in 8,000 state/private-owned spots. "In Brooklyn, people'd take the subway," O'Malley said. "We had to reckon with the automobile." Inside, up to 500 vended. Charbroiled hamburgers and French dip sandwich (roast beef and ham) led the menu. It sold out for the Giants.

"Later the rivalry faded for a time," Doggett said, "but at first it was like back east." Mays regularly hurt the Bums—except when "Jocko Conlan umped. For some reason he wouldn't call Willie safe." Once Jocko lost John Roseboro's belt in the dimly lit Coliseum. "Did the ball go over [the inner fence]?" he pined. "No," lied Willie, avenging, "it went through a [fictional] hole." John got a ground-rule double. Another fly neared right fielder Felipe Alou. "Lost it in the sun," Alston explained, "but Mays covered so much ground that he caught the ball in right, threw to the plate, and kept the guy from scoring." A writer asked if the play was planned. The only plan—Mays's—was God's.

Slices of a season: the early 1960s. Scully hired a stenographer to answer hundreds of weekly letters. Allen's secretary split mail into pro and con. Vin's little of the latter involved "people who call you a big jerk or dunderhead." On Radio Appreciation Day he was "showered with gifts," said the *Times*. Another day many of the 85,065 in attendance tried to hear what Scully had to say. For three innings he said nothing. "The radio went dead. Finally, I renewed contact by talking into a telephone."

One game a batter topped the ball, dropped his stick, left for first, and had the ball hit the bat. Arguing, Milwaukee skipper Birdie Tebbetts protested the game, saw Scully, and stopped near his booth: "Vinny, do you have a rule book?" Catching it, Birdie checked the rule, then said "something along the lines of 'Darn it,'" Vin smiled. Before Tebbetts could tell the umpires, Scully announced that Birdie had withdrawn the protest, chirping that he was wrong.

Ex-Brook Roger Craig saw Scully in Arizona: "I can't pitch out here. My spitter dries halfway to the plate." At Vero Beach, Vin awoke to a wail of "Go-go!" Sleeping, roommate Leo Durocher was still coaching third. Once the Lip bawled at Conlan, kicking him in the shins, being booted back, and rekicking Jocko, finding shin guards under his pants.

Another night—"a particularly dull game, so I started looking for some color"—Scully began perusing the National League *Green Book*. There it was! Umpire Frank Secory's same-date birthday: August 24.

On a whim, Vin took a chance. "I said over the radio, 'I'll count to three and everybody yell, Happy birthday, Frank.'"

Scully: "One, two, three."

The Coliseum's cast of thousands: "Happy birthday, Frank!"

Vin aired the second 1960 and 1962–63 All-Star Games with Allen, Curt Gowdy, and Joe Garagiola, respectively. The National Sportscasters and Sportswriters Association of America named its first "Best Sportscaster": Mel, beating Scully, Blattner, Dean, and Nelson. Each bigs team's No. 1 Voice shared a WNEW New York 1960 preview show: To Vin, "It's great to be back." Dodgers official Arthur E. (Red) Patterson differed, pouring salt in the Apple's wound. "Back in New York, we could go to work quietly at this [off-season] time on such things as yearbooks, spring training plans, and press brochures. Here the fans demand baseball action of some sort just about the year round."

As much as any player, Vin linked a canal (Gowanus) and ravine. Archives contain his August 25, 1960, reply to a letter about Brooklyn's "Atlantic Nine of 1868." The historian longhand wrote:

> The Atlantics were from the Williamsburg section of Brooklyn first organized in 1857. They were part of an Association of 24 teams from New York and New Jersey. A pitcher with the Brooklyn Stars was supposedly to have thrown the first curve against the Atlantics in 1865. The first steal of a base was against the Atlantics in 1865. The Atlantics used the first bunt in 1866. The Atlantics beat the Cincy Red Stockings on June 14, 1870, in the most celebrated game of the time. Cincy had won 78 straight without a tie until this game. Sincerely, Vin Scully.

Next month Bob Costas, 8, moved from Long Island to Los Angeles, his TripTik the car radio. Prince meant western Pennsylvania; Gillespie, the upper Midwest; Caray, Cardinals Nation. In Nevada, Costas heard Scully. The Portable Vinny was becoming The Franchise. "We can hear the Dodgers," Bob's father said. "We're almost there."

NEAR CINCINNATI, Costas learned why Mark Twain vowed to return for the apocalypse because the city lagged 20 years behind the time. Wireless as metaphor: Waite Hoyt's tense was past. The ordinary announcer says, "Ground ball to the shortstop, who catches it and throws to first." Whatever else he was, the Reds' 1942–65 Voice was not ordinary: "The shortstop caught it, threw to first, and the runner beat the throw." Reason: "accuracy!" Waite said. "As I speak to you, what happened a moment ago is gone."

Hoyt grew up in Brooklyn, pitched for seven teams, and found "the secret to success — getting a job with the Yankees": 157-98 in 1921–30. Retiring in 1938, the minstrel's son, Palace Theater singer and dancer, and part-time mortician turned to Reds radio, missing the 1945–55 first division. "Scully was a *good*-news broadcaster," he huffed. "The Reds made me a *bad*-news announcer."

On August 6, 1961, Wills hit his first homer in 1,167 bigs ups. Rusty, he raced to first, finally heard the crowd, looked up, slowed down, and

almost tripped. "I get home, expecting my teammates to meet me on the
top step of the dugout," Maury said. "Instead, they're all lying on the
ground like they had fainted." Ten days later, Cincy blanked L.A., 6-0 and
8-0, before a Coliseum league twi-night record 72,140. "Drysdale [thrice]
knocked Frank Robinson down," said Hoyt, "then hit him and got tossed."
A three-game Reds sweep took the lead—for good.

Robby became MVP. Vada Pinson hit .343. By September 26, Cincinnati neared its first post-1940 flag. "We fly home after clinching a tie,"
said manager Fred Hutchinson, "drive downtown, and thousands line
the road." In Fountain Square, loudspeakers blared Bucs-Dodgers play-
by-play. L.A.'s elimination—Gilliam flied to Bob Skinner at 11:26 P.M.—
uncorked joy in Lynchburg and Loudonville and Springdale and Sardinia.
A Dodgers title would have put Vin on Series television. Instead, Garagiola
joined Allen, Hoyt doing radio.

Scully returned to a secret life. "He'd have loved to be a song-and-
dance man," Ben Platt mused. In December, O'Malley was named Beverly
Hills B'nai B'rith Man of the Year. The would-be hoofer did a skit, "Is
This Your [Walter's] Life?" In Washington, Kennedy soon ended a first
year as President, his "picture of total urbanity," a writer said, "the first
true reflection in the Presidency of America at the turn of mid-century, a
country of city dwellers, long gone from Main Street": like Vin.

Each liked the ancient Greeks' definition of happiness: "the full use
of your powers along lines of excellence," hating the second rate in others
and themselves. Each was a middle-brow: Sinatra, Fitzgerald, Crosby.
Mrs. Kennedy called Jack's favorite song "Hail to the Chief." Vin could be
heard singing a Broadway tune. A group of Nobel Prize laureates became
"the most extraordinary collection of talent," said JFK, "ever gathered
together in the White House—with the possible exception of when Thomas
Jefferson died alone." Increasingly, Scully's collection domineered a booth.

By 1961, Vin later said, "they were turning the dirt at Chavez Ravine,
and so we all knew this golden palace on the other side of the horizon."
Koufax set a league single-season (269) strikeout record. The Coliseum
closed September 20: Dodgers 4, Cubs 3 in 13 innings. Since 1958, O'Malley's
temporary den had drawn a nonpareil 8,400,676. Ahead: what *Le Figaro* of
Paris, praising Kennedy, termed "a certain feeling of possibility."

6

YOU'RE THE TOP (1962–1966)

"OUR HOUSE IS A VERY, very, very fine house," sang Crosby, Stills, Nash, and Young. Urban, smart, and comely, Dodger Stadium was a very fine house.

In 1956, touring Japan, Walter O'Malley eyed ground-level suites— "dugout boxes"—between each dugout. By 1962 they joined the Ravine's five-tier seating, Santa Ana Bermuda grass, red brick and clay infield and warning track, and palm trees beyond the outfield. A 1960 aerial photograph, Frank Finch wrote, "shows Dodger Stadium beginning to take shape." Eventually, it cost twice the original $12 million estimate. "This will be a monument to the O'Malleys," the Irish Tory vowed of baseball's first privately financed park since Yankee Stadium in 1923.

Emil Praeger's original 85,000-seat plan with center-field fountain enclosed the hollow. O'Malley ditched it for a 56,000 unobstructed-seat capacity, close-up view of downtown and the San Gabriel Mountains, and terrace parking near any seat. "Say your ticket's on the third level," said Walter. "A parking space [actually 16,000] is a few hundred feet away." Hilda Chester's heir—"The Dodger Mom"—awaited each game's start. "She was always first in line," Buzzie Bavasi smiled, "then rode an escalator" to the orange-red, gold, or blue-colored deck. A pitcher liked length (330 feet, lines; 380, alleys; and 410, center) and foul ball–friendly turf. Added Jerry Doggett: "Ebbets Field, it ain't."

A 10-foot wood fence linked left-center and right-center field. The scoreboard touted Farmer John's sausage links and Phillips 66 motor oil. The concrete infield sired wacky hops. The sky was blue; weather, warm; aisles and seats, spick-and-span. Even the address penned baseball: 1000 Elysian Park Avenue, after its first park, Hoboken's Elysian Field.

ON MONDAY NIGHT, April 9, 1962, testing the organ, O'Malley and Rosalind Wyman walked the entire club level. "We had a wonderful time," she said. "We looked it over and said, 'There it is. Would you believe what we've gone through? And it's finally here!'" Next day a parade moved through Center City. O'Malley's Golden Gulch opened vs. Cincinnati: 52,562 watched; others became lost, had faux tickets, joined a freeway parking lot, or watched on television. Vin emceed pregame, Kay O'Malley and Podres tossing the first ball and pitch, respectively. First hit/run: Cincy's Eddie Kasko. Homer: mate Wally Post. Dodgers hit: The née-Duke of Flatbush. Run: Gilliam. The park brooked a Brooklyn twist: Praeger forgot to include water fountains. "Foul poles were in foul territory," said Jim Murray. "How would you homer? The National League ruled them fair, then moved the poles next year so they were."

The April 11 *Times* headlined, "Reds Crash Dodger Stadium Party": 6-3, Bob Purkey beating Podres. Koufax then won, 6-2, Gilliam the first Angeleno to go deep. A day later Pete Richert K'd six straight batters. In "some ways," The Franchise mused, "the Dodgers seemed a revolutionary"—actually, retro—"team. Pitching. More pitching. Plus Maury was in the process of changing how the game is played." To Scully, "Jackie Robinson [was] a runner. He had defiance. He ran like he had a chip on his shoulder. He was the only player I ever saw who could steal better when he was mad." Wills was "a nice little guy who steals bases. When Maury runs, it's all downhill." The Mouse That Roared forged baseball's extreme makeover.

"For years it'd been all power," chirped Wills. "I'd steal second and Jim Gilliam sacrificed me to third and I'd come home on an infield out." Ty Cobb held the bigs's stolen base record: 1915's 96. Maury swiped 104, became MVP and Associated Press Athlete of the Year, and wowed been there, done that. Casey Stengel spanned Tris Speaker and Tom Seaver. "Don't care who's hitting," he said. "I wanna see him [Wills] slide. He has the most amazing slide I ever saw." One game he homered twice, Vin skipping repetition (statistic) for reaction (stunned teammates'). Frank Howard had 31 taters. Tommy Davis led both leagues in batting (.346), hits (230), and team-record ribbies (153). Scully, as he said, had himself a ball: "This team is even more exciting to watch [than the '50s Dodgers]. It just runs and runs and runs."

Cy Younger Drysdale was 25-9, K'd 232, and pitched 314 innings. "He had to work a little harder," said catcher Roseboro, "but he was 100 percent meaner than Sandy, and everybody knew it." In 1960, Mr. K walked 100 in 175 innings. "[Even] batting practice," jibed a writer, "was like Russian roulette with five bullets." Planets then realigned. On June 30, 1962, suburban Claremont's Dave Fantz, 14, started feeding late-inning Dodgers-Mets tape into a reel-to-reel recorder. Forty years later, Fantz's nephew found the 40-minute tape "in a box, spent hours digitizing it to improve the sound quality and transfer it to CD," the *L.A. Times* wrote, "ignored advice from friends and co-workers to auction it off to the highest bidder, and happily handed it over to the company [Dodgers] that signed the artist [Vin]."

The artist daubed Koufax's ninth-inning coda: Gene Woodling's walk, force outs by Richie Ashburn and Rod Kanehl, and Mantilla, "capping Sandy's biggest night, maybe even more important to him than his [1959] 18 strikeouts against the Giants." Felix slapped "a 1-2 fastball . . . to Wills, he has it, goes to [Larry] Burright—no-hitter!" Koufax vanished under mates near the mound. "[Ron] Fairly with his arms around Sandy, pushing him toward the dugout! Other Dodgers leaping over the mob of players to just touch him."

Poetry: "And a shower of blue pillows down on the field," Vin said. "Sandy Koufax pitches a no-hitter for the Dodgers . . . the first Dodger left-hander to pitch a no-hitter since way back in nineteen hundred and eight."

Prophecy: "A sheepish grin on his face, and first of all, he will go on television back to New York—and perhaps Sandy's mother and dad back there stayed with the ballgame to watch their son pitch the *first* no-hitter"—more to follow.

Litany: "So Sandy Koufax joins a list of . . . Dodgers who have pitched no-hitters. They go like this—way back—oh, let's start at the turn of the century," naming 10 since 1906.

Finally: "To that great list, add the name Sandy Koufax, who gets another ovation as he goes jumping down into the Dodger dugout!"

Later, a photographer said: "Smile." Sandy: "I can't. I'm too nervous, too scared, and too tired." Next month Raynaud's phenomenon, numbing the pitching hand's palm and fingers, shelved him for nine weeks. The Dodgers led after July 7, then morphed like Kelso into a spavined nag. On September 30, Mays's 47th homer edged Houston, 2-1. The Jints then heard Scully from Chavez Ravine. St. Louis's Gene Oliver's dinger beat Podres, 1-0, New York's two expatriates ending the regular season tied.

"The rivalry in those days was still a carryover," said Drysdale. "And it was a heavy rivalry." As Peggy Lee sang, we had been this way before.

"WHERE IS WHAT I started for so long ago?" asked Walt Whitman's poem "Facing West from California's Shores." "And why is it yet unfound?" The Dodgers found Eldorado three time zones away. The Apple's other emigrant "went along for the ride," said Russ Hodges. "Given what went before, we didn't have a choice."

The 1954 champion Jints drew only 1,155,067. New York was changing, said future Voice Lon Simmons: "People at the ballpark got mugged." A two-foot-square Polo Grounds piece of sod moved West. Hodges trudged along, joining Simmons, 33. "When you're young, everything means more," Lon said. "You couldn't get closer to my emotions than the Giants' first years."

The '58ers played at 22,900-seat Seals Stadium. "On the street you heard baseball from a dozen directions," said a flagship affiliate KSFO official. "A restaurant had the radio on. People at the opera'd wear ear plugs." A holdout muttered, "Good God! People will think we're Milwaukee!" then shorthand for popping a civic cork. Upon a homer Russ cried, "Bye, bye, baby!" Baghdaders by the Bay cheered their own. "[Unlike Mays,] Cepeda, Felipe Alou, and Jim Davenport weren't New York's," said Simmons. Attendance doubled. "People loved the bandbox." Hodges, in turn, became Seals's seal.

"How ya' doing, everybody?" he began each game. The Giants' next home did not do well. Candlestick Park debuted April 12, 1960. The temperature dived at night. Wind mimed Mariah. "Distant, generic," said Vin, treating it like a dangling participle. The trick was looking past. Cepeda's swing was quick and wild. Willie McCovey's spun from longer gams than Lauren Hutton's. Juan Marichal high kicked like Gwen Verdon meets Gower Champion. Mays was Mays. Candlestick hosted the first 1961 All-Star Game: National League, 5-4. "All people remember," said Doggett, "is [Frisco's] Stu Miller, balking when a gale moved him." Headlines read "Miller Blown off Mound!" Reading the Miracle of Coogan's Bluff, the '62ers hoped to encore.

The best-of-three playoff opener was an 8-0 Jints runaway. As we have seen, the O'Malleys then won (8-7) baseball's longest (4 hours, 18 minutes) regulation game. Next day Wills got his fourth straight hit, stole second and third base, and scored on a wild throw — "the [1950s] unBrooklyns!" laughed Vin — giving L.A. a 4-2 seventh-inning lead. "All that effort for *what?*" Mays remembers asking: four ninth-inning Giants runs. Willie flung the last out into Dodger Stadium's bleachers. Like 1951, champagne left one clubhouse for the other.

"A funny thing happened to us while we were switching channels," said the *Times*. "The Dodgers fumbled away the pennant." The collapse cost Vin his fifth Fall Classic: "Losing feels worse," he said, "than winning feels good." Hodges had a reason to drink — not that he needed one. "The only way we won't drink is if we tie," he told a colleague. Curfew promptly extended an extra-inning game. "We're just gonna break a rule," he said. God broke the mold of many of the age's playmen.

IT IS CLEAR THAT in growing up in the 1950s and early '60s we were lucky, however vague and selective recall may be. "An amazing age," said Jack Buck, "of announcers" humane, more often human, capable of envy, also capable of art. Red and Mel. Prince and Brickhouse. Ernie Harwell and Byrum Saam. CBS's Dean and NBC's Wolff. Each could then be said to rival Vin in identity.

One announcer especially grasped the symbiotic relationship among the Dodgers, Giants, and 1962 Metropolitan Baseball Club of New York, Inc. "They were our parents," Lindsey Nelson mused of the expansion Mets. Even uniform colors tied Bums blue and Jints orange, touching the Apple's need for a ready and unifying eloquence.

In 1958 Mayor Robert Wagner forged a committee chaired by lawyer William Shea. Its aim: get *another* team to move to New York. Spurned by the Reds, Bucs, and Phils, Shea announced a prospective third major—

Continental—league. "It had heft," said historian Jerome Holtzman. "Threat of player raids and anti-trust suits made the National League expand." In 1961 the New York State Senate OK'd $55 million for the Queens site that O'Malley snubbed. Ground broke on Flushing Meadows Park. The expansion draft broke *old* ground. "[New manager] Stengel went for veteran New York players," mused Holtzman. "Craig, Hodges, Neal." Their temporary home was older: the Polo Grounds, gussied up with $250,000 in city cash.

The *Times* rumored that "Scully is secretly planning to shed his Dodger microphone and steal back to New York to report the exploits of the Mets." Instead, hiring Nelson, they got a princeling/professor of lyric lilt and country gabble. In 1962 Casey's "Metsies" gathered at St. Petersburg. "We got to work on the little finesses," Stengel said. "Runners at first and second, and the first baseman holding a runner, breaking in and back to take a pickoff throw." New York lost, 17-1. "The little finesses," he grasped, "ain't gonna be our problem."

A solution was Brooklyn, coming home. On May 30, a full house 55,704 hailed the Dodgers. "Even at the Polo Grounds, so many had Brooklyn caps," said The Franchise. Others had had enough. Lost in thought, Vin walked his childhood field before the game. A voice interrupted. "Hey, Scully, why don't you go back to L.A. Who needs you?" *E pluribus unum.* Shea Stadium was christened April 16, 1964, with Dodgers Holy Water from Brooklyn's Gowanus Canal and Giants Holy Water from the Harlem River at the point it passed Coogan's Bluff. Next day's pregame opener starred ex-Jints and ex-Bums. Mets lose, 4-3, to Pittsburgh.

Yarns still stitch the Amazins'. "The early Mets played for fun," said Nelson. "They weren't capable of playing for anything else. People loved us because we typified all the frustrations of the world's losers. If we ever advanced to mediocrity, it would be fatal." They did; it wasn't. Craig was hardship's poster child, losing 18 straight games. First baseman Marvin Eugene Throneberry conjured Alphonse at the plate and Gaston in the field. A mate dropped a fly. "What are you trying to do?" flushed Marvelous Marv. "Steal my fans?" A *New Yorker* cartoon showed several dejected Mets entering the dugout. A bystander says, "Cheer up. You can't lose them all."

In 1963 the question was whether Koufax ever would.

"As a person, modest, quite retiring, didn't like to be the center of attention," Vin said of Sandy. "On the mound, overwhelming. The only pitcher I ever saw who, within his first three pitches, I'd think to myself, 'Wow, this could be a no-hitter.'" Roseboro nodded. "If you've ever had a ball come about 90 miles an hour at your head, it screws up your thinking patterns. You have to think about safety before you think about hitting the ball hard."

On May 11 Koufax retired Mays to end the seventh inning. Relocated to La Jolla, California, Tom Oliphant sweated an 8-0 no-hitter. "If Uncle Wilbur is outside watering the lawn," Scully said, "you might tell him it's OK to turn off the hose and come inside for a while." Forty-five years later, his circuitry still made the *Boston Globe* columnist glow. Afterward, a writer asked what Mr. K was thinking. "About the bawling out I'll get from my parents," he said, icing an elbow. "I was supposed to leave them tickets at the gate, but I forgot." Sandy wed a 25-5 record, bigs-low 11 shutouts and 1.88 earned run average, and National League–record 306 Ks. Ron Perranoski was 16-3 with 21 saves. Los Angeles hit just 110 homers but had a post-1945 best 2.85 ERA. Restless, O'Malley never stopped trying to burnish the Dodger brand.

"A [June] testimonial was given to Scully during [a] Dodger-Giant game," wrote the *Times*'s Don Page. "More than 52,000 fans paid to visit the Taj O'Malley, and, it seems, about 40,000 brought transistor radios." Danny Goodman began baseball's first "novelties" department, vending a portable. "Everybody knows that no Dodger fan would be without one," Dick Young said, guessing that many left early because "they feel they can walk out, listening, without missing a thing." O'Malley staged a "Stadium Club Safari," flying 25 members to Dodgertown for nine days of sun, gin, and clinics, including Vin's "How to Keep Score," and increasingly teased baseball's first pay-cable Subscription TeleVision (STV): "It'll have a $5 installation, [$1] weekly charge, and our park's lowest ticket price [$1.50] per game." The service began July 17, Triple-A Albuquerque's Frank Sims announcing. Just 2,500 subscribed. "The technology and penetration weren't there yet," Doggett said. "For once Walter was *too* ahead of the curve."

For a decade, the Dodgers had been ahead of St. Louis. In 1942 and 1946 the Cardinals beat 104-50 Brooklyn and won a best-of-three playoff, respectively. "Then the rivalry changed," said Scully, receding to 1950s

Bums dominance, reviving in August 1963. Stan Musial, 42—"How good was he? Good enough to take your breath away"— homered his first up as a granddad. The Swifties went 19-1 to draw within a game. L.A. arrived for a three-set series, Murray's "Ghostly Echoes" column evoking 1962. Stan homered in the opener: Dodgers, 3-1. A day later Koufax blanked the Birds. Next door to Vin sat a Voice more often than not antipodal.

Scully exuded mellowspeak. Harry Caray screamed *we* and *come on* and *let's score a run*! Vin seemed baseball's man of letters. The Redbirds' polemicist was as subtle as a Joe Louis jab. "Two opposites, showing how there's no one road to popularity," said Doggett. "Find *who* you are, then sell *what* you are." It might be! The bigs's 1945–97 Jackie Gleason. It could be! The Maestro of the Seventh-Inning Stretch. It was! God breaking the mold *before* making Harry Christopher Caray. "Holy Cow!" lives, even now.

"Thank God I came along when I did," said Caray, airing America's once-southernmost and once-westernmost team. *Webster's* defines fan, derived from Greek fanatic, as showing "extreme zeal, piety, etc." Said a paper: "The greatest show, no ifs or buts, is to hear . . . Caray going nuts." On September 18, 1963, 124 KMOX network outlets from Webster, Iowa, to Cleveland, Tennessee, heard him broadcast the Dodgers' series final.

St. Louis led, 5-4, as just up-from-Spokane rookie Dick Nen batted. "Here it comes," Caray called a ninth-inning pitch. A soul-wracking stillness ensued. "Oh, my God," he finally said, using then-sacrilege. "It's over the roof!" (L.A. won in the 13th inning.) The Dodgers went over the moon, soon clinching their 11th pennant.

In 1989 Musial attended a seminar. "Stan," the moderator said, ".331 lifetime, what do you think you'd hit today—watered-down pitching, expansion?"

The Man replied, "Oh, .285, .290."

"Stan, you're a modest guy," he jousted, "but what are you talking about, .285, .290?" Musial said, "What the hell, I'm 69 years old."

In October 1963, Scully was 35.

WHITEY FORD's 24-7 record helped take the Stripes' fourth straight pennant. "For years he'd been the World Series," said Mickey Mantle of record wins (10), losses (8), starts (22), opening-game starts (8), innings (146), strikeouts (94), walks (34), and scoreless innings (33⅔ straight).

"Then Koufax comes along," ending his supremacy. The Classic shocked the Yankees—and their quarter-century marquee.

In 1958 Mel Allen aired the Milwaukee-New York Series. A wire arrived sent four hours before Game 2. "Allen, you Yankee-lover, shut up." Nelson differed: "The best of all time to broadcast the game"—depending on your view, a Saladin, random chatterer, or surpassing personality of the big city in the flesh.

CBS TV's 1957 prime-time *Person to Person* profiled Mel's cachet. Another first: *Variety*, naming him "among the world's 25 most recognizable voices." *Sports Illustrated* hailed "the most successful, best-known, highest-paid, most voluble figure in sportscasting, and one of the biggest names in broadcasting generally," airing each 1946–63 Series on network wireless or television. "How about that!" turned national idiom, binding stardom of name and game.

Bill Glavin, a teacher, grew up in Albany, at one time or another hearing the Dodgers', Yanks', Jints', or Mets' network. "Each year, the Nuns arranged for the Series to be piped into class over the loudspeaker. You'd hear from people you never knew —'The Duke [Snider] parked one' or 'Damn Yankees!'" Bill shook his head. "Games were daytime. You'd talk about it, hear or see it, then argue afterward." In 1963 he heard Allen's then-record 21st Classic, including nine vs. New York's bête noire. "Man alive," Mel said later, "I couldn't believe so many involved the Dodgers."

In 1953 O'Malley cornered him before the Series' opener. "Walter asked me to take care of his boy," Allen, 40, told Vin, 25. "Don't you worry about a thing." Two years later, Scully relayed a Jimmy Durante quip to writers Arthur Daley and Frank Graham: "Rooting for the Yankees is like rooting for U.S. Steel." In 1963, steel breaking, he voice-overed his second Series highlight film: "a monumental time for the franchise," Vin said later. "If you had any connection to the Dodgers, probably the sweetest moment in their history—not only to beat the lordly Yankees, but beat them in four straight."

The Grand Event began with Mel, deemed broadcasting's gold standard. It ended with Vin's coin supplanting him.

"It is no longer a Subway Series," Scully began baseball's more sepia than officially "color" film. "The Dodgers, once located in Brooklyn, now belong to Los Angeles." Ford and Koufax, "two of baseball's greatest southpaws," posed before The Stadium opener. A Marine color guard raised the flag. Musial threw out the first pitch. The Chairman of the Board's was a called strike to Wills.

Koufax began with a trailer of coming Ks: Tony Kubek, Bobby Richardson, and Tom Tresh. Next inning Frank Howard "connects with a powerful swing," said Scully. "There goes the ball. What a blast—almost hitting the wall [457 feet from home plate]! Howard is held to one of the longest doubles in Stadium history." Bill Skowron's single scored Hondo: 1-0. Dick Tracewski safetied to center field. "Johnny Roseboro [then] wallops a drive to right! If it's fair, it's a homer! And it is! The Dodgers have stolen the Yankee home run thunder," ultimately putting it in trust.

Mantle and Roger Maris strikeouts commenced the second inning. "That's five in a row!" Vin cheered. "Tying a [1943 Mort Cooper] Series record!" Nine of the first 12 Yanks fanned. By the ninth, Koufax, facing pinch-hitter Harry Bright, had tied Erskine's 1953 Game 3 K mark (14). "I guess I'm the only guy in baseball to have sixty thousand [*sic*, 69,000] cheering for me to strike out," Bright complied. Said Scully: "The fans are pulling for . . . the Brooklyn boy to break the record. . . . Koufax has his strikeout record—and the Dodgers have a 5 to 2 victory."

A day later Wills singled, was picked off at first base, but reached second on Joe Pepitone's errant throw. Gilliam singled and Willie Davis doubled. Skowron later homered to the opposite field: "Those right-field stands were a favorite target," Vin mused, "before the Yankees traded him to the Dodgers." Tripling, one Davis, Tommy, scored the other. Perranoski saved Podres, 4-1: "A surprised lead for the supposed underdog." Thereafter: shock and awe.

The Series' program cover showed two hats superimposed over Dodger Stadium. In Game 3, a sellout 55,912 watched batters fade. With two out, Tommy Davis slashed a first-inning ball to second. "Richardson gets in front of the ball, but it spins off to his left [off his shin] and caroms away! . . . Gilliam scores!" In the ninth, "Pepitone hits a long [two-out] drive to right. Fairly goes back. Back, back, and pulls it down near the fence!" L.A., 1-0. Next afternoon New York brought suitcases to Dodger Stadium. Howard began closing them. He "sends it rocketing into left field!" said Scully of the first man to hit the loge level. "It's back, back, away back into the corner of the second deck!"

The Fall Occasion "is accorded the greatest coverage of a sports event," he continued. Peacock Radio's starred Joe Garagiola and the man who shot a hole-in-one, invented a bottle-can opener, sang a duet with Pearl Bailey, and was baptized in the Jordan River. In *One Flew Over the Cuckoo's Nest*, Jack Nicholson plays a schizophrenic straining to hear Game 4 wireless. "Yep, the voice was mine," said Harwell. "Wish I got a residual." Instead, Ernie got to air Mantle's seventh-frame game-tying dinger. On NBC TV, Allen did, too, wheezing, "Going, going, gone!" To Vin, his serial nasal condition mimed "a wire closing the throat's trap door." Mel left the booth, swigging coffee and lemon juice. Scully took over, seldom looking back.

Gilliam led off the Dodgers' seventh inning by slapping to third base. "But Pepitone loses [Cletis Boyer's throw] in the white-shirt background," Scully said. "It hits him on the arm, and gets by him, bouncing down the right-field line!" Willie Davis flew to Mantle, scoring Junior. Mel returned in the ninth, rasping, "The Dodgers out in front, 2 to 1. Bobby Richardson the batter. Struck out, doubled to center, and grounded to short." He could barely speak. "The Dodgers on the verge! Ball one, low and inside. Good fastball. A one and one count."

"That's enough," Tom Gallery said.

"Wait a minute. One ball, one strike," Allen said hoarsely. Seizing Mel with two hands, NBC Sports's mandarin led him from the booth.

"Two and one the count to Bobby Richardson," Vin resumed, pinch-speaking, "and, Mel, we all understand . . . just hang in there." With two out, Elston Howard reached base on an error. Hector Lopez then dribbled out to Wills. "All bedlam," said Scully, "breaks loose on the field."

Like a ghost, Allen returned postgame. "In a moment we'll review the highlights of the game for you," he said, still unsteady. "Home runs by Howard and Mantle accounted for two of the runs and an error by Pepitone and a sacrifice fly gave the Dodgers the winning run and a sweep in four games, the first time the Yankees have been swept in four straight!"

Mel paused. "And that's the way it went today at Dodger Stadium as the Dodgers are now the world champions!"

How it went for one Voice differed from the other.

"I ALWAYS THOUGHT of Mel as a good-natured man who was consumed by the business," Vin said later. "I looked at him as a warning to me that I never wanted to get so caught up in being an announcer that I forgot

I was a man." Allen's last Rose Bowl was 1963. "His voice shrieked, rasped, bellowed, and sputtered," rued the *Times*, "as he flogged the NBC network with inaccuracies and clichés." Next year's Peacocks demoted him. That December, with no reason, not even a release, the Yanks fired their apotheosis. "Mel gave them his life," said Barber, "and they broke his heart."

The Stripes unofficially approached Scully. "Have you ever thought about coming back to New York?" asked an advertiser. "I'm happy in Los Angeles," Vin said; to Young, "playing a strong Yankee offer to get a raise." Replacing Mel, Garagiola got a telegram: "'Hope you stay on the job as long as I did.' I told him, 'I didn't know there were still guys like you around.'" Childless, unmarried, Allen began a decade of curiosa. Scully began a decade less of *SportsCenter* cynicism, *Inside Sports*'s Brad Buchholz wrote in 1998, "than something else—let's call it a sense of gentle humility—that transcends the smart-aleck posture of the day": as current as when "[1963] patrons delighted in carrying their portable radios into Dodger Stadium just to hear Scully's call."

That June a balk rule controversy referenced the pitcher pausing one second while stretching: "It's just hard," Vin noted, "to know how long that is." One night he got a stopwatch. "When I start the watch," Scully said on air, "I'll say the letter *A* and when you think a second has elapsed, you say *B*." The crowd twice boomed *B*. "Only Vin," mused Larry Stewart, "could get his audience at the park to be a straight man."

In 1961 the American League had expanded to Los Angeles. "News from the Angels camp was wholesome and happy," *Sports Illustrated* said. "It was one for all, all for one, and we're going to win our share [actually 70-91]." The Halos won little of Vin's audience, leaving Wrigley Field to become O'Malley's tenant. Ex-Dodgers flagship KMPC hired a familiar, easy name. "The Angels couldn't get *Diz*," Bud Blattner joked, "so they got *me*!" He had skill, vim, and a past as *pod-nuh*'s keeper. The Dodgers had tradition, cash, and Scully, treating the Halos, a writer said, "with tolerance rather than recognition."

One day Baltimore changed pitchers during a game at Chavez Ravine. "That's what we call it," said Angels owner Gene Autry: "No Dodger Stadium for us!" Fans began to applaud. Orioles' Voice Chuck Thompson told himself, "Wow, these are really great fans here in California, cheering Baltimore." Next day the O's again changed pitchers. Again fans cheered.

Thompson says, "What in the world is going on?" Binoculars surf the stands. A light goes on.

Thousands of Angelenos are wearing earplugs. "But they're not listening to our game," said Chuck. "They're tuned to *Scully*": a prolific pulling up of chairs.

THE 1962–65 HALOS drew one-third of O'Malley's gate—3,392,244 vs. 10,076,114—but paid 50 percent of toilet paper and cut and watered the grass. Autry owned a number of hotels. "I'd have a hell of a time getting people who rent rooms to water the posies. It's the responsibility of the landlord." O'Malley felt Gene a sponge. "The Angels play as many games in our 'hotel' as we do. Are we supposed to let everything die when they're at home?" The '64 Dodgers were dying on their own.

Attendance was 2,228,751 vs. 1962's major-league record 2,755,184. Allan Roth left for NBC baseball. Swimming upstream: Sandy, no-noing Philadelphia, 4-0; Nicholas Volpe painting Union Oil portraits of Big D, Mr. K, Gilliam, Roseboro, both Davises, and largely forgotten Wally Moon; and actor, licensed pilot, gourmet cook, and future bigs owner Danny Kaye—"a Renaissance man, and more," said Vin—singing a ditty written in 1962 by wife Sylvia and Herb Baker. It began, "So I say D. I say D-O. D-O-D. D-O-D-G. D-O-D-G-E-R-S!" and ended, "The team that's all heart. All heart and all thumbs. They're my Los Angeles—your Los Angeles—our Los Angeles—Do you think we'll really win the pennant?—Bums!"

Another pennant would have to wait. A continuum lay ahead. Nobody had thrown three no-hitters: Koufax threw four. 1962, National League–low .197 enemy batting average; 1963, MVP; 1964, league-leading winning percentage (.792) and earned run average (1.74); 1965, 26 victories, .765 percentage, 382 Ks, and fourth-straight league-best ERA (2.04).

"In this time," said first baseman Wes Parker, "he was hands down, without a doubt, the greatest pitcher in baseball history." Roseboro added: "I think God created one Sandy Koufax." One was sufficient for 1965's Buster Keaton Dodgers: minimalist, often silent, and rear view in time and place.

"FORGET THE STUPID ROBINS," Don Page wrote that March. "Spring hasn't arrived until you hear the first red-crested Scully." His '65ers flaunted the bigs's first regular switch-hitting infield (Parker, Jim Lefebvre, Wills, and Gilliam). Wes reminded Vin of TV's *Dr. Kildare*: "the kid you'd like to see ringing your doorbell when your daughter starts dating." Another, first baseman/outfielder Fairly, "should have a brother named Frank Merriwell." The Mouse swiped 94 bases. Tommy Davis broke his ankle. Replacing him after 12 years in the minors, Lou Johnson went deep a team-high 12 times. The Dodgers scored a third-worst 608 runs. Pitching had to compensate, and did.

On June 15 the Ravine swayed to the album *Sounds of the Dodgers*, written by *Herald-Examiner* Melvin Durslag; score, Sammy Fain; producer, Jackie Barnett; music, played by Eddie Freeman's orchestra. Durante sang "Dandy Sandy"; Stubby Kaye, "Soliloquy of a Dodger Fan"; Wills, "Somebody's Keepin' the Score"; and Willie Davis, "That's the Way the Ball Bounces." "Dodger Stadium" became a fight song. Vin narrated "The Story of the Dodgers." *Sounds*'s jingling noise—more than 100,000 copies sold—pleased O'Midas. August 22 showed what Alston said he learned in 23 years as skipper: "You make out your lineup card, sit back, and strange things happen."

Batting at Candlestick, Juan Marichal took a strike. Returning the ball to Koufax, Roseboro "threw it," Juan charged, "too close to my ear." John removed his mask, took a step toward Marichal, and felt a bat hit his head. "Baseball's most famous on-field fight," said Vin, proved worthy of the rivalry. Roseboro launched a hook; Mays applied a bear hug; Jint Tito Fuentes waved a bat. Warren Giles fined Marichal $1,750, suspended him eight games, and was called "a gutless so-and so" by Wills. Taking Sandy long, Willie swung the game. "While the Giants won the battle," The Franchise harmonized, "the Dodgers ultimately won the war."

By September 9, 1965, the now-perfect pitcher had done everything but throw a perfect game. Later, Salon.com's Gary Kaufman read the transcript of Scully's last half inning, taped after Vin, phoning KFI, had the station record it. "It read like a short story," he wrote. "It had tension, rising and falling drama, great turns of phrase. It was, and still is, the best piece of baseball writing I've ever seen. And it came off the top of his head, at a moment when, like the man whose feat he was describing, he knew he had to be the top of his game. I've since heard a tape of that half-inning. There's not a single misstep. He never once stumbles for a word, makes a false start or trips over himself."

True, or not? Read, and judge.

"THREE TIMES IN HIS sensational career has Sandy Koufax walked out to the mound to pitch a fateful ninth where he turned in a no-hitter," Vin began. "But tonight, September the ninth, Nineteen Hundred and Sixty-five, he made the toughest walk of his career, I'm sure, because through eight innings he has pitched a perfect game." Sandy "has struck out 11, he has retired 24 consecutive batters, and the first man he will look at is catcher Chris Krug, big right-hand hitter, flied to second, grounded to short. Dick Tracewski is now at second base and Koufax ready and delivers: curveball for a strike. Oh and 1 the count to Chris Krug. Out on deck to pinch-hit is one of the men we mentioned earlier as a possible, Joey Amalfitano. Here's the strike 1 pitch to Krug: fastball, swung on and missed, strike 2. And you can almost taste the pressure now. Koufax lifted his cap, ran his fingers through his black hair, then pulled the cap back down, fussing at the bill. Krug must feel it too as he backs out, heaves a sigh, took off his helmet, put it back on, and steps back up to the plate.

"Tracewski is over to his right to fill up the middle, Kennedy is deep to guard the line. The strike 2 pitch on the way: fastball, outside, ball 1. Krug started to go after it and held up and Torborg held the ball high in the air trying to convince [umpire] Vargo, but Eddie said no sir. One and 2 the count to Chris Krug." It was 9:41 P.M., Vin said, September the ninth. "The 1-2 pitch on the way: curveball, tapped foul off to the left of the plate. The Dodgers defensively in this spine-tingling moment: Sandy Koufax and Jeff Torborg. The boys who will try and stop anything hit their way: Wes Parker, Dick Tracewski, Maury Wills, and John Kennedy; the outfield of Lou Johnson, Willie Davis, and Ron Fairly." Unforgettably: "And there's 29,000 people in the ballpark and a million butterflies. Twenty-nine thousand, one hundred and thirty-nine paid.

"Koufax into his windup and the 1-2 pitch: fastball, fouled back out of play. In the Dodger dugout Al Ferrara gets up and walks down near the runway, and it begins to get tough to be a teammate and sit in the dugout and have to watch." Detail befit a ledger board. "Sandy back of the rubber, now toes it. All the boys in the bullpen straining to get a better look as they look through the wire fence in left field. One and 2 the count to Chris Krug. Koufax, feet together, now to his windup and the 1-2 pitch: fastball outside, ball 2 [crowd booed]. A lot of people at the ballpark are starting to see the pitches with their hearts. The pitch was outside, Torborg tried to pull it over the plate but Vargo, an experienced umpire, wouldn't go for it.

Two and 2 the count to Chris Krug. Sandy reading signs, into his windup, 2-2 pitch: fastball, got him swingin'! Sandy Koufax has struck out 12. He is two outs away from a perfect game."

In *Rooster Cogburn*, an aging scamp tells John Wayne: "Been everywhere, done everything." Amalfitano, who had, pinch-hit for Don Kessinger. "From Southern California, from San Pedro. He was an original bonus boy with the Giants. Joe's been around, and as we mentioned earlier, he has helped to beat the Dodgers twice, and on deck is Harvey Kuenn. Kennedy is tight to the bag at third, the fastball, a strike." An egg timer reminded Red Barber to give the score. Lacking one, Vin did. "Oh and 1 with one out in the ninth inning, 1 to nothing, Dodgers. Sandy reading, into his windup and the strike 1 pitch: curveball, tapped foul. Oh and 2. And Amalfitano walks away and shakes himself a little bit, and swings the bat. And Koufax with a new ball, takes a hitch at his belt, and walks behind the mound." Pause: "I would think that the mound at Dodger Stadium right now is the loneliest place in the world. Sandy fussing, looks in to get his sign, oh and 2 to Amalfitano. The strike 2 pitch to Joe: fastball, swung on and missed, strike 3!"

The 1959 American League batting titleist neared the plate. "He is one out away from the Promised Land, and Harvey Kuenn is comin' up. So Harvey Kuenn is batting for Bob Hendley." Vin had never taped a Koufax no-no. Hoping to archive the game, he again observed the clock. "The time on the scoreboard is 9:44. The date, September the ninth, 1965, and Koufax is working on veteran Harvey Kuenn. Sandy into his windup and the pitch, a fastball for a strike! He has struck out, by the way, five consecutive batters, and that's gone unnoticed. Sandy ready and the strike 1 pitch: very high, and he lost his hat. He really forced that one. That's only the second time tonight where I have had the feeling that Sandy threw instead of pitched, trying to get that little extra, and that time he tried so hard his hat fell off—he took an extremely long stride to the plate—and Torborg had to go up to get it.

"One and 1 to Harvey Kuenn. Now he's ready: fastball, high, ball 2. You can't blame a man for pushing just a little now": Scully, as Everyman. "Sandy backs off, mops his forehead, runs his left index finger along his forehead, dries it off on his left pants leg": Classicist, or Impressionist? "All the while Kuenn just waiting. Now Sandy looks in. Into his windup and the 2-1 pitch to Kuenn: swung on and missed, strike 2!" Peroration:

"It is 9:46 P.M. Two and 2 to Harvey Kuenn, one strike away. Sandy into his windup, here's the pitch: Swung on and missed, a perfect game!" Hitting his mute button, Vin next spoke 38 seconds later.

"On the scoreboard in right field it is 9:46 in the City of the Angels, Los Angeles, California. And a crowd of 29,139 just sitting in to see the only pitcher in baseball history to hurl four no-hit, no-run games. He has done it four straight years, and now he caps it: On his fourth no-hitter, he made it a perfect game. And Sandy Koufax, whose name will always remind you of strikeouts, did it with a flurry. He struck out the last six consecutive batters. So when he wrote his name in capital letters in the record books, that *K* stands out even more than the *O-U-F-A-X*."

LATER, THE *Scribner Encyclopedia* called "Scully's work during that game" as flawless as 27 up and down. "It is considered by many to be the best radio broadcast in baseball history," writing poetry without a pen. "I mean, *hear* this," said Joe Castiglione, Red Sox voice since 1983. At 37, another man might stress over prematurely peaking. Scully deemed each game an empty canvas on which to draw.

"You come into the booth, and you get your paints and brushes, and you mix the paints," Vin said. "On TV, the picture's there, so you don't have to do all the brush strokes. You're shading, subtle things. On radio you look at the vacant screen, and you begin with a broad swath here and a fine line there—vivid tints and bold pastels." After three hours, "you say, 'OK, that's the best I can do today.' You fill the canvas, trying to put things together," even as no 1965 team pulled away.

On September 1 Cincinnati led by percentage points. Mate: Nineteen days later Frisco held a four-game lead. Checkmate: L.A. won 13 straight, ending the season vs. Milwaukee at the Ravine. Brewtown's Bob Uecker gawked at its staff. "We'd rate 'em like divers. A pitch under the chin, hold up a sign—5. Fastball in the ribs—10. That was their secret. They'd only score three runs a game—but we couldn't score three in a series." In 1965 Uke hit a no-misprint .400 vs. Koufax. "There he was, the greatest stuff since Doubleday—and I'd hit a home run or smack a double. That alone should have kept him out of the Hall of Fame."

By 2009 the Dodgers vaunted 48 Cooperstowners, six world titles, 18 pennants, and eight Cy Young, 10 MVP, and 16 Rookie of the Year awards. "Some mirror to look back through," said Doggett. By contrast,

Milwaukee's broke. The '63ers drew 773,018 vs. 1954–57's 2 million yearly. Resigning, Earl Gillespie saw handwriting on the wall. Only a temporary court order kept the 1965 Braves from marching to Georgia. "What a mess," said new mikeman Merle Harmon. "They had to play that year in a city which knew it was losing them."

Harmon brooked a no-win choice. "If I praised the Braves, people said, 'Don't root for traitors.' If I didn't, die-hards said, 'Don't mess up another club.'" Milwaukee vied till September, "baseball afraid we'd make the Series and our park'd be empty." On September 22, 1965, the Braves played their last game at County Stadium. "Given what had come before," said Gillespie, "the opponent was ironic" — L.A.

Since 1957 the National League had severed Milwaukee, New York, and Flatbush. On Saturday, October 2, the ex-Brooks beat the future Atlantas, 3-1, clinching at the Ravine. Alston then posed a question scenting of the Daffy Dodgers.

"Vin, tomorrow [closing day] doesn't mean anything, so how about managing?" Walt asked, Scully later told a Dodgers luncheon. "You tell me on the air what to do. I'll listen in the dugout, with earphones on, and give directions to the guys."

The kicker was the team: "full of champagne," soused, Vin knew. Told he had the final off, Fairly didn't go to bed.

"My God," Scully gawked, seeing him early Sunday, "your eyes look awful."

"You should see 'em from this side," said Ron, entering the clubhouse to learn of Parker's stomachache. He would play, after all.

Fairly singled his first at-bat: "a dear friend, more than a little drowsy," Scully said, "as I gave the word for him to steal second." By now, The Portable Vinny "was letting fans in on the news that I was managing. 'For those of you with radios, let's have Fairly steal. [A novelty: Ron had two swipes all year.] Watch Fairly's face when he looks at third [base coach Preston Gomez] and gets the sign.'"

Listening, Alston hawed into the pinch-skipper's ear: "Dummy, when you want to go you've got to call it quicker than that!" Ron got the sign too late to steal. "Walt often said, 'If it's a good play and doesn't work, try it again,'" mused Vin, who did.

Disbelieving, Ron did "a double-take. He didn't know what was going on, but the fans, who did, were going crazy." Thrice Johnson fouled a pitch as "beet-red" Fairly slid—to Scully, "sloshed"—into second. Said Ron, later: "Stick a fork in me, I'm done."

Receding, The Franchise scrapped the steal sign. "OK, Alston," he chuckled, "I got you this far. You're on your own." Writer Bob Verdi noticed. "With customary respect for his profession and for baseball, [Vin] relinquished his task quickly, fearful that he was overstepping. He did not want to play God or seem bigger than the game itself. Fairly trundled into second . . . and Scully went back to . . . [being]" baseball's West Coast state of mind.

"Nationally, he isn't as well known as some of the others," wrote *L.A. Times*man Sid Ziff, "but only because he has never covered the big football games, the Kentucky Derby, or the National Open. It's just as well because if the Dodgers ever did let him roam they'd never get him back." The American League's 1965 Series Voice was antipodean. "When [Ray Scott] intoned, slowly, formally, simply, 'First down, Green Bay,'" wrote *TV Guide*, "10 million spines would quiver."

In 1956 CBS TV had begun weekly pro football. "Until then," Ray said, "America did everything Sunday *except* watch TV—drive, family, hit the beach." Columbia changed how we spend it. Born in Johnstown, Pennsylvania, Scott flooded the Super Bowl (four), NFL final game (nine), and regular season, barking "Starr. Dowler. Touchdown. Green Bay" (a.k.a. Titletown). CBS, Melvin Durslag wrote, "didn't make a move to any big game without him."

Ironically, another game was Ray's *affaire de coeur*. "My father preferred baseball, no contest," said son Preston. In 1961 the Washington Senators-turned-Twins hired Scott: to him, a natural evolution. Like 1958 L.A., the Twin Cities felt the bigs craze. "For a while they cut Ray some slack," said team publicist Tom Mee. "People were so pleased to have this national celebrity as a local announcer"—arguably a larger name on baseball's 1965 Fall Event than the best announcer in the sport.

Since 1949 the Yankees had made 14 Series. On July 11, 1965, Minnesota trailed, 5-4. "The Yanks were aging," Ray mused. "We're in first, and we'd beat 'em the first two of a three-game series." Harmon Killebrew faced Pete Mikkelsen in the ninth inning. "A drive deep to left!" Scott cried. "Way back! It's a home run! The Twins win!" The dynasty was dead; my radio seemed to quiver. September 26 knit new team/old town. "The Twins have won 98 games," Ray said in Washington. "Number 99 means the pennant. . . . He struck him out! . . . Final score: the Twins 2, the Senators 1! The Twins have won the American League pennant!" Jim "Mudcat" Grant went 21-7. Tony Oliva hit .321. Zoilo Versalles became the franchise's first MVP since Roger Peckinpaugh in 1925.

The Series was Vin's sixth. By contrast, Ray said, "as an announcer I'd just taken up the game." Scott was a baritone; Scully, tenor. The West Coast harbored glitz, skin, and cash. The Upper Midwest resembled Mayberry devoid of accent. Dodger Stadium was baseball's summer Hermitage: "as large in L.A.," wrote Dick Kidson, "as are the strawberries at Farmers Market." Metropolitan Stadium was austere, almost skeletal. Vin had a story for every pitch. "Scott's style was like football's," said 1961 colleague Bob Wolff. "Gradually he realized baseball needs more talk."

Again Vin voiced the highlight film, lauding "the Land of 10,000 Lakes, from one of which tributaries the mighty Mississippi flows through the Twin Cities." Vice President Hubert Humphrey's first pitch opened the first Series of transplanted teams. Behind, 1-0, "the huge Twins first baseman [Don Mincher] connects solidly with all his power." Later "Versalles gets around on one. He pulls it down the line. It's another homer!": final, 8-2. Next afternoon "Bob Allison makes a sensational catch of Jim Lefebvre's drive down the left-field line." One K, Jim Kaat, clipped another, Koufax, 5-1.

The Classic repaired to California, "Dodger fans hoping they can turn the tide," said Scully. In 1999, the *Wall Street Journal* termed the Ravine "like reverting to" 1965: architecture, hot dogs, and organ music, a gated village vs. the then-counter culture, as Timothy Leary said, "turn[ing] on, tune[ing] in, drop[ping] out." Claude Osteen and Drysdale won, 4-0 and 7-2, respectively. Sandy then blanked Kaat, 7-0. "Though I never saw Bob Gibson," Twins skipper Sam Mele said, "Koufax is amazing, the best I ever saw." The scoreboard read: "And now [back] to the Twin Cities."

Vin's airplane seatmate was All-American, Heisman Trophy's, and ABC Radio's Tom Harmon. A flight attendant asked, "Aren't you on television?"

"No, but *he* is," Tom said of Scully.

"Incredible," said The Franchise. "You mean you don't know who this fellow is? Go ahead—tell her."

"I am," said Tom, proudly, thinking of daughter Kris, "[actor-singer] Rick Nelson's father-in-law."

Allison's Game 6 blast put Minnesota up, 2-0. Later, "Grant rips into the first pitch," Vin said. "It's back, back, away back for a [three-run] home run!": first American League Series–dinging hurler since 1920's Jim Bagby, ironically, against the Dodgers. The Twins' 5-1 verdict left Alston in a hash: Mr. K, on two days' rest, or Big D, three? "Sandy took longer to warm up," Walt said, "so he starts, then Don from the pen." Koufax's foil, again Kaat, won 283 games, was a fielding paladin and last original Washington Senator, and as Vin dubbed Gibson, threw "as though he's double-parked." A quarter century later, the high-voiced, good-guy analyst said of Sandy: "Next time I'll pitch against a mortal."

In the fourth inning, "Johnson hammers a long drive down the left-field line!" Scully highlighted. "It may be foul! No, it strikes the foul pole screen and drops back on the field!" Parker's bouncer over first then scored Fairly. Next inning Scott yielded play-by-play. Frank Quilici hit a one-out drive: "Johnson going back and over—and it's off the fence! It's a double!" Vin said. Rich Rollins walked. "So Koufax is struggling. It's almost impossible to do it on one pitch in the big leagues. Today he does not have a curveball." With two out, Versalles batted, Gilliam "guarding the line to cut down the chance of an extra-base hit at third."

Sandy threw 1-2 heat. "Ground ball, backhanded by Gilliam! To the bag for a force! Oh, what a play!" said Scully. "And that would have been a double and at least one run batted in." Instead, Koufax began the home ninth, up, 2-0. "Vin Scully," Ray observed, "is wending his way to the Dodgers dressing room in anticipation of a possible Series-winning celebration." Earl Battey fanned after Killebrew's one-out single. "Koufax reaching back," Scott said of Allison's 2-2 count. "He did it! And so the Dodgers win the 1965 World Series!" —to the *Times*, "The Days of Vin and Roses."

In the clubhouse, "high atop the safety of a trunk," he noted, Scully interviewed No. 32. Three days earlier Koufax had said, "I feel 100 years old." Vin: "Today, how do you feel?" Sandy: "A hundred and one." After 18 teams in 13 years, Johnson was "a living storybook," said The Franchise. The Dodgers were "wild, ecstatic, euphoric, you name it."

Next day Vin began a Hawaiian holiday. Mr. K won a Series MVP Corvette. "Yeah," said a writer, "and he'll use it to stand on when he washes his Rolls-Royce." Soon he could afford a Bentley, too.

"WE MUST ALL hang together," said Benjamin Franklin of the Declaration of Independence, "or surely we will all hang separately." Holding out in early 1966, Koufax and Drysdale hung together for 32 days. Each asked for $1 million through 1968. Bavasi bid $120,000 for 1966 alone. Ultimately, Koufax got $125,000; Big D, $110,000. Don finished 13-16. Sandy was 27-9, had 317 Ks and a 1.73 ERA, and won a third Cy Young Award.

Unlike 1965 the Dodgers led just eight days before September. Alston demolished a clubhouse table. Wills and Tommy Davis jousted in the dugout. The team that fought together then won eight straight together. Could it beat the Pirates, fronting since July? Their gravelly, unpredictable Voice felt not. To Bob Prince, a great play sparked, "How sweet it is!"; homers, "Kiss it good-bye!"; a triumph, "We had 'em all the way!" A segue might weave from U.S. Steel via presidential politics to golf with Bing Crosby. "Oh, by the way, Clemente grounded out, Stargell flied out, and that's the inning." Once Bob made a joke to a woman in a bar. Her husband pulled a gun: thus, the nickname Gunner. Some thought Prince a maniac. It is fair to call him maniacally riveting.

In May 1966 Bob spotted Pirates trainer Danny Whelan holding a wiener painted green. "There," he gibed, "is a [TV] picture of a grown man pointing a green weenie at Lee May." May popped up. Trucks put the Weenie on their aerial. Serta Mattress made a model to help it endure a doubleheader. On August 2 the Dodgers played at Pittsburgh. "Let's put the Green Weenie on Drysdale!" Prince told *his* transistored crowd. A roar commenced. Big D stood, sneering. Finally Augie Donatelli said to throw.

"How can I pitch with these nuts going crazy and that skinny bastard up in the booth?" said Drysdale.

"I don't know, but pitch," said the umpire. Donn Clendenon homered. Leaving, Drysdale shook his fist.

The Dodgers clinched, 6-3, October 2, at Philadelphia. Prince's consolation prize was airing NBC Series Radio. The American League entry was Baltimore's ex-St. Louis Browns. Frank Robinson won the Triple Crown. The Orioles' Luis Aparicio, Dave Johnson, and Paul Blair were foolproof up the middle. Boog Powell and Brooks Robinson spun infield corner security. Said B. Robby: "It didn't matter. The Dodgers looked at us like hired help."

The Fall Classic began October 5, Vin airing NBC TV. He soon discovered that good help is not always hard to find.

SINCE 1953, Allen, Blattner, Buck, Dean, Garagiola, Merle Harmon, Nelson, and Wolff, among others, had televised network baseball. In 1966, the Peacocks, buying bigs's exclusivity, asked Curt Gowdy to replace them all. Unlike Vin, the Wyoming Cowboy was a small-town boy. Unlike Diz, he roused little response to personality. "The game is the important thing," Curt said. "A Voice is no better than his script."

The Rocky Mountaineer's style was home style, becoming a sports generation's paradigm: 16 All-Star Games, 13 World Series, 24 NCAA Final Fours, seven Olympics, eight Super Bowls, 14 Rose Bowls, Pan-American Games, *The American Sportsman*, and sportscasting's first George Foster Peabody award for radio/TV excellence. "Putting a town into a piece about [him]," a writer said, "is like trying to establish residence for a migratory duck."

Through 1975 Curt *was* as much as *did* network baseball. "The good news is his preparation," said Blattner. Bad: "If only the Good Shepherd did play-by-play, even He'd be overexposed." Gowdy frowned on hype and buzz. The late '60s and early '70s smiled. "As spectacle, baseball suffers on [TV]," wrote Harry Caray. "The fan at the park [talk, drink, take Junior to the john] rarely notices the time span between pitches. [Not] the same fan at home." Not responsible, Curt became accountable.

Local teamers split the pre-1966 Classic. "NBC's new pact changed everything," said sports head Carl Lindemann. "Getting exclusivity, we were going to showcase our network boy." Curt televised half of each game: Vin and Chuck Thompson, the other half in L.A. and Baltimore, respectively. Harwell, Bill O'Donnell, and Jon Miller had or would air the Orioles. Only Chuck defined Charm City. There was something about his voice—"I don't care what he says," laughed Jon, "as long as he says it"— that fetched "a guy sipping a cold beer on his back porch," said Costas, "keeping up with his team."

According to Lindemann, Scully disliked only telecasting at Dodger Stadium. Carl noted his doing network *radio* in Baltimore. "What about *TV*?" The Franchise countered. "My [California] fans won't be able to see me." The NBCer never forgot the chill. "Here's Vin, beloved, reluctant to accept not being on TV daily." Game 1 bred tit for tat. Scully did the first

4½ innings: "Just wonderful," said Lindemann, "with Gowdy supplying color." Curt then inherited a clunker made duller by Vin's reticence to speak. "Just sits there the last 4½ innings." Only Dodger bats were as still.

Each Robinson tapped Drysdale for a Game-1 dinger. Reliever Moe Drabowsky K'd 11 in 6⅔ innings: Baltimore, 5-2. A photo shows Willie Davis, in the dirt, rising, hands on hips, to argue a force out. Next day his Series-record three muffs sunk Sandy, 6-0. Paul Blair and F. Robby homered off Osteen and Drysdale, respectively, to twice win, 1-0. "They had some young pitchers that were amazing," said Tommy Davis, "and they just overpowered us": fewest Series runs (2), hits (17), total bases (23), and batting average (.142), and most straight scoreless innings (33).

The Dodgers barnstormed Japan for a month, glad to get away, not glad to come back. On November 18 Koufax retired because of an arthritic elbow, having struck out 1,128 in the last 1,292 innings. "I don't regret for one minute the 12 years I've spent with baseball, but I could regret one season too many." A photo at the Beverly Wilshire Hotel shows him in narrow tie, white shirt, and dark suit, next to attorney William Hayes, wincing. One writer mixed film and stage: "He left at *High Noon*, a Hamlet in mid-soliloquy."

Postscript: Four years later Vin and Curt emceed an off-season TV baseball awards dinner from Los Angeles. "They were picked to co-host," said Lindemann, "and with their bad blood, we kept 'em apart." Oddly, to prize 1980s' Scully, one must grasp 1960s' Gowdy. Initially NBC dismissed how Curt's voice was not a fever-swamp. He was fair, accurate, and had a Chip Hilton delivery. Surely that would suffice. Instead, the network's 1966–68 A.C. Nielsen *Game* and Series rating fell 10 and 19 percent, respectively. Only All-Star Game numbers nixed a view that baseball was too bland for a camp and inchoate age.

Curt never scrimped on study, touting, "It's the ballgame, stupid." Why did he become a fall guy, then and now? Ubiquity, for one thing. "Imagine what a viewer felt," said Nelson. "Mel, Buck, Wolff, and Diz in the last decade—and one guy replaces 'em?" The *Sporting News* got so many letters—"atrocity . . . a pallbearer . . . baseball is not dead, no thanks to Gowdy"—that it routed them to NBC. Viewers tired. Lack of hoopla hurt. To Curt, Vin's elegance was as alien as damming a Wyoming stream.

"We learned a lot about what worked, and didn't," said future NBC Sports president Arthur Watson. The Peacocks remembered in 1982.

"THE FATHER I NEVER HAD," Vin often said. As Scully bloomed, Red Barber burned. On September 22, 1966, the day CBSer Michael Burke became Yankees president, 413 pocked the last-placers' 65,010-seat Big Ballpark in the Bronx. Deeming it "the perfect place for Burke to start, nowhere to go but up," Red asked WPIX TV to pan the stands. No shot. Barber vainly asked again. "I later found out [Yanks radio/TV head] Perry Smith told them not to show the seats." Report, he recalled from teletype. "I don't know what the paid attendance is today, but whatever it is, it is the smallest crowd in the history of Yankee Stadium, and this crowd is the story, not the game."

Next week, asked to breakfast, Barber expected a new pact. Burke skipped sugar: "There is no reason to be talking pleasantries." Red was fired—and reborn. "I'd become a servant to the microphone," he said later. "On my own, I'd have gone back for what who knows how long." The next quarter century became a valentine: seven books, dozens of radio/TV gigs, and feathers in the cap for excellence, still a stickler for preparation.

In 1978, this mix of "old courtliness and the flintiness of the utterly independent man," wrote David Halberstam, joined Allen as the first Voice to enter Cooperstown. In 1981 Barber began Friday commentary on National Public Radio's *Morning Edition*. Depending on date and mood, he drew cats, cooking, or squirrels eating birdseed, once segueing from Geraldine Ferraro to Mary, Queen of Scots, to caddies at the British Open. Time of discourse: three minutes. Red skipped an egg timer.

Barber died in 1992, "still trying to speak correctly and trying not to get my tenses fouled up." In a eulogy, Steve Kelley wrote, "Some people are meant to be immortal. Their voices and their visions are meant to continue from generation to generation." Owning himself, Red could not be bought.

"Scully brought intelligence, industry, imagination, and, above all, integrity to the assignment," his mentor said. "I have to be careful about him. He's my boy." With Barber axed, the boy became even more on his own: as it happened, a good place to be.

7

DON'T FENCE ME IN (1967–1975)

SUMMER 1968. Judy Collins's recording of Joni Mitchell's "Both Sides Now" hits No. 8 on *Billboard* magazine's best-selling chart. The mid to late 1960s vaunted war, riot, EST, and Zen; hawk vs. dove; hard hat vs. hippie; the Silent Majority vs. the pop intelligentsia. Scully lived both sides, too.

On one hand, he got a second straight National Sportscasters and Sportswriters of the Year award in Salisbury, North Carolina. The other: Dodger Stadium braved its first rained-out game. Worse, in 1967 attendance fell a million to 1,664,362. "Five years they had 2 million or more," said Jim Murray. "Now . . . they were playing to the grounds help." Yin: L.A. lacked a TV network. Yang: All KTTV games were futuristic "color." Minus: 1969 radio outlets fell to eight. Plus: 1970 video added Sunday road games to Giants coverage. "Increasing television," O'Malley observed, "but not giving away the product." It worked, said Horace Stoneham, having seen what didn't.

In New York, the Jints had telecast their entire home schedule. In "Baghdad," they limited exposure to Dodger Stadium—"every game there," Horace said, "nothing home. Terrific balance"—till the 1968 A's invaded Oakland, sacking baseball in the Bay. "Suddenly, our attendance falls, since we're dividing a finite market," said Russ Hodges, retiring in 1970. Vin never matched—who did?—his Call.

"Hartung down the line at third base, not taking any chances. Lockman with not too big of a lead at second, but he'll be running like the wind if Thomson hits one." Fate threw. Thomson hit one. "I don't believe it! The Giants win the pennant!" Like Rodney Dangerfield, the late-'60s Angelenos would have been content to win respect.

"MY MOTHER KNEW nothing about baseball until the Dodgers came to Los Angeles," conceded scouting director Ben Wade's wife Betsy. "She fell in love with Vinny, and then fell in love with the Dodgers," not easy in eighth-place 1967–68. Terming Vin "disenchanted in L.A.," the *Sporting News* said the Yankees again "made inquiries about his [availability]." Gilliam retired, Wills and Tommy Davis left, and Koufax's speeding bullet slowed as an NBC analyst. Only Drysdale remained.

On May 31, 1968, having tossed 44 straight scoreless frames, Big D faced the Giants. "Dick Dietz waiting," Vin said of a bases-full, no-out ninth. "Big pitch by Drysdale—into the windup he goes. Two-2 pitch. Curve—hit him!" ending the streak—Don's "string of pearls." Or "did it hit the bat? It hit the bat, said [plate umpire Harry] Wendelstedt. Hold everything!"—especially the Stonehams, smothering the man in blue. Dietz, skipper Herman Franks, and coach Peanuts Lowery claimed a hit batsman. "And now Wendelstedt gesturing with his arm as if to say Dietz stuck his arm in front of the pitch," voiding a base: thus, run.

"Dick Dietz is still at the plate! The bases are still loaded. Drysdale, for the moment, still has his scoreless streak! Let the personnel and the years change. They are still the Giants and the Dodgers, no two ways about it." Dietz popped "into shallow left . . . Oliver tags. [Jim] Fairey for the catch! *He's not coming!*" Don got the next two out. On June 8, the last active Brooklyn Dodger broke Walter Johnson's 1913 record 56 scoreless frames (eventually, 58 2/3). "Ground ball wide of third. It's Boyer who has the chance! He's done it!" Tiers pulsed, then stilled: L.A. drew its still-worst attendance: 1,581,093.

A listener wrote Scully: "For the edification, clarification, and elucidation of my lovely wife, please explain that when you say a batter 'checks in' at a certain figure, you're referring to his batting average and not his weight." Scoring 2.9 runs a game, the '68ers checked out. In November, a Westwood Shrine Club–backed testimonial dinner at the Beverly Hilton International Hotel wooed O'Malley, Bavasi, and Alston; Drysdale, Koufax, Reese, and Hank Aaron; and actors Milton Berle, Dan Dailey, Buddy Hackett, and George Jessel, among others, to mark The

Franchise's decade in Tinseltown. Many recited Koufax's Perfect Game: "It is 9:46 [P.M.] in The City of the Angels." Prose was telling: Scully's eyes were on the clock.

"How much more time do I have for trying something new? Could I have become a moderator? An actor? A singer? A fellow never knows what he can do unless he tries." By 1969 Vin had missed only two Dodgers games, aired seven World Series and four All-Star Games, been NBC Television's 1966–67 series *Occasional Wife* narrator, and begun hosting its quiz show *It Takes Two*. "Laurence Olivier was once asked what makes a great actor and he said, 'The humility to prepare and the confidence to bring it off,'" said Scully. "Believe me, I'm loaded with the humility to prepare. I've always been afraid of going out and sounding like a horse's fanny." *This Is Your Life*'s Ralph Edwards took him aside. "The critics are going to find this 'inane.' They find every game show inane. To them, the game show is the lowest form of entertainment. Play it cool." Vin played it crowded.

Each year he added 190 (games) to 165 (*It Takes Two*s): a schedule akin to rush hour on I-405. One day Scully taped four *It*s in beautiful downtown Burbank and aired a 12-inning "cliff-dweller" (Jints skipper Wes Westrum). Next day, another four—and a twi-night doubleheader. Could the Dodgers wave a flag? Vin asked on radio. (From 1967–73, no.) At NBC: Miss, how many feet of thread knit a pair of stockings? (Miss didn't know. Did Scully care?) Was Maury Wills, reacquired from Pittsburgh, has-been or halcyon? (Has, becoming a worse NBC analyst than Koufax.) How many pairs of shoes does a male adult alligator sire? (There once was a girl from Nantucket . . . oops, wrong card.) Where were we? Burbank? Chavez Ravine? A time for taping? A time at bat? "I'm glad I did it all," Vin said a decade later. "It's just that with that schedule, I'd hate to do it again."

It Takes Two died in 1970, despite Vin, a writer said, "being the closest thing we have seen to Art Linkletter for emceeing charm." On Monday, January 15, 1973, CBS TV's weekday afternoon *The Vin Scully Show* debuted, "featuring interviews with personalities from the entertainment world," read the *Sporting News*. "It was a talk show," said the host, "and really something. I was scheduled around the soap operas and actually nobody knew it was on and nobody really knew when it went off." A bawdy ploy survived each series.

"As a novice around NBC," read *TV Guide*, "Scully was a target of studio practical jokers, who carry their levity to the show. On one occasion, a sedan, once used for a rub-out in a George Raft movie, was driven on-stage. Scully was to open the trunk to find the answer to a question on bootlegging." Unknown to Vin, crews, actors, and administrators, including *Laugh-In*'s entire company, crashed *It Takes Two*. Innocently, "Scully opened the trunk. His jaw fell. Reclining within, unseen by the audience, was a delicious redhead, who had starred in *Playboy*. She leaned on an elbow, staring soulfully at Scully. She was as naked as a jaybird."

Fordham had not prepared Vin for ladies who had on not a stitch. "[He] was speechless. His first impulse was to remove his coat and cover the lady, which, you must admit, is a knightly thought, but he realized this would stir suspicion among the audience. Nervously, he lifted the answer from the trunk and closed it. The plotters in the wings roared." Canceled after 13 weeks, *Show* joined *It Takes Two* in Vin's psychic attic. His new door opened to welcome an old friend.

As 1965–68 COMMISSIONER of baseball, William D. Eckert was a terrific Air Force lieutenant general. Inept and inarticulate, he made baseball seem related to Caligula's horse. "[It] is a game meant to be played on real grass and during lazy afternoons, with children, old men, and an occasional housewife watching," barbed New York's advertising firm of Kenyon and Eckhard. *Fortune* magazine sacked "the beat-up national sport." Not long ago, read the *Wall Street Journal*, "baseball ranked with apple pie, the flag, and motherhood as an American institution. If you weren't enthusiastic about it, you risked being considered unpatriotic. Not now." In late 1968, "football passed baseball as the top favorite sport," pollster Lou Harris said, "and has since held its front-runner position. The problem is that baseball has become too dull." By 2 to 1, "fans agree that 'there are too many times during a baseball game when there is no action.'" Who better than Vin to turn inaction into art?

Baseball cashiered Eckert December 6, 1968. *Times*man Bob Oates soon floated a successor. "Scully has been with the club for many years on both coasts," he wrote. "About half his baseball career has been spent in America's largest city and half in the country's most explosive population area. He would bring . . . a first-class mind as well as the self-confidence to act when necessary and the self-control to abstain from action in other circumstances." Oates likened Vin to Pete Rozelle, NFL head since January 1960. "Scully's knowledge of baseball now is at least as great as Rozelle's knowledge [then] and the problems are similar." In early 1969 Bowie Kuhn got the job, the 24 big-league owners unanimously picking him. The Dodgers got the willies, fearing Scully was about to scram.

"He has never hit a fair ball for the Dodgers on the field, but he has never uttered a foul one off it," said Murray, noting Vin's talk/quiz show dalliance. "He has seen and described almost every ball thrown or caught by hundreds of Dodgers." In 1958 he was "almost the one thing certifiably major league about the Dodgers. No matter where the team finished Scully leads his league. Popular with show-biz types, he has had such drop-in stars as Rowan and Martin and Johnny Carson." Regulars were Dick Smothers and Henny Youngman. Mr. K once visited. Asked the most consecutive batters he retired in a no-hitter, Annette Funicello guessed 88. Murray wrote that she was either bad at arithmetic or baseball.

"It was a time in my life when I was looking to express myself in other ways than I'd known," Vin mused, loving baseball, but hating lobbies. "I'd done baseball—nothing else—for two decades. I was trying to show I could say something besides 'ball two, strike one.'" Scully wouldn't leave—or would he? In 1969 Big D tore a rotator cuff. "It's all over, baby," he said, retiring after 209 victories, a 2.95 ERA, 29 homers, and a National League–record 154 hit batsmen. Ted Sizemore became Rookie of the Year. The league expanded to San Diego—and Montreal.

In May, Vin and Doggett paid a French cabbie $6 an hour on their first visit to the ex-Dodgers' farm. That summer Willie Davis tilled franchise history, hitting safely in 30 straight games. On September 3, 0 for 3, he failed to bunt safely in the seventh inning. "With the Dodgers ahead [4-0]," said Vin, "Willie may not get another [streak-extending] chance." Next inning, New York's Tommie Agee and Donn Clendenon homered to tie the score. Even the home skipper was nonplussed. "Osteen . . . throws him [Ron Swoboda] out—and Walter Alston was on the field! He was heading to take Osteen out, when Swoboda hit the first pitch back to the box!" The bottom half inning put *Los Angeles* in a box.

"If the pitcher makes out," Scully reasoned, "or whoever bats for him [Willie Crawford], then Willie Davis will be the number three hitter in the ninth inning—unless the Dodgers get a run and win it, of course." A hit might save the game. An out might salvage Davis. "If he [Crawford] makes the last out in the eighth, Willie Davis will get another shot." Crawford rolled out. The ninth-inning Mets went meekly. Wills's single began the Dodgers' ninth.

"For more of the fun for the folks in the stands trying to figure out about Willie Davis," said the insider, "if [Manny] Mota sacrifices Wills to second, will they pitch to Willie? Left-handed pitcher [Jack DiLauro] on the mound. He's a left-handed batter." Mota sacrificed. Davis batted to "an ovation," having "one thing in his favor"—DiLauro's arm! "If there's a right-hand pitcher, the odds figure for sure they would walk him intentionally. But what will they do with a left-hander?" Catcher Duffy Dyer rose behind the plate. "And let's see. If he does not go in a crouch, they're going to put him on. Dyer looks over at [Mets manager] Gil Hodges. He's not in a crouch . . . and now he goes in a crouch!" Davis "has one last swing—or *is* it the last swing?"

DiLauro threw a "soft curve—and it's a base hit to left! Here comes Wills; he will score!" Forty-four seconds later The Franchise resurfaced. "Day after day, and year after year, the Dodgers remain the Dodgers. And through all the lightning bolts, the thunder, the heartbreaks, the laughs and the thrills, it's comforting to know in this whacky world, the Dodgers are *still* the Dodgers." Incredibly, "Willie Davis, on one last shot, when the question was in doubt if he would be even allowed to swing a bat, gets a ninth-inning game-winning base hit to extend his hitting streak to 31 [ending a day later]. What a finish."

On July 20, 1970, pitcher Bill Singer finished a Dodgers no-no: the team's then-15th. "Looks into Jeff Torborg," observed Scully. "[Byron] Browne waiting. . . . Fastball! Popped in the air, foul! It's Torborg who has a play. It's Torborg who's got it!" Singer's nickname was "Billy No-No." "The no-no is because of how he runs. When Bill Singer runs, his head shakes from side to side. And Don Drysdale once said, 'Here comes Billy No-No.'" That year a Dodgers "yes" made Peter O'Malley his dad's successor. The new president inked Vin to "a long-term contract"; retired Sandy, Campy, and Robinson's No. 32, 39, and 42, respectively; and began to revive "the Dodger way," said Scully. "From within."

Tom Lasorda was 1969–72 Dodgers Triple-A manager: to Davey Lopes, "our common bond." Another infielder, stiff-legged Ron Cey—to Lasorda, "Penguin"—crowed over being "part of Tommy's system." In 1973 Alston's likely heir became his third-base coach. "I want my team to think baseball the way my wife shops," gibed the "Dodger Blue" originator. "Twenty-four hours a day." Lasorda saw a sign reading "Scully For *Voice* President." To Major Tom, Vin was "Mr. Dodger," accenting the surname.

"I use the word Dodger with high esteem," said Lasorda, "because it's a word that is synonymous with baseball. If a person said I'm with the Padres, you'd say, 'what seminary do you belong to?'" Indians: "What reservation?" Giants: "You're not that big." Vin recollects an age in transition: "We weren't what we'd been," or would be again. One constant sat beside him. Scully being Scully, it was easy to forget how another Voice called the team.

In *I Love Lucy*, Ricky Ricardo loses his job. He calls himself a "has-ran," then "also-been." Lucy corrects him: "has-been." For a long time Jerry Doggett felt like an also-ran. "I wasn't even a has-been," he laughed. "Hadn't done enough."

In 1930, Missouri-born Doggett, 14, joined his divorced mom in Illinois. "I wanted to write about sports, but didn't have the ability, so I tried to talk my way through." In 1938 radio school led to East Texas League Longview. "Eighty dollars a month. Then, it seemed like a million." By 1941 Doggett made Dallas of the Texas League. Ultimately, rights fell to a rival station, whose owner, Gordon McLendon, wanted Dizzy Dean. Greed saved Jerry's job. "When Diz's talks collapsed, I didn't know how to react. I wasn't used to a happy ending."

In 1950 Doggett became Liberty Broadcasting System's *Game of the Day* travel, scheduling, and play-by-play director. "It went into every area without a big-league team," he said. "The reaction was just enormous. I hoped we'd go on forever." Instead, Liberty went to Chapter 11. Adrift, Jerry retrenched Texas League and Southwest Conference football and basketball and, above all, helped NBC's Nelson on TV golf. Tom Gallery remembered when Bavasi phoned in 1955.

"Desmond's drinking again," Buzzie said. "We're replacing him, and I've got four finalists' tapes." The Peacocks' sports head interrupted: "Take Jerry's. Don't bother with the others." Finally, after the bus rides and flea-bags, success—or was it? The Dodgers' Andre Baruch left for CBS Radio. Helfer reupped for 1956. In February, Jerry was to join him—except that O'Malley changed his mind. "Friends [of Connie's]," wrote Dick Young, "are elated to hear he will be back at the mike." Dazed, Doggett recouped his Dallas job: "A Giants team, and I'd been talking to the Dodgers!" That summer Bavasi again called after Desmond's last Dodgers binge: Could Jerry hop a plane?

On Labor Day, he debuted—a Bucs-Bums doubleheader—returning next month to Texas, an also-ran no more. In 1957, Doggett, Vin, and Helfer sang their season-long farewell: "Scully will be the only Dodger broadcaster invited to accompany the Brooks to Los Angeles," claimed the *Journal-American*'s Max Kase, "if and when." The third man "didn't know if I was going." Finally O'Malley nodded. "Having lived in Texas," Jerry noted, "I'd always wanted to live in California." The has-been would air more golf, minor-league L.A. hockey, Cotton and Gator Bowls, and second 1961 All-Star Game.

In 1962 Doggett spurned the expansion Houston Colt .45s' lead microphone. That March he eyed "a jewel [Ravine]. I'm sure hearts were breaking in Brooklyn. But Walter was as pleased as you could be." Name-dropping pleased a publicist: Dick Clark, Doris Day, Danny Kaye, Gregory Peck, Frank Sinatra, and Robert Wagner. "If celebrities go to Dodger Stadium," Vin said, "Dodgers went to Hollywood." Drysdale did *Lawman* with John Russell and Peter Brown. Roseboro was stranded on *Gilligan's Island*. Wes Parker admitted to "a *Brady Bunch*." Pitcher Don Sutton's "most embarrassing moment in life was the *Dating Game*." A black Arkansan made *Hogan's Heroes*. "I was a German sergeant. You know me!" said Willie Davis. "Imagine me being a German sergeant!" The team's biggest name made baseball lush and humming, a place to leave the world behind.

"Some know him as Vin Scully," Kaye would say. "I know him more intimately as Vincent Edward Scully." Doggett knew him as "the best broadcaster to come down the road," forging the bigs's longest team—32 years. Chuck Thompson noted mikemen "spending more time with each other than a spouse. Some teams off-air are incompatible." Vin and Jerry ate, shopped, and worked together. "We haven't got married yet," mused The Franchise. "We've got to pick out silver and get ready."

Did John Barrymore have an *alter idem*? We recall the star, not cast. Baseball's Ed McMahon knew that would apply to him—a courtier, not clown. "I was an average announcer whose greatest break was to work with Vin," Doggett said, retiring in 1987, a decade before his death. In turn, Vin "loved him as a brother. Jerry was remarkable in the sense that he didn't have a jealous bone in his body. He's the best partner anyone ever had."

Earlier the partner penned his requiem. "My life shows it pays not to give up"—also, to be second banana to the best banana on the tree.

VIN AND DOGGETT's radio/TV midpoint was 1971. On January 26, 1972, Scully's wife Joan, 35, died in her sleep at their Pacific Palisades home of an apparently accidental overdose of medication for a severe cold and bronchitis. "From the first day I can remember, I was brought up thinking about death," Vin would later say. "It is a constant companion in our religion. Tomorrow is so uncertain," itinerant, like baseball's life.

"Think of what the broadcaster does," said Scully. Leave a plane, find the hotel, and migrate to the park. Dugout talk precedes a game. Tedium succeeds it. Increasingly, Vin worried that "being out on the road as much as I am, I am killing the most precious thing I have—time. You never know how much of it you have left. I get very Irish when I'm on the road too long," the road having changed.

"In the old days you had the same players together coming out of the minor-league system," he said. "There was a common experience. What you have today is a collection of players, not a team." Gone: train rides ("getting together in the dining car"), card games ("players in their shorts"), even roommates ("like an Army barracks"). Now, you get "on the bus single file, you get off, and everybody has the tendency to kind of scatter": apt, since by then Vin's life had diffused.

"I felt like jumping off a building," Scully called his "series of severe twists." Instead, he "reorganized"—reprioritized—spurning ABC's and NBC's *Monday Night Football* and *Baseball,* respectively; wedding football Rams owner Carroll Rosenbloom's secretary Sandra Schaefer in 1973; and weighing apples, oranges, and professional plums. "The uncertainty, plus my loyalty to the Dodgers, was one reason I'd turned down chances to do more network assignments." Sandra had two children, Todd, 10, and Kelly, 5. "Adding to my three, we had *The Brady Bunch*. With the bigger family, I thought I ought to work a little harder." Working *better*: the Dodgers' farm.

In 1973 Steve Garvey, Lopes, Bill Russell, and Cey began baseball's longest-running infield. Next year Garvey became L.A.'s first post-Koufax MVP, Mike Marshall graced a bigs-record 106 games, and Bill

Buckner batted .314. An opposing player neared a most Ruthian line. On September 29, 1973, Hank Aaron hit homer 713. "The year ended with him one short of Ruth's career record," said Braves Voice Milo Hamilton. "That winter [author] George Plimpton asked what I'd say when he broke it," later writing *One for the Book.* "I said, 'I gotta be spontaneous,' but I kept preparing, planning what I could say."

Hank's first 1974 swing tied the Babe. Then, on Monday, April 8, "sitting on 714," Milo said, Aaron hit at Atlanta–Fulton County Stadium. "Here's the pitch by [L.A.'s Al] Downing . . . swinging. . . . There's a drive into left-center field! That ball is gonna be . . . outta here! It's gone! It's 715!" clearing the fence into reliever Tom House's glove. "There's a new home-run champion of all time! And it's Henry Aaron! Henry Aaron's coming around third! His teammates are at home plate! Listen to this crowd!"

Scully would have turned atheist before "preparing, planning. I didn't want any part," telling Plimpton, "I would worry if I prepared something that I would be so anxious to get to my pearls of wisdom that maybe he *wouldn't* hit the home run [Buckner climbed a hurricane fence] and I would have started *saying* it!" On a rainy night in Georgia, Vin peered at Aaron, waiting. "The outfield deep and straightaway," he began on new flagship KABC. "Fastball! There's a high drive into deep left-center field! Buckner goes back! To the fence! It is gone!" Rising, Scully moved to the back of the booth, poured a glass of water, and hushed for nearly half a minute. "I didn't want to talk over the noise," he said later—still eight, under the wireless.

In Dobbs Ferry, New York, future CBS Radioer Peter King, 17, was "rehearsing for a student concert, and mad because I can't see Curt Gowdy," televising on NBC. Luckily, Armed Forces Radio broadcast via shortwave, "so I lug my radio to school." Serendipity sang at 9:10 P.M. "I leave rehearsal, go to the restroom and find that Vin's, not Milo's, network is being carried. Amazingly, Aaron picks this *minute* to homer. The crowd's nuts, Vin's silent, and I think, 'Wow, what better way to broadcast?' Then I finish my business" as The Franchise resumed *his.*

"What a marvelous moment for baseball. What a marvelous moment for Atlanta and the state of Georgia. What a marvelous moment for the country and the world," Scully said: like din, parallel structure all around. *"A black man is getting a standing ovation in the Deep South for breaking a record of an all-time baseball idol* [emphasis added]. And it is a great moment for all of us, and particularly for Henry Aaron, who is met at home plate not only by every member of the Braves but by his father and mother." Embracing, Hank said he felt 10 years younger. "For the first time in a long time that poker face . . . shows a tremendous strain and relief," Vin mused. "It is over." Conjecture wasn't.

By 2009, 33 men, including Scully and Hamilton, had won the National Baseball Hall of Fame and Museum's Ford C. Frick Award for broadcast excellence. Seven times Milo left one bigs team for another. Aaron was a solace. "Milo's call is heard more often," Jon Miller said. "It was a better sound bite, focusing on the event, a highlight that plays well later." Vin stressed context, "setting the scene and atmosphere, noting civil rights, using the crowd as a person," unlike Gowdy, workmanlike on NBC.

That fall the Wyoming Cowboy again found facing Scully more of a problem than an opportunity in disguise.

LIKE 1971–72, Vin and analyst Bob Gibson aired the 1973 Mets-Reds best-of-five League Championship Series on the Robert Wold Company's syndicated radio network. A December *Sporting News* ad hyped "The Vin Scully Playoff Highlight Tape—a Christmas gift for every baseball fan." To Vin, a better gift would "be a Dodgers flag," Murray wrote, "putting him on [NBC] TV's Series." A year later L.A. won the LCS vs. Pittsburgh. "And so, above all, our heartiest congratulations to every one of the 25 players," said Scully. "It has been a long year. And at no time did they quit on themselves, and it has sure paid off. Screwball [from Marshall]! Got him! Swinging! The Dodgers are the champions of the National League!"

Gowdy, Vin, and the A's Monte Moore did a leeward All-California Classic. A rare highlight was Oakland's Reggie Jackson's fly ball. Sal Bando "should come and score," Vin said. "[Joe] Ferguson took it [from Jimmy Wynn], with the better arm. Here comes the throw! They got him! Oh, what a play!" Another: Game 2's ninth inning. "The Dodgers with a one-run lead," said Curt. Scully: "Screwball!" Gowdy: "That's it, getting him [Angel Mangual]." In Game 5, Marshall stopped warming up to watch the A's crowd hurl trash at Buckner. "In a case like this," said Joe Rudi, "you expect the pitcher to throw a fastball." Mike did. Joe found the seats, Oakland winning, 3-2. Moore had now aired more '70s Series— three—than anyone but Gowdy. Where had baseball gone wrong?

"There are three kinds of lies," said Benjamin Disraeli. "Lies, damned lies, and statistics." Truth was simpler: Scully's Peacock future flowed from 1974. "Vin made [Curt, Monte, and Tony Kubek] sound like college radio rejects," said the *New York Post*'s Henry Hecht. The *Chicago Tribune* read, "For 25 years, he's been living, breathing proof that a good play-by-play man can be on the ball club's payroll and still deliver sparkling commentary totally devoid of the hambone, hometown histrionics usually associated with such house men's Frick 'n Frack."

On October 16 the Federal Communications Commission (FCC) passed a rule requiring "formal pronouncement—really a confession," wrote the *Sporting News*'s Jack Craig, "that when a team has any control, direct or otherwise, over selection of announcers, the public be notified in each broadcast. The rule stems from more than a year of research by the FCC on the relationship between teams and stations that supposedly creates biased broadcasting." It seemed irrelevant to Scully.

"As excited as he might get," said Kaye, "one never gets the feeling that Vin is rooting for the home team." Rather, Craig observed, "he is candid, explaining concealed weaknesses as well as reciting known strengths of the athletes." At the *Boston Globe*, "several office hands turned down [Gowdy/Moore's] TV sound [from Oakland] in order to pick up Scully on [NBC] radio. He speaks quickly yet with clarity . . . and an instinct to talk of things that are of most interest to fans."

Radio/TV acolytes "fell all over themselves," said the *Tribune*'s Gary Deeb, "with praise for his crisp, crystal-clear voice, superb diction, and well-rounded vocabulary." Oates cited "four assets in particular": intelligence, personality, "the understanding that can only come from long involvement with the game and its players, and the ability to synthesize and verbalize [it]." Gary Kaufman loved "his flow. The words run into one another." The Voice was still enchanted by the crowd. "That's why I've never had to work to maintain my enthusiasm. I still get goose bumps when the crowd sings the National Anthem or I hear the roar before the first pitch. Maybe it means I haven't grown." Approbation had.

"Fans say they'd rather have Scully managing the club than Walter Alston," said the *Times*, forgetting Fairly. Jerome Holtzman hailed "positively the best baseball announcer I've ever heard." The *Sporting News* added: "[He] always appears to live up to his reputation as a peerless . . . play-by-play man."

"Someone told me I had done a good job at the Series," said Vin, having last televised 1966's, and then, "I figured after eight years, I had to." Frank Finch understood: "If you want to see the game, listen to Scully."

DAILY, ERIC NEEL LISTENED. His parents were divorcing. The future *ESPN The Magazine* sat on a stool, in his grandpa's L.A. kitchen, hearing a transistor radio. "I was scared and I didn't really trust *anyone*," he said. "Except Vin. He'd say, 'Hi again, everybody, and a very pleasant good evening to you, wherever you may be,' and my life would come back on line." Alone, at six a castaway, "I swear the way [Scully's] smooth, round Irish lilt wrapped itself around me, it promised, almost every summer night, to keep me safe." CBS TV sports head Robert Wussler understood.

In 1975 Wussler inked Vin to a three-year football, golf, and tennis pact. "I could still do the Dodgers," Dad said as daughter Catherine Anne was born. "Network baseball was never a big deal [CBS didn't carry it]. I was happy as it is," invoking journalist-turned-scriptwriter John McNulty's "the money's good, and there's no heavy lifting." For a time, it seemed enough.

"I've been describing people in motion for 25 years," said Scully. "Why, I did the Rose Bowl parade one year with [actress] Elizabeth Montgomery. I'm basically a reporter." For football, "I'll apply the same principles: as much preparation and accuracy as possible." Vin enrolled in "Faulkner University," asking "dean" Rams assistant coach Jack Faulkner to consider him "an empty computer before the invention of the wheel. . . . I'd like to get in fifty hours of classwork. The last time I was around football, most teams were in the straight T and the defenses were relatively simple. Now they've got split backs, split ends, over defenses, under defenses, opposite-right formations and everything else."

Novelist Graham Greene referenced "the heart of the matter." Scully's was "players and backgrounds, weaknesses, strengths, upbringing, everything." Baseball was composite study. "Football is cramming," he said, attending ex-NBA forward Jerry Lucas's memory school. "You need to memorize the names and numbers of many players. I'm going nights to an eight-week course. I've already had four lessons," laughing, "or five, I forget."

Vin read "eight books on tennis" by Billy Talbert and Tony Trabert; played Santa Monica teaching pro Bob Harmon; then aired Jimmy

Connors-Rod Laver, CBS *Tennis Classic,* and *Challenge of the Sexes* with co-host skier and freestyler Suzy Chaffee "in events like bowling, gymnastics, pocket billiards, skydiving, and swimming," wrote Kay Gardella, "pitting men and women against each other to see which of the sexes dominated athletically."

Deeb typed a Nostradamus key. "I guess Scully must be the oldest [then 47] 'new face' on national television. For the first time, CBS Sports has a major personality it can hang its hat on." Vin would do "the key commentary on this spring's Masters golf tourney [true]; call play-by-play of top NFL games next fall [amen]; show up often on the CBS *Sports Spectacular* [bingo]; and be behind the mike at next year's Super Bowl [stay tuned]."

Play word association. "Today, in a test," wrote Deeb, "a sports fan might respond to 'NBC' with 'Curt Gowdy.' And to 'ABC' with 'Howard Cosell.' But it is likely that 'CBS' would draw a blank." Columbia bet that Vin would fill it. No longer were other sports something to take or leave.

Vin's boyhood home, from a 1930s bridge catwalk: Washington Heights in northern Manhattan. Scully played stickball, listened to college football, and watched baseball at the Polo Grounds. Later, crossing the Harlem River, he attended Fordham Preparatory School and University. *Bettmann/Corbis*

As a child, Vin loved the Giants. Their bête noire played at Ebbets Field, where anything could happen, said famed Dodgers Voice Red Barber, "and did." You could walk a Brooklyn street, hearing Red all around, and not miss a pitch. *National Baseball Hall of Fame Library*

In 1949, Vin met Barber, also CBS Sports Director. Soon Scully did network football from the roof at Fenway Park. Impressed, Red made the 22-year-old tyro a Dodgers announcer. Vin became "the son I never had." *National Baseball Hall of Fame Library*

In 1947, Jackie Robinson left Montreal for Brooklyn, cracking baseball's color barrier. Scully admired what Hemingway termed "grace under pressure." Jackie knew that "if he failed," said Vin, "it may have set back the cause for years, maybe forever." *National Baseball Hall of Fame Library*

In 1954, his fifth big-league season, Scully became the Bums' lead announcer, succeeding Red Barber. Jerry Doggett, *left*, later joined him. They broadcast the Dodgers together for 32 (1956–87) years. *National Baseball Hall of Fame Library*

In 1953, Vin, 25, aired his first World Series; 1956, the last half of Don Larsen's perfect game; a year earlier, the final out of Brooklyn's first and sole world title, then hushed: "If I'd said another word, I'd have broken down and cried." *our3doxies Classic Photos*

Broadcasters gather, mid-1950s spring training. *Front, left to second from right*: Dodgers' Vin, Connie Desmond, and Al Helfer. *Back, in middle, left to right*: Yankees' Barber and Mel Allen. "I was a kid, really," said Vin, in his hometown, doing what he loved. *Mel Allen Estate*

In 1957, the Dodgers moved to Los Angeles. Vin looked on, torn. The 1958–61ers struck gold in the gaping Coliseum. Thrice the 1959 Series topped 92,000, *above*. That May 7, 93,103 lit matches for crippled Roy Campanella. Said Vin: "Let there be a prayer for every light." *National Baseball Hall of Fame Library*

Vilified for leaving Brooklyn, owner Walter O'Malley had the last laugh a continent away. His 1962–66 team drew more than 2 million yearly and won three pennants and two World Series. In 1965, skipper Walter Alston, *right*, let Vin manage the season's final game. *National Baseball Hall of Fame Library*

Opening in 1962, drop-dead gorgeous 56,000-capacity Dodger Stadium tied five-tier seating, Santa Ana Bermuda grass, a view of the San Gabriel Mountains, and palm trees beyond the outfield: baseball's first privately financed park since Yankee Stadium debuted in 1923. *National Baseball Hall of Fame Library*

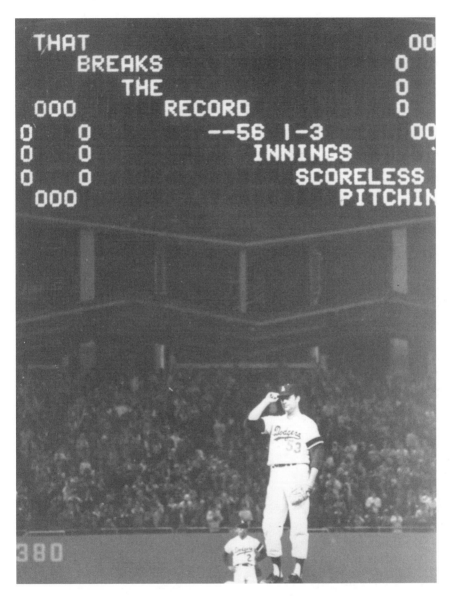

Perhaps Vin's Everest play-by-play was Sandy Koufax's 1965 perfect game. In 1968, future Dodgers broadcaster Don Drysdale threw a then-record 58⅔ straight scoreless innings. In 1993, Big D died suddenly at 56. Scully announced it "as best I can with a broken heart." *National Baseball Hall of Fame Library*

Scully aired Bill Buckner's 1986 error, Kirk Gibson's 1988 leviathan, and Henry Aaron's 1974 crossing a most Ruthian line. In Atlanta, Vin said: "A black man is getting a standing ovation in the Deep South for breaking a record of an all-time baseball idol." *National Baseball Hall of Fame Library*

In 1982, shown with announcer Ralph Kiner, Scully, only 54, received the
Hall of Fame's Ford C. Frick broadcast award. "I wanna sing, I wanna dance,
I wanna laugh, I wanna shout, I wanna cry, and I'd like to pray," Vin, sans
notes, told pilgrims filling Cooper Park. *National Baseball Hall of Fame Library*

In the late 1960s and 1970s, Vin took a road less traveled: CBS Radio baseball and network TV football, golf, tennis, and quiz and talk programming. He liked Laurence Olivier's secret of success: "The humility to prepare and the confidence to bring it off." *National Baseball Hall of Fame Library*

Scully had been known for local, not network, baseball. That changed in 1983. Vin became NBC TV's play-by-playman—Joe Garagiola did analysis—airing 3 World Series, 4 All-Star Games, 7 LCS, and *Game of the Week*. Goethe said, "America, you have it better." Baseball did. *National Baseball Hall of Fame Library*

In 1990, baseball improbably ended *Game*. Vin rejoined CBS Radio, having never left the Dodgers. On September 24, 2000, the American Sportscasters Association named Scully "Sportscaster of the 20th Century." As ASA head Lou Schwartz presented the award, the Chavez Ravine crowd roared "Vinny! Vinny!"—hoping to always pull up his chair. *American Sportscasters Association*

8

WHERE YOU LEAD (1976–1982)

WOULD RADIO'S MAN be as good on television? Would baseball's thrive on baseball-free CBS? In the mid-1970s, inquiring minds wished to know. Once Scully described a frustrated batter accidentally "hit himself on the head with the bat. I've seen golfers do that." Vin filled his first network golf daybook in 1975. "And Jack Nicklaus breaks a tie that he had with Arnold Palmer," he said. "Nicklaus now stands alone atop the heap, atop Mt. Olympus, if you will, as he wins his fifth Masters." Dick Young liked "the thrilling presentation of one of the most successful tournaments ever played when Nicklaus, [Tom] Weiskopf, and [Johnny] Miller came down the stretch." Scully's stretch had been the seventh inning's. Part of him still wished it were.

"[Hearsay] is that Scully had pondered seeking the [1975] NBC *Monday Night Baseball* job, but nixed it when he heard that Joe Garagiola was aboard," Jack Craig wrote. "I'm not Joe Show Biz," countered the Funny Man, "just a sweatshirt guy running at top speed to stay even. Those guys on the bubblegum cards, they're mine." Already Joe's card listed TV's *Memory Game, Sale of the Century, The Today Show,* 1961–64 *Major League Baseball,* and 1972's Monday pregame *Baseball World of Joe Garagiola.* In 1974 he aired the All-Star Game with Gowdy, then collared Carl Lindemann. "[Curt] kept cutting me off. I couldn't say a word."

Next year Joe added Saturday, Monday, the Reds-Pirates LCS, and Classic play-by-play. Like a farmer, Lindemann felt the wind. Garagiola was "one of the most likable voices in broadcasting," the *New York Times* said, and pitchman for baseball's TV angel, Chrysler Corp., "maneuvering behind the scenes," mused Carl, "to get Gowdy off baseball altogether." Vin sympathized. "[He and Garagiola] apparently should not be invited to the same party," said Craig, asking if "when viewers hear him more often, and away from baseball, [Scully] may lose his image as an absolute untouchable."

To Vin—like O'Malley, cautious—Dodgers security spired. "The only way I would divorce myself," he told the *Los Angeles Times*, "would be with a firm, no-loophole [network] contract which would pay me a reasonable amount of money and would give me more time at home than I have now." Columbia might provide it. "The reason I took the sports assignment . . . is to scout around," not wanting network *and* local. "You're away every weekend during the baseball season, then football and golf."

The quandary "keeps me awake. I go back and forth." The club was "kind. They know [why] I'm working [network] this year. I could have left them this winter. But I wouldn't do that. I'd give them a year's notice." Fordham's *fils* fenced with conscience. Six children. Network jack. Homebody, meet Traveling Man. When is the smart thing wrong? "All the guilt," he said. "Then thinking, no, this is for my family." A theologian would like the discourse. Vin merely pined for life to stabilize and sort out.

"No more two-week road trips," the *Tribune* reassured in early 1975. By fall, fine print reared. "My [NFL] schedule has me going east almost every weekend [to national games]," Scully rued. "Aren't there any games out here I can do?" The *L.A. Times*'s Larry Stewart answered: "National telecasts are usually the first game of a doubleheader and because of the early starting time normally originate" from, say, New York. Moreover, the O'Malleys went ungently, balking when CBS named Vin and analyst Hank Stram to September 21's Cowboys-Rams. Reason: Dodgers same-day TV.

Lindsey Nelson had spent 14 years balancing local ball and network pigskin. "You have to lay down the ground rules far in advance." Vin's newest child was seven months old. At some point, Stewart said, "CBS or the Dodgers will lose out to the family."

Network grass wasn't necessarily greener—at least, as we shall see, for now.

By 1976 THE EXCEPTION to all-stars-are-national had "worked periodically for CBS the past year," said Craig, "so the rest of the nation has discovered what the Dodger faithful already knew . . . his sheer talent, with an added boost from the fact that his home base is the media metropolis of Los Angeles." Baseball's status quo was breaking up, change's effect unsure.

Since 1957, NBC Radio had aired the Fall and Mid-Summer Classic. The LCS hung in limbo. Buying exclusivity, CBS showed how even a brief wisp of Scully could top being at the park. "Our analysts are almost irrelevant," Dick Brescia, Columbia's then-senior vice president, said of Sparky Anderson, Johnny Bench, and Al Downing, among others. "I care about play-by-play."

In 1977 Brescia approached Vin at the All-Star Game. "Tell me what you see in the booth."

"What do you mean?"

"What's in there? What's in the booth?"

Scully asked Dick to explain.

"I see one guy without whom nothing happens till you say a word," Brescia said. "That's how important your job is." In radio, "the announcer's the show. The slow pace is perfect. If you've got a bad Voice, the game stinks. Great Voice, bad game or not, you win."

Vin added the 1979–82 Series to 1977–78's All-Star Game: "our *best* announcer," Dick mused, "and our *typical* announcer." His roster became a Hall of Fame assembly line: at one time or another, including Cooperstown's Gowdy, Harwell, Jerry Coleman, Jack Buck, and Harry Kalas. CBS's 1976–82 Star and Classic audience rose by 37 and 45 percent, respectively. By 1985's Saturday *Game of the Week*, Vin, on to bigger things, had been succeeded, if not replaced.

TV was chancier. ABC ended NBC's monopoly by buying 1976–79 *Monday Night* and every-other-year All-Star, LCS, and Series coverage. "Good luck to 'em. We've still got a lot left," said Garagiola, inheriting Curt's play-by-play. Joe's rise changed *Game*. "Non-players grow up with baseball myth," said Nelson. "To ex-jocks, it's a career." Scully and Caray denoted wine and beer, respectively. Garagiola and Tony Kubek blared meat and spuds—as tony as a paper plate.

"A great example of black and white," said NBC executive producer Scotty Connal. A pitcher throws badly to second base. "Joe'd say, 'The second baseman's fault.' Tony answers: 'The pitcher's fault.'" Few doubted that honesty was their policy.

"He's got an expensive toy," Tony said of Yankees owner George Steinbrenner. "Baseball's tough enough without an owner harassing you." Irked, The Boss memoed NBC about "biting the fan that feeds it."

Tony: "George likes to use people as pawns."

King George: "Kubek will not get player interviews."

Tony shrugged. Joe's job was to report; his, illumine. What was ABC's? "It'll take something different for *Monday Night* to work," said sports president Roone Arledge, not intending it to become how his network blew the routine 6-4-3. Scoring yawns and lulls, *Post*man Henry Hecht suggested Warner Wolf, Prince, and Bob Uecker, then Cosell and Keith Jackson, "be locked in a room and forced to spend 100 hours a week listening to Scully."

The Dodgers marked the National League Centennial by asking fans to name their "'most memorable personality' in the history of the [L.A.] franchise." Vin routed Big D, Mr. K, and Wills. It was easy to see why. Pittsburgh's Rennie Stennett gave out cigars, vowing, "It's a boy!" Said Scully of a baby girl: "He only missed by one." Pete Rose "just beat out a walk." A grounder neared Davey Lopes. "He's set to jump . . . and didn't have to."

John Milner almost reached the wall. "Milner doesn't get enough of it and here's Dave Kingman, who doesn't have to get enough of it." King Kong promptly homered. "So Milner hits a long out and Kingman hits one out long." Let us hail a day long remembered.

EACH YEAR VIN RECALLED June 6, 1944—D-Day—the Allied invasion of Hitler's *Festung Europa*. "Having been associated a little bit with World War II, the flag means a great deal," he said. "There are many of us who feel the flag is sacred." On April 25, 1976, two slugs intent on defaming it left the Dodger Stadium bleachers.

Ted Sizemore took a ball. "And wait a minute, there's an animal loose, two of them, alright," Scully began. One "had something folded under his arm," said Cubs center fielder Rick Monday. Vin wasn't "sure what he's doing out there." Haltingly, a slug laid the U.S. flag out like a picnic blanket, spreading lighter fluid. Said Scully: "It looks like he's going to burn a flag!" Wind doused his first match. The animal lit a second. Racing,

Monday dodged thrown fluid, taking "[the flag] away from him." Like the other 25,550 in attendance, Scully would have booked the slug on a purgatory cruise.

"That guy was going to set fire to the American flag! Can you imagine that?" Vin bayed, flesh and blood, not catchphrase or caricature. "You've gotta lose him in a hurry!" Chavez Ravine then turned to its object of adulation. "Rick will get an ovation, and properly so. Rick Monday, quick thinking, gets a round of applause in center field." The message board read: "'Rick Monday—You Made a Great Play!' And now, a lot of the folks are standing. And now the *whole ballpark*! And he's going to get a standing ovation!"

At this point an unsunshine patriot began singing "God Bless America." Dodger Stadium soon throbbed to teary carolers. "A moment none of us will forget," said Scully. Pavarotti never sounded better.

To VIN, BASEBALL'S 1976–78 sound track replaced the National Anthem "with 'We're in the Money.'" Five times the '70s Dodgers finished second to Cincinnati. "I don't manage this team," said Sparky Anderson. "It's managed by Rose and Morgan and Bench and Perez." In 1976 the Big Red Machine led the league in 15 offensive categories, swept the LCS, and crushed the Yankees. That winter KABC's network rose to 15 outlets; O'Malley OK'd Vin's all-home radio and partial road TV schedule, pleasing CBS; and Darrtown (pop. 179), Ohio's leading citizen retired after seven pennants, four world titles, and a 2,040-1,613 record.

"It took me a long time to get here. It didn't take me that long to decide when I thought I'd had enough," said Walter Alston, reminiscing about a once-tripped-on-his-shoelace, falling-from-the-turnip truck naïf.

Vero Beach, 1954, Walt's first year as manager. Before a game Scully asks, "What's today's lineup, skipper?"

"'Pee Wee Reese, Gilliam, Snider, Hodges, through Campanella,'" said Alston. "Batting eighth is Charlie Jones."

Vin paused. "Who's that?"

Leaving, No. 24 feigned a meeting. "Well, Vinny, if you're going to broadcast the Dodgers, at least you ought to know the players"—camp numbering about 250.

Scully began asking, "Are you Charlie Jones?" of one player after another. Two decades later Jones was still missing, like Walt the year

Brooklyn basked in bliss. "It's late '55, a truly momentous time," said Vin, "and I mail a Christmas card to 'Mr. and Mrs. Walter Alston, Darrtown, Ohio, the manager of the world champion Brooklyn Dodgers.'" The card returned, address unknown.

Scully became "a guy [who'll] get to using those big words. I told him a few times that I wasn't sure whether he was complimenting or insulting me," laughed Alston, third man to skipper the same team for 20 years (others, John McGraw and Connie Mack). The fourth bled Dodger Blue. "The first time I saw Tom Lasorda he was catching batting practice," said Monday, symmetrically traded to L.A. in January 1977. "Thirty minutes later, I saw him on the mound throwing batting practice. Thirty minutes later, he was in the outfield with us. I thought, 'who is this guy?'" Rick quickly learned.

In 1929, General Motors former director John Raskob wrote about saving and investing stocks: "I am firm in my belief that anyone not only can be rich but ought to be rich." The '77 Angelenos made bigs history with nearly 3 million in home attendance. Their LCS foil hoped to *alter* history. The sans-ever title 1950 Phillies lost the Series; 1964, blew a 6½-game September lead; 1976, lost a playoff to The Machine. Vin denoted easy listening; Harry Kalas, a wrecker razing cars. "It's like Harry had opera training," said team VP Larry Shenk. "No one can call a homer like him." To the Main Line, Brandywine, and Center City, "It's outta here!" was outta sight.

By 1977 the Chicago-born, Iowa-schooled, Army-trained, and ex-Astros announcer synthesized a region's hope, grief, and sufferance. LCS Games 1-2 split. In Set 3, L.A. trailed, 5-3, in a two-out, no-on ninth. "We're thinking Series," said Phils skipper Danny Ozark, until Vic Davalillo bunted, Bruce Froemming blew the *out!* call, and Manny Mota skied to left. "Luzinski going back!" said Kalas. "And this ball is trapped! . . . It's a double for Manny Mota! Coming in to score: Davalillo. . . . It's now a 5-4 ballgame!" Bill Russell singled to score Lopes: a 6-5 ex-Bums crusher. Next day Steve Carlton lost, 4-1. Philly's Veterans Stadium wilted in the rain.

On October 11 the Stripes and Dodgers began their first North American rounders tournament since 1963. "How big were they?" jabbed ABC TV's Cosell. "The opener led our [*News Tonight*] newscast." Vin would have relished it. "It's amazing to me when I go back to New York," he said. "Of course, those were the golden days. The last time I was there

I had a man with a kid come up to me. He said, 'Son, this is Vin Scully. Remember?' He was 12. I said, 'Hey, pal, I've been gone since '57.' All he wanted to talk about was Campy and Robinson and Pee Wee and Hodges and Newk. It's been a remarkable number of years." If not remarkable, Vin's World Series absence stung.

Baseball's new TV pact let the network pick Classic mikemen. "In ABC's first [1977] Series," said Phil Mushnick, "they wanted [football trucklers] Jackson and Cosell." Then-*Los Angeles Examiner*'s Stewart blew a fuse: "There are two things wrong with ABC's coverage. A) Scully is not involved. B) Cosell is. ABC . . . went to great lengths to use Cosell, who admittedly doesn't like baseball and obviously doesn't know much about it, on the Series." He doubted if Arledge cared. "The public is outraged that you have forced Cosell down its throat and, particularly here in Los Angeles, it is outraged Vin Scully is not behind the mike with the Dodgers in the Series."

Bowie Kuhn recoiled at The Franchise being odd man out. "He preferred the participating teams' announcers to work the Series," said Stewart, noting ABC's crumbs for Scully: two innings on each home game. In response, Vin's "lawyer and business advisor, Ed Hookstratten, insisted Scully turn down ABC's offer." Insult hurt, but taught: the bigs's Secretariat dumped for two Mr. Eds.

Vin had minimized network ball. "I'd hear from fans in New York, where they remembered me, or other places aware of my work, and they'd say, 'Gee, why aren't you on?'" He was flattered, but unmoved. "I was happy"—and newly wise. In 1971 Scully had warned then-Fordham student Ed Randall, "You have to get to the apartment house before you can get inside the apartment." Another Series would require a network key.

Go FIGURE. VIN misses the 1977 Classic. The Dodgers' new third man airs it on CBS Radio. To Scully, statistics were "used much like a drunk uses a lamp post: for support, not illumination." Ross Porter treated them like a power company. At three, on his daddy's knee, "I'd hear him read baseball stories, pique my interest," said the Okie. "I'd sit in the family car at night listening to games": his hero, strangely, Harry Caray, who treated statistics like beriberi.

In 1953, Porter, 14, joined Class D Shawnee. Later, he left the University of Oklahoma via WKY Oklahoma City for L.A.'s KNBC TV's *The John*

McKay Show, Golf with the Pros, and high school hoops. "Sandy [Koufax] once turned down a basketball scholarship, and was now under contract to NBC. They didn't know what to give him, so he did my color." Ross did NBC roundball and football, taking a 1973 and 2001 Emmy, 1970 and 1972–73 Associated Press awards, and 1969, 1972, and 1976 Southern California Golden Mikes.

Porter discreetly welcomed another first-in-his-class. "I'm an addition to the team, not Vin's replacement," he said. "I thought, wow, with Vin, the Dodgers'll make me run water!" Instead, Porter ran to the Oktoberfest. In Game 6, Yankee Thurman Munson reached. "Here's a drive to right field and deep!" Ross said of next-up Reggie Jackson. "Smith going back! It's gone!" No. 44 later faced Elias Sosa. "Set. The pitch. Drive to right field and deep! Way back! Going, going, gone! Another home run for Reggie Jackson!"

Charlie Hough knuckled an eighth-inning toss. "Jackson, with four runs batted in, sends a fly ball to center field deep! That's going to be way back! And that's going to be gone! Reggie Jackson has hit his third home run [on three straight pitches] of the game!" said Ross, voice deep and disembodied. Cosell added: "[Including Game 5] four straight homers!" New York led, 8-4, as "[Lee Lacy's bunt was] popped up! Torrez has got it! And the Yankees are the world champions for the 21st time—and for the first time in 15 years."

In 1977 Peter O'Malley began Sunday and "selected weeknight" TV coverage. Next year L.A.'s $1.8 million rights fee led the league. On April 14, its core handled the Ravine's Opening Day first ball. The twirler allowed to "going out early and see if I can reach the field from the radio booth. I really don't want to stand in the first base box and throw the ball. But I better make sure I can reach the field," said Vin, who did. "I wouldn't want to conk anyone on the head."

In 1975 the Dodgers and Columbia aped radio's 1940s *The Bickersons.* By 1978 they sang Sammy Cahn's and Jimmy Van Heusen's "Love and Marriage." CBS inked Vin through 1982. "Tonight," Stewart wrote, "you can see and hear Scully working the Dodger season opener in Atlanta and tomorrow and Sunday you can see and hear him anchoring CBS's coverage of the Masters." Vin bubbled, packing for Augusta. "Atlanta is a half-hour plane ride away from Augusta. I'm getting variety now with network work," loving, as always, baseball's.

Mr. K was best all-time pitcher; Mays, "best all-around"; Jackie Robinson, "fiercest competitor," Scully told Doug Krikorian. Lasorda was best ambassador. "On my tombstone," he said, "I want to have the Dodgers' schedule. That way I'll work for them even after I've died." Major Tom was bounced six times from 1977–79. "I don't get to hear Vinny as much as everyone else. So when you see me getting thrown out, it's only because I want to go into the clubhouse and find out if he can still do the job." Baying "Herrrrrre's Vinny!" Lasorda called him baseball's Johnny Carson "because he's gone so much."

In 1978 the past year's plot reran: pennant, Classic loss, Porter on CBS, and Vin's Series MIA. The Phillies again lost a four-game playoff. "The 1-0 pitch," said ABC's Al Michaels. "Hit into center field for a base hit. Ron Cey being waved in! And it allows the winning run as it gets by Maddox!" The Stripes and Dodgers visited a 10th time since 1941, Los Angeles taking an 11-5 opener. "There's one into left-center field! It's another one!" cried Garagiola of Lopes twice going deep.

Next night L.A. led, 4-3, ninth inning, two out and on. "It's the kind of situation an announcer lives for," Vin would say. "Baseball *mano a mano*." Jackson fouled four pitches vs. reliever Bob Welch. Finally: "Struck him out!" said Joe G. "Ballgame over! Bob Welch! A marvelous performance!" New York then won four straight. "Popped up behind the plate!" said Bill White, first black to air a Series, his second for CBS Radio. "Coming back, Munson! Throws the mask away! . . . The Yankees have won their second straight world championship!"

Strains part, then reconnect. O'Malley led a decade-later National League president search committee. "It's his [White's] if he wants it," said one owner. Ultimately, he did, becoming the bigs's first black league head. Said Doggett: "One part of Robinson would be proud. The other would have wondered what took so long."

AT LIBERTY, VIN "took it easy" in October. "It's just a case of understanding the situation. Baseball sold the rights to the network, and the network wants to use its own announcers." Later, he dubbed the 1977–78 Series "a blur to me. I was preoccupied [with the NFL]." Flying to a football gig, Scully passed over Yankee Stadium. A woman in the next seat eyed him with puzzlement. "How can *you* be up *here* while *they're* playing down *there*?" Angelenos missed him. "That's because I didn't have to fight the curve."

Vin's fastball spiked a late-1978 interview. "When you do the play-by-play, you don't say, 'A black man hit a ball to a white man.' They're all the same color." Even uniforms were color-blind. "In L.A., fans will applaud a visiting player who makes a good play. You get a good feeling that . . . is [often] lacking"—especially in the East. "It's almost animal. Where you go to a ball game in threatening weather, you get to the park on edge." At the Ravine, "the weather is so nice, and . . . park so relaxing, that it soothes. They don't have the pressures of confinement in a small city, or the friction." One difference was cultural. Another, generational. "[Most] letters are from youngsters who want to become broadcasters. In the old days they wanted to be ballplayers." Most now wanted to be Scully.

March 1979: Vero Beach. Vin did Dodgertown: "If this isn't heaven, I can't wait to see what is." Azalea, jade practice fields, and roofless dugouts at 6,500-seat Holman Stadium—"Walter's idea," Scully said, "so folks'd feel near their guys"—lit village green Capra celluloid. Each St. Patrick's Day, O'Malley held a dinner. Singing "Danny Boy," Vin brought down the house. Rochester, New York, Mayor William Johnson recalled Robinson in the 1940s. "This was such a special place in America, especially given the Dodgers' pioneering role in spurring integration," he said. Each year the black urban expert visited Vero like a pilgrim does Lourdes. "With luck, you'd sit in the stands next, say, to Koufax. Once there, you were hooked forever."

Don Drysdale Drive adjoined Roy Campanella Boulevard. To reach the field, you took Duke Snider Street to post-1981 Vin Scully Way. "Dodgertown did not invent spring training. It only perfected it," wrote *Sports Illustrated*. By 1979, The Franchise's spring schedule meant an occasional Channel 11 game. "I was busy with the network: tough at the start, but it came eventually," said Scully. "Preparation and study take you only so far, then you have to apply it": a lesson for the Dodgers, losing their most games since 1968.

Leaving: Mota, after a bigs record 146th pinch-hit. "The 41-year-old Dominican star waiting," began Porter. "Looped to right field! There it is! Mota did it!" Arriving: Rookie of the Year Rick Sutcliffe. Dying: O'Malley *père*, August 9, 1979. "He created the Dodgers himself," said Steve Garvey.

"The attitude. The marketing skills. The stadium in Los Angeles. And the foresight to move from Brooklyn to Los Angeles." Vin thanked his patron for letting Scully be Scully. "He let me grow, make mistakes." In turn, "Walter [told] you Scully has been responsible for selling more Dodger tickets than Koufax, Drysdale, and Wills combined," Krikorian wrote, "creating a passionate community loyalty to the team far beyond what you would expect from mere pennants and world championships."

Vin's warp-speed schedule included a Friars Club lunch to which Cey wore a cowboy hat. "Maybe he's heard about the rumor that Houston wants him." A listener heard Vin on his first CBS Radio Classic—to quote its highlight film, *Fantastic Series 1979*. In Pittsburgh, a faux turf patch marred center field. In Baltimore, football yard lines evoked retired John Unitas. Garb rivaled roller derby's: Birds, white and orange; Bucs, striped, yellow, or black and gold. It didn't matter on the wireless. "You didn't see the ugliness," said Doggett. "All you got was Vin."

Baltimore led the opener, 3-0, "to the merriment of [a] wild flock of fans," Scully said. Doug DeCinces dinged "deep into the big black sky": Orioles, 5-4. Next night Pittsburgh's Bert Blyleven tossed a lob. "Eddie Murray *times* it. Then *admires* it." Trailing, "the Birds [later] had to peek at a human scarecrow, Kent Tekulve": Pirates, 3-2. Sister Sledge sang their theme, "We Are Family." Losing Games 3 and 4, the Bucs seemed dysfunctional. Willie Stargell a.k.a. Pops then "demonstrates his paternal power": Pittsburgh, 7-1 and 4-0.

Helicoptering from D.C., President Carter watched the final: a softball-playing Georgian whose staff played country hardball. A (Steel) City man batted in the sixth. "Willie Stargell, and, of course, he always makes the opposition uneasy, especially in this kind of situation," mused Vin's play-by-play. "One-nothing, Baltimore, and a man aboard. Stargell at the plate. McGregor comes to him. And there's a high fly ball into deep right-center field! Back goes Singleton, away back to the wall. It's gone! He's done it!"—Bucs, 4-1.

"Pops has hit it out!" said the man who hit it out each night.

LIKE 1974, THE *New York Times* noted "fans turning off [network] TV's [Jackson, Cosell, Michaels, and Drysdale] sound . . . and onto [Scully's] commentary." Through 1982 Vin averaged 48 million listeners—one in three Americans 18 or older—on the Mid-Summer and Fall Classic. He also aired the 1980 no-no of a man who in 1973 inhaled today's "surround sound": Scully in the Round.

"There were maybe 22,000 fans in the stands at Dodger Stadium and I think half had their radios with them, listening to him," then-Astro Jerry Reuss told the *Houston Chronicle*'s David Barron. "You could hear it from high in the left-field stands all the way around to the stadium club." The future Dodger knew that Vin was telling a story "because his voice was getting higher"; whereupon Jerry "got some rosin and let him finish"; after which the crowd chuckled. "That's when I got back on the mound and delivered my pitch."

Reuss won a last-weekend 1980 game to grease a Western Division playoff vs. Houston. July's All-Star Game—Nationals, 4-2, their ninth straight victory—bared the Ravine's new "Diamond Vision Scoreboard" of line score, lineup, and replay. In October, the 'Stros braved an odd LCS double play: fly to right field, relay to the pitcher, and toss to third base, where a stray runner was put out. As CBS went to break, "Scully summed it up quickly," wrote the *New York Times*'s George Vecsey, "using the scorecard symbols for the three participating fielders: *Just your basic nine-one-five double play*, Scully said, knowing that real baseball fans would understand the staccato eloquence of his call."

"For the first time in 60 years," Vin would say, rehighlighting, "two teams that have never won a World Series [Royals and Phillies] meet in baseball's showcase." Philly began by accentuating the affirmative: 7-6 and 6-4. Keith Moreland's designated hitter safety "backfires on its American League founders." As Scully knew, reliever Tug McGraw's "cool, calm, and collective countenance" was none of the above. Kansas City's "favorite 12-year-old [came] home in a glittering World Series premiere."

George Brett and Mike Schmidt homered. Amos Otis, "known as A.O., gets ready to send this ball AWOL." Next day "the pride of the show-me state shows 'em," tying *l'affaire*. The first all-artificial turf Classic then swung: McGraw acing K.C.'s Quiz (Dan Quisenberry), 4-3. The Quakers returned to Philadelphia, Kalas re-creating Tug's last out: "World champions of baseball! It's pandemonium at Veterans Stadium! All of the fans are on their feet. This city has come together behind a baseball team! Phillies are world champions! This city knows it! This city loves it!"

Vin augured Philly's day-later parade. "The Ghosts of Phillies Past are finally laid to rest." Next year presaged ground shifting under baseball's feet, though it seemed oblivious at the time.

BORN IN CAYAMBE, Ecuador, and schooled in philosophy, engineering, letters, and journalism at Central University of Quito, Jaime Jarrin learned radio at a local 750,000-watt commercial station. "Hearing my voice, a friend asked if I'd considered being an announcer," he told XM Satellite Radio's 2007 *Voices of The Game*. Actually, he had "the bug to fly. I even enrolled in aviation school, but didn't stay," migrating to Southern California in 1955. The 19-year-old had never heard of baseball. "I unpack in time for the Dodgers-Yankees Series, and can't believe the interest. I'm like, 'Wow, what's going on here? What *is* this game?'"

Jarrin became Pasadena's Spanish KWKW sports/news director as broadcast Latinos seemed mostly prop, joke, or foil. Desi Arnaz vowed to 'splain a thin' or two. Carmen Miranda's come-on was a befruited head. *The Cisco Kid* made English elementary. Pancho: "Oh, Cisco." Cisco: "Oh, Pancho." Radio/TV Hispanic bigs were even rarer. "Mostly we didn't exist," said Jaime. "Those who did were called un-American."

In late 1955 he set out to grasp, if not call, the game. "I'd watch the [Pacific Coast League] Angels and [Hollywood] Stars, and later the Dodgers when they came West." In 1958, Jarrin spurned the big club's play-by-play. "I still wasn't ready. That entire year I read every book I could on baseball." Debuting next year, "I figured I'd do about six or seven years, then go back into news or boxing or soccer. Famous last words."

Wearing headphones, "I started in baseball by staying in studio," translating Vin and Doggett "when the team was on the road. I'd re-create. Vin prepped me, noting in advance the weather or terms that might give me trouble." On XM, he recounted "copying" Scully's rhythm, envying Vin's "talent for choosing the right word in the right place." In turn, The Franchise liked his extempora. "I was in awe. Jaime'd immediately interpret me."

Emigrating, Columbian journalist Sandra Hernandez "listened to two things on the radio": Spanish soaps and "our evangelist," ferrying the Dodgers—"*Esquivadores*"—to barrio, tract, and farm. *La Voz de Oro*—"the Golden Voice"—continued to ferry news: Winston Churchill's memorial service, Pope John Paul II's U.S. visit, a gunman holding a plane and 56 hostages on an airport Tarmac until Jaime arrived to negotiate, and John F. Kennedy's murder.

Where were you November 22, 1963? Part of Jarrin is still there. The Texas School Book Depository. Crumpled roses. Mrs. Kennedy's bloodstained suit. Lyndon Johnson's swearing in, the widow at his side. Three days later Jaime deplaned in Washington at 6:30 A.M., "not a soul around, only soldiers with machine guns patrolling the streets." By chance, he bumped into a friend, L.A. councilman Eduardo Roybal.

"What are you here for?" said Roybal.

"To cover the funeral."

"What do you need?"

"Everything."

In thirty minutes, Jaime had a jeep with "two soldiers, a radio technician, and equipment." By 1:30, he stood in the Capitol Rotunda, 40 feet from the casket. "I was broadcasting when Mrs. Kennedy came in with John Jr." Jarrin hopped a jeep to Arlington National Cemetery, missing John-John's salute, the riderless steed, and caisson trek. "I got there just in time to broadcast the family's entrance—the most difficult assignment I ever had."

"THE DODGERS WERE the first major-league team," said Scully, "to pay attention to the Spanish-speaking market"—also to broadcast bilingually. By the late 1960s, Jaime aired them from San Diego and San Francisco. In 1970 he won a radio/TV Golden Mike Award for interviewing President Richard Nixon and Mexico's Gustavo Diaz Ordaz. "The White House press secretary [Ron Ziegler] told us that there would be no personal interviews," said Jaime, for whom luck again beat a path. "They walked near where I was standing." Alone, Jarrin asked Milhous to address his Spanish-speaking audience, "knowing that I was running the risk of having the Secret Service take me out of there by force." Nixon made *Espanol* perfectly clear. Jaime "knew then that Ordaz would have to talk," and did.

In 1973 he inaugurated L.A.'s Spanish Network. Leaving studio, Jarrin went each game live: "finally, first class," moving uptown, not upstairs. "*La pelota viene como una mariposa,*" he chimed: the ball moved like a butterfly. "*Se va, se va, se va* ": in any language, going, going, gone. "*Es el momento del matador, el momento de la verdad*" prefaced a 3-2 sacks-full pitch—to Jaime, the bullfighter's Rubicon, in a game of life or death.

By 1980 Hispanics totaled 25 percent of Dodgers attendance. Next April, a 20-year-old Mexican rookie made the team. On Opening Day, Fernando Valenzuela faced Houston. "So [he] has this crowd just *dying* to salute him," Vin cried in the ninth. "With two out, a full count . . . Valenzuela delivers! Screw ball! Got him [Dave Roberts] swinging! What a way to start! Fernando Valenzuela, in his first big-league start, pitches a shutout! And a little child shall lead them!" Soon the San Fernando Valley seemed to signify his name.

By May 1, No. 34 had four shutouts, a 0.20 ERA, and a .348 batting average, stirring a vain demand for more home video. "Almost all TV had been road," Jaime mused. "Now, especially with more [legal and illegal] immigration, the interest was unbelievable." Fernandomania became a physical burgeoning in all its diversity. "I'd translate English into Spanish for him, then back again. I must have seemed an oddity." Vin dubbed the Ecuadorian "Numero Uno," adding, "Jaime and I agree that it's the game, not us. There's so much going on, and the more you know, the more interesting it is."

For a decade, Cosell had styled baseball a dodo in a warp-speed world. "So he says that baseball is dull and slow," said The Franchise, "completely missing the point. Hell, bridge is slower than blackjack. But the guy who plays bridge loves it *because* it's a bit slower: a game for thought." The average person "hasn't played much football. He doesn't think he knows as much as Tom Landry or Don Shula." Almost everyone, including Bridget, Vin said, had played baseball—"even nuns. The baseball fan is generally more knowledgeable." A man who synthesized Vin's Gaelic mix of grace, pain, and cheer agreed.

"You're brought up with it," said 1954–2001 Cardinals Voice Jack Buck. "With baseball, you're telling bright people inside dope they don't know because they're not there." Scully felt that "most baseball fans know what it's like to have a ground ball take a bad hop and hit you in the mouth." By 1981 the Dodgers had tired of October's black eye, their last title 1965. "We had the feeling," said Jerry Reuss, "that this might be our last chance." Fernando's 8-0 start abbreviated the odds.

Los Angeles led Cincinnati by half a game at the June 12 players' strike, later taking the first and, pray God, sole Intradivisional Series. Trailing the LCS, it revived at Olympic Stadium, Montreal's spaceship-shaped sterile cuckoo. The final was Sunday, October 18. In Minneapolis, CBS's Vin primed for football, "Everybody telling me, 'what a shame you have to be here.'" Eagles general manager Jim Murray cornered him pre-kickoff: "What a tough assignment. Your head is here doing football, and I know your heart's in Montreal with the baseball game."

Vin brightened: "Maybe it will rain in Montreal."

"If that game's rained out, so you can broadcast it tomorrow," Murray laughed, "I'll really believe there is a Dodger in the sky." The sky opened. Scully flew to Montreal, "so I was there when what happened, happened."

Baseball bans postseason local television. Vin did radio in a 1-all ninth. The Grand Old Flagsman swung. "A fly ball to Andre Dawson and deep. Dawson to the track! Dawson to the wall! It's gone! Home run by Rick Monday, and the Dodgers go wild."

Once more, with feeling: L.A. went forth against—the Yanks. "We're too good to lose again," Lopes vowed. Pride precedeth the unfall.

A sign in the Bronx bespoke past distress: "Don't the Dodgers ever learn?" New York's Bob Watson became 17th to homer his first Series up. Next night Jimmy Cagney, 82, threw out the Yanks' first ball. Inverting 1978, the Stripes quickly led, 2 games to 0. California confused them. "Murcer tries to lay one down," said ABC's Michaels in Game 3. "And Cey makes a diving catch in foul ground! Throws to first! Double play!" Lasorda and Pedro Guerrero huddled before hitting. "A few words of advice, for Pete's sake," Vin added, highlighting. "The Legend of El Toro" lived, 5-4, "on heart and hope."

L.A. reversed a 6-3 day-later deficit. "As the game enters its fourth hour," reliever "Steve Howe tries to maintain [and did, 8-7] a new balance of power." Next afternoon, behind, 1-0, the O'Malleys struck: "A high fly ball to left. Back goes Piniella! It's gone!" Scully said on CBS. "Pedro Guerrero hits a home run into the left-field bleachers!" Steve Yeager encored. "Swung on! *Another* high drive! Back goes Piniella! Way back! It's gone!"—2-1. Bridge or blackjack: L.A. drew a fourth straight in New York. "Watson hits a high fly ball to Landreaux! This is it!"

The team plane left straightaway for California. "Looking to celebrate," Vin and his wife returned to Manhattan's Carlyle Hotel. "It was kinda late, so I said to the bartender, 'Can I have a bottle of champagne?'"

"I'll tell you what, Mr. Scully," said the barkeep. "I'll put it in a bag and I'll give it to you. But I don't want [hotel resident] Mr. Steinbrenner to see it." The brown baggers took an elevator to their room, opened the bottle, and toasted the Dodgers. In retrospect, the bash had just begun.

SCULLY'S *ANNUS MIRABILIS* began January 5, 1982, by telephone from America's most famous village. "He has a natural talent combined with a splendid voice and a fluid delivery," said Hall of Fame head Ed Stack, naming Vin, at 54, easily the youngest Frickster. "Scully has elevated the business of broadcasting baseball to an art." Another broadcaster called from the world's most famous house. "You were a good [Pacific Palisades, California] neighbor, you were a great sports announcer, and you were a darn good friend," said Ronald Reagan, having re-created the '30s Cubs for WHO Des Moines.

"It's different now than when I was broadcasting baseball," he began. For one thing, Reagan marked a homer by crying, "And he gets a case of [sponsor] Wheaties!" Another: "Back then, it might be a slow roller to the shortstop, but you'd say, 'It's a hot shot to short . . . he's got it . . . he whips the throw to first . . . got him!'"

"Mr. President," Vin laughed, "is this an audition? I'm on shaky grounds when I hear you do that."

"No," said Reagan. "I was just trying to show the audience how tough your job is."

Vin's nod did not surprise a then-Tallahassee columnist. "In my opinion, Scully is the best baseball announcer we have, and one of the best in football and golf," wrote Barber, praising, as he seldom had, baseball's "best owner, too." Walter O'Malley had become "irked by Scully's CBS absences . . . [taking him] from the Dodgers from time to time. . . . He told me so at Vero. . . . When Walter got irked, as I very well knew, he wasn't going to lose." Red felt that he would have made Vin choose: L.A. or CBS. Son Peter grasped that "Scully was valuable enough when he was with the baseball team, and that his [network] appearances added to his stature with the baseball audience."

Comparatively iffy was Vin's stature at CBS. Columbia had kept the Masters, bought the Bing Crosby and Bob Hope pro-ams, and aired a record 19 tournaments in 1979. As 18th-hole/main Voice, Scully anchored 17-15's Jack Whitaker, Ben Wright, and Pat Summerall, respectively. Sunday's round often abutted 7 P.M.'s *60 Minutes.* "We'll have highlights for you at 11:30 after the news," Vin said. "And now good-bye to our viewers in the East and Midwest." Pro: felicity. Don January "played with all the passion and verve of a meter reader." Con: *Golf Digest*'s 1977 TV poll put Vin behind Dave Marr, Byron Nelson, Ken Venturi, Henry Longhurst, and Jim McKay.

The Ol' Redhead shrugged. "The only reason that Scully is not more widely promoted by CBS as a star is that the big shots at CBS operate out of New York," he wrote, "and if you don't hang your hat in The Black Rock on The Avenue of the Americas you are somewhat provincial." Fact was somewhat simpler: To Vin, CBS increasingly seemed more Big Fib than Black Rock. Gary Deeb had "taken it to the bank that Scully will be behind the mike at [the 1976] Super Bowl." Soon Vin felt taken, said a friend, "having been promised CBS's main football job."

After Hank Stram, Scully worked with, among others, Alex Hawkins, previewing the 1978 Dallas-Denver Super Bowl. Hawk: "[Cowboys quarterback] Roger Staubach kinda runs like a sissy." Vin: "Did you ever play football without a helmet?" Next year he called the National Football Conference title game with ex-coach George Allen. Irv Cross then left *The NFL Today* studio to become Scully's analyst. Other teams: rookie full-timer John Madden, with Gary Bender; Allen, joining Lindsey Nelson; and Tom Brookshier and a Voice likely vaulting higher, quicker, than any former jock.

Born in Florida, Summerall graduated Arkansas '52, was a 1953–61 Cardinals and Giants kicker/end, and taught school off-season. Retiring, Pat chose the 4-3 over 4+3: CBS Radio and TV, 1961 and 1967, respectively, becoming a blue-chip consortium. In 1994 he joined Fox TV's new pro football coverage. The *New York Times* parodied him calling *Old Man and the Sea*. "Marlins. Sharks. Harpoon. Broken knife. What a struggle. John?"—analyst Madden. The NFL's Hemingway did not plan on being sacked by baseball's F. Scott Fitzgerald.

In his book, *The Game Behind the Game*, producer Terry O'Neill replayed the shuffle. By 1981 CBS Sports had decided to bet the ranch on Madden as its football bookplate. Who was a better fit: Scully or Summerall? Each worked four games with John, Pat's just the facts, ma'am, deemed more in tune with the diuretic color man. CBS denied promising Vin a Super Bowl. Several insiders affirm that it reneged. "Summerall played his strengths," said one. "What mattered was that he was football's guy. Pat wouldn't yield, and CBS wouldn't push."

On January 10, 1982, Vin called "The [last-minute] Catch": Frisco 28, Dallas 27 in the NFC title game. "[Joe] Montana . . . looking . . . looking . . . throwing in the end zone! [Dwight] Clark caught it!" Summerall did Super Bowl XVI two weeks later. In turn, Scully vetoed Columbia's "last, best, 10-year, $7 million" offer," said the *Sporting News*. A CBS don told *TV Guide*: "He feels that he was lied to, and he doesn't want to work for us. It's that simple," closing Vin's lid on TV's Network of the Eye banked on floating clouds.

THAT MAY 5, The Franchise got the George Foster Peabody Pioneer in Broadcasting Award for Excellence in Sports Broadcasting, following Bert Parks, Lowell Thomas, and radio's Bob and Ray. "While your style and grace are often imitated, there is only one Vin Scully," wrote Kuhn, sensing him coming home. Scully arrived August 1, 1982, getting the Hall's Frick Award. An antithesis presented him.

"Today is Father's Day," Mets 1962 radio/TVer Ralph Kiner once said. "So to all you fathers in the audience, happy birthday."

American Cyanamid Co. was a Mets TV sponsor. "We'll be right back," Kiner went to commercial, "after this word from American Cyanide."

Near another break, he vowed, "We'll be back after this word for Manufacturers Hangover." Ralph's depiction of Marv Throneberry seemed to apply equally to himself: "He never made the same mistake twice. He always made different ones."

Howard Johnson became Walter Johnson; Gary Carter, Gary Cooper; Milt May, Mel Ott; Tim McCarver, Tim MacArthur. The General often said, "Chance favors a prepared man." Prepared, Kiner introduced Vin at the Hall with "many adjectives . . . used to describe Scully and his style. And his entertaining, precise, proficient, charming, friendly, outgoing, smooth, relaxed, warm, knowledgeable, intelligent, literate, concise, well-prepared, colorful material."

The crowd laughed. The Franchise rose. Ten thousand pilgrims filled Cooper Park, including Dodgers players, execs, staff, and Vin's mother. "I guess a vital portion of the human existence is when man is visited with misfortune," he commenced. "He invariably will look his eyes to the heavens and say why me? Why with the millions and millions of people in this world am I asked to carry a cross, and yet if I'm to be honest with you and myself today I have to ask the same question when good fortune came my way—why me? Why with the millions and millions of more deserving people would a red-haired kid with a hole in his pants and his shirt-tail hanging out, playing stick ball in the streets of New York, wind up in Cooperstown? Why me indeed?"

Applause braced the air. "I don't have the answer . . . but I do know how I feel," said Scully. "I wanna sing, I wanna dance, I wanna laugh, I wanna shout, I wanna cry, and I'd like to pray. I would like to pray with humility and with great thanksgiving." He thanked Bridget and Allan Reeve; wife Sandra and their children, "who pay the bill of loneliness and separation while I'm away"; Barber and Desmond, "who cared about that skinny redheaded kid . . . and made sure that he would do reasonably well"; Doggett and Porter; the O'Malleys, including "Walter and Kay— bless them both"; writers "who have been more than generous to me over the years"; and his bicoastal team. The anecdotist then closed.

"There is a legend in the West of an Indian Chief who was wont to test the manhood of his young braves by making them climb up the side of a mountain as far as they could in a single day. And at daybreak on the appointed day four braves left the village." The first returned in late afternoon with a spruce sprig to show how high he traveled. Later, two brought a branch of pine and alpine shrub. "But it wasn't until late that night by a full moon with the stars dancing in the heavens that the fourth brave arrived. 'What did you bring back?'" asked the Chief. "'How high did you climb?'"

"The brave said: 'Where I was there was no spruce or pine to shield me from the sun, there was no flower to cheer my path, there was only snow and ice and barren rocks and cold hard ground. My feet are torn and bloodied. I'm worn out and exhausted. I'm barehanded and I have come home late.'" A distant "look came into his eyes, and he said, 'I saw the sea.'"

Scully paused. "For thirty-three years the good Lord has allowed me to do what I have always wanted to do, broadcast my favorite game. He has allowed me to climb my mountain, and today, thanks to the Ford C. Frick Award, I thank you for sharing this moment with me because, believe me, today I saw the sea."

Vin denied "ever even thinking about [Cooperstown], to be honest." The Springfield, Massachusetts, *Republican* had. Its cartoonist remembered "Scully's mellow tones coming over Armed Forces Radio in 1965 making duty in Vietnam just a little bit easier to take." To a columnist, "he has done what he probably never dreamed to be possible. He has become a better baseball broadcaster than Red Barber, or anybody." Jon Miller then aired the Red Sox. "The very fact that Miller often will imitate him during one of his broadcasts is high tribute to this great baseball pro." Jilting gimmick—"How about that!" "Hey-Hey! "Holy Cow!"—Vin had "a reputation for being consistently good, and for being especially proficient under pressure."

In 1982 the would-be Music Man got Vin Scully Night, fourth National Sportscaster of the Year award, and star on the Hollywood Walk of Fame between, aptly, Tommy Dorsey and Ferlin Husky. Danny Kaye hosted a 30-minute KTTV salute. An anonymous San Diegoan sent a rose: "This bud's for you." One thorn was a minor June accident: Vin's car, sideswiped by a van. Another: replacing CBS. "You don't go out and buy a network," Scully said. "On the other hand, our kids were growing up. I was doing relatively fewer Dodger games [46 TV and 81 radio]. If any network approached me for baseball, it was easier to not reject the offer whole cloth." Three threads began a quilt: Dr. Dick, an Unordinary Joe, and new bigs medium.

As we have seen, the Dodgers had already tried pay-cable television. "Didn't work," said Doggett. "Not enough homes were [cable] wired. Others thought, 'Why pay for what we see for free?'" The '82ers aired 12 ON-TV games, Al Downing doing play-by-play. Few cared: Free local coverage remained TV's anchor. For a fee you could access cable programming. "The problem was availability," Jerry mused. "Without [a system], the customer was out of luck." Belatedly, baseball pined to please—thus, grow.

In 1976 Ted Turner bought the Atlanta Braves, upped their TV schedule, and renamed WTCG Atlanta SuperStation WTBS. "The Braves'll tie the sticks to the big-time," he hoped. Cable soon swelled baseball's stage; baseball, swelling cable's. "TBS was just one offering," said Ted. "People didn't know how it could sell the Braves a world from Georgia." In 1982 Atlanta began the season a bigs record 13-0. Suddenly, people knew.

The streak became "the 'two-by-four' that hit America between the eyes," said Braves Voice Ernie Johnson. A Storm Lake, Iowa, sign read "The Atlanta Braves: Iowa's Team." In Valdez, Alaska, a Braves Fan Club chapter pooled cash, bought a screen, and named its bar "The Braves' Lounge." In a decade, WTBS households leaped 7,000 percent. Basic subscription cable now wires 9 in 10 homes.

"The greatest thing to happen [to baseball] since Bat Day," the *Philadelphia Inquirer* wrote. A letter to the *Sporting News* thanked cable for "getting baseball back in the hearts of rural America." Tim McCarver, Skip Caray, and, above all, dad Harry became its billboard. Scully became its beneficiary, in a most circuitous way.

"LOOK AT THE LANDSCAPE if you're at [1982] NBC," said Vecsey. "No one could foresee SuperStation growth": TBS, WGN, New York's WOR. ABC yearly did 13 to 18 random games. CBS liked its non-baseball menu. NBC baseball had built a middling audience, little post-mid-'60s ballyhoo, and niche as Avis to football's Hertz. Could the Peacocks jump-start *Game of the Week* after a decade-plus in the garage?

Originally, NBC felt that Garagiola's devotion to the quaint and personal might halt *Game*'s hemorrhage. His mother could not speak English. Dad worked in a brickyard. Their son learned a salute to the flag, catch in the throat, tear in the eye Americanism. Best friend Yogi Berra lived "a pickoff away" on St. Louis's Dago Hill. Joe made the Cards, 1946; retired as a player, 1954; next year, joined KMOX St. Louis, becoming his own best subject matter. "You can't imagine the thrill," he said of a .257 lifetime average, "to walk into a clubhouse and wonder if your uniform is still there."

Dago Hill became terra firma. Baseball: "It's not like going to church." Dead air: "I'm Italian. I like to talk." Strategy: "An idiot could pick up" the signs. St. Louis forgave Joe's sharp voice. Harry Caray taught him how to use the diaphragm. "I had a lot of help, and needed it," said Garagiola. "Off my first play-by-play, I wouldn't have hired myself." Emceeing, the ribster became Berra's *ex officio* ambassador. "I'll ask him, 'What time is it?' Yogi'll say, 'Now?'"

Joe wrote 1960's best-selling *Baseball Is a Funny Game*. "One day I'm a dumb jock and the next I'm a writer." In 1962 he told Bob Wolff: "You work your side of the street [interviewing players], and I'll work mine." Wolff liked his partner's verse. "He'd say, 'The guy stapled him to the bag.'" A runner's "smilin' like he swallowed a banana peel." Due diligence followed. "After the game, we'd replay each pitch. 'I said this, you said that, and I shoulda said this.'"

This often meant a long-running belly laugh. Joe's 1952 Pirates finished last in runs, doubles, triples, home runs, Ks, walks, shutouts, ERA—and wins (42-112, 54½ games behind Brooklyn). "It was the most courageous team in baseball," said baseball's Leno. "We had 154 games scheduled, and we showed up for every one." Diction was a yuck. One year Garagiola, Berra, and Dizzy Dean joined the Missouri Hall of Fame. "What do you want? Good grammar or good taste?" Another was studied nonchalance. "I'm an expert on two things—trades and slumps."

Never catching a no-no, Joe aired Nolan Ryan's fifth in a 1981 *Game* from Houston, "pressure building!" as L.A. batted in the ninth. "This may be it [game-ending grounder]," he said, correctly. Scully's yeastier call portended NBC. "And what a moment as Nolan Ryan tries to become the first pitcher to have five no-hitters." The KTTV camera bared Ryan exhaling. "Yeah, we're all with you, Nolie, huffin' and puffin' now. Breaking ball, hit to third! Over to first! He's got it!"

How far did Yogi go in high school? "Nine blocks," said his pal. Joe's *Game* didn't go as far as before NBC dry-gulched Gowdy. "Saturday had a constituency," recalled Scotty Connal, "but we couldn't boost it." Millions still missed Ol' Diz. Local-team TV increasingly split the audience. On one hand, Garagiola-Kubek seemed as reliable as a jeep. The other: Ratings fell from 1974's 7.3 to 1981's 6.3. (One point reflects 1 percent of all households with a TV set.)

The Peacocks cast about to start, not stall, them. In 1979, Arthur Watson Fordham '52 had become NBC Sports head. The first Californian he conjured surprisingly wasn't Vin.

"OH, MY!" Dick Enberg's trademark idiom etched working as a $1-an-hour Central Michigan University student janitor; graduating, Doctor of Health Sciences, Indiana University; and coaching and teaching at California State University. "I wanted to be the best professor around—that, and never give the same test twice," he said. "Sportscasting was just a way to supplement my salary." Soon the part-time mid-'60s boxing and Western Hockey League Blades announcer left blue books behind.

In 1966 the renamed California Angels left Dodger Stadium for hard-by-Disneyland Anaheim Stadium—the Big A. By 1969, Dick, 34, added Halos play-by-play to Rams radio and UCLA TV hoops. "Our new park was a jewel," he said, "but Vin just dominated. Do your best work, and you're still run out of town."

Enberg's Michigan youth was heavy with farmland shot by Ansel Adams. "Wonderful folks, and towns. You feel the generations, like Vin raised on Barber. Most guys love detail on a game-winning hit. Not Scully: 'Here comes the *tying* run—and here comes the *winning* run.' That's from Red. It was enough to give you an inferiority complex"—ironic, since Dick's booth was sublime.

Joining it in 1969 and 1973, Dave Niehaus and Drysdale, respectively, aped what Dave called Vin's "posture of don't cheerlead or make excuses." One change was dialogue. "Almost all guys spoke to the listener," Niehaus said. "We needed to be different, talk with each other." Dick got the Angels to install toggle mikes. "Lets you hear a partner, push the button down, and respond. Pioneering then: Everybody does it now."

"I'm going to have dinner tonight at Singer's house," Drysdale once said.

"Bill Singer, the pitcher?" Niehaus said.

"No, Dave," said Don. "The singer is Frank Sinatra."

Yearly the Halos sang off-key. "Never in contention," said Enberg, "so you stress personality." A batter hit between shortstop Jim Fregosi's legs. "Water *over* the bridge," mused skipper Lefty Phillips. In 1972 California got a Mets pitcher for Fregosi. Nolan Ryan's seven no-hitters included Dick's boyhood team. "At 8, I hitch-hiked to Briggs [later, Tiger] Stadium. Years later [July 15, 1973] I'm in the booth, and nobody can touch the ball." Detroit's Norm Cash finally ditched a bat, using a clubhouse chair leg. "The plate ump didn't notice" till Ryan threw.

"Get a bat," said Ron Luciano.

"Why?" Cash huffed. "I'm not gonna hit Ryan anyway."

Dick hit the big time with TV's syndicated *Sports Challenge*. "The [ex-jock] people on these shows were idols to me as kid. Now I'm asking them questions." Enberg aired the game show *Battle*, produced PBS's *The Way It Was*, and joined NBC in 1975. Vin finally seemed far away.

FOR A LONG TIME, Gowdy was as close as any television. Replacing him, Dr. Dick examined the Granddaddy, Super Bowl, other football, and NCAA basketball; ministered to Wimbledon, the French Open, Breeders Cup, and Masters; and became the first sportscaster to visit the People's Republic of China. Not even Curt kept more balls in the air. "Had to, but hated to," said Enberg, leaving the Angels in 1978. "After all, baseball's my favorite sport." In 1982 Watson gave him the backup "B" *Game* and Halos-Brewers LCS. "I'd recall the '50s, when I was growing up and Milwaukee was everything. When things move me, it's clear to viewers." With Joe, he did the Series. Enberg was warm, open, and oblivious to dominoes.

That fall backup Merle Harmon, "his contract," Craig wrote, "calling for too much money compared to events available for him to call," fell to a cheaper prodigy. Bob Costas later eclipsed the bare and statistical. Then, he was content to join Kubek—"I'd grown up with Tony"—dropped from the primary *Game*. Garagiola was named "A" game analyst. On December 9, 1982, Scully became the Peacocks' duce for a reported $1 million yearly.

"NBC is proud to hire baseball's best announcer," said Watson, announcing a new $550 million big-league pact. "Vin reflects the importance we place on the game," abruptly and unexpectedly. NBC's 407 percent fee hike required return on investment. Scully also benefited from Dick midwifing his rise. "Neither was a shock jock," mused a friend. "Enberg's raves showed a Scully-type's potential." Being a baseballer helped. "Curt was linked to football," said Harwell. "People liked Vin's identity." Finally, recollecting CBS, Scully likely saw redemption at NBC.

Sadly, Vin's Cortez found no room at baseball's inn. Enberg was in Europe "when I got the news," ironically "having taken a slew of material to read for '83. I understood the business, but it still broke my heart." Later he rejoined Angels video. "Even friends asked why I did local baseball after NBC," said Dick. "I gave the most honest answer I could—I love the game. I miss it."

In 2002, flying from Buffalo to Los Angeles, he learned of the Halos' first flag "after, of all things, doing a football game." Dick began to weep. Fearing trouble, the next-seat passenger caressed a crucifix and held his hand. Laughing, Enberg calmed her. "I told her why it meant so much—the Angels—after all these years!"

Oh, my! After all these years, Vin was still announcing.

9

CLIMB EVERY MOUNTAIN (1983–1989)

In 1979 Hank Greenwald became a Giants broadcaster, saying "the best way to learn baseball is to watch, read," and laugh. In Montreal, he noted how "when you ask for the non-smoking section, they send you to Buffalo." Philadelphia: "It's such a rabid baseball town, even trucks are named for Connie Mack." San Diego: Ken Caminiti left a game with "stomach problems. Why shouldn't the guy with all the hits and RBIs also have the runs?"

Five times Hank's Jints placed last or next to last. One fall he turned 50. "It's funny. When the season started I was only 43." A foul splashed Candlestick Park's sea of empty seats. Greenwald gave the section number. "Anyone coming to tomorrow's game might want to stop and pick it up." Another night San Francisco drew 1,632. "Sixteen thirty-two! That's not a crowd. That's a shirt size."

Puck could be profound. "There's not a lot going on in baseball," Hank noted, adding what Vin would not: "Your job is to create the illusion that there is." In 1987–88 he braved the pathetic-playing, Billy Martin–drinking, Steinbrenner-meddling Yanks. Taxed, Greenwald at least knew what he had. In New York, celebrity bred credibility. "It's amazing," he said, "how a couple years with the Yankees can validate your career."

It may profane to say that Scully's NBC suzerainty validated his career. By 1983 Vin owned Southern California, had a plaque in Cooperstown, become a media doyen, and proved impervious to fad. Still, "for all his fame," Jack Craig wrote, "[much of America] deems Scully an unknown entity, [hearing] snatches of his radio work in postseason baseball and with the Dodgers. Not everyone lives in Los Angeles." A wider audience would finally *hear* what it had only heard *about*.

To America, the 1980s wed flag-waving, the Evil Empire's collapse, supply-side economics, and Reagan's "special triumph," as Wright Morris wrote of Norman Rockwell, "in the conviction his countrymen share that the mythical world he evokes exists." For Scully, they meant proving himself, said *Scribner*, "the greatest broadcaster in baseball history." The decade was good to Pacific Palisades. Its success was not inevitable in early 1983.

"Skeptics could wonder how well [Vin] will do on TV [vs. radio] on a network [vs.] local level," the *Sporting News* observed. "It will require two large egos, talkative ones, to share one microphone," knowing they had some patching up to do. In 1963 The Franchise and Funny Man aired the All-Star Game. "Before we went on the air, I said, 'Joe, you played a long time, but I've broadcast as many games as you've played and then some,'" said Scully. "'So if you're gonna talk 'inside baseball,' you tell the *fans* the 'inside baseball.' But don't tell *me*."

Vin termed Garagiola "not quite the lovable bumpkin that many people accept him as. He didn't get to be a big-league catcher by being a lollipop," baring "a consuming ego in the broadcast booth." To Lindsey Nelson, Garagiola was "the single most ambitious man I ever met," not intending praise. Strangely, Bob Wolff found 1962–64's pal less Rottweiler than Cocker Spaniel: "We worked well together." Joe wrote a note if Wolff couldn't see a pitcher warming up: "'Smith to the left, Jones to the right.' That way I could say it: He wanted me to look good."

If Vin and Joe flew right, they would likely fly high. "Garagiola grasped who the star was," said a friend. Scully was Arcturus; Joe, Ursa Minor. "Some people were hoping we'd be the odd couple, always sniping at each other. But they forgot that Joe and I are two old pros. We drove in from the airport together, dined together, and went out to the ballpark together. It's like a dance team. You have to work together to learn each other's style." Pause. "A team either grows or it stagnates. And I feel we grew as the season progressed."

His color man agreed. "They thought we'd fight for the microphone, and that we'd have super egos that wouldn't fit into the booth. All I asked was to wait until we worked together. You can take it to the bank," he said of "meshing." Before long the *New York Times* observed: "That the duo of Scully and Garagiola is very good, and often even great, is no longer in dispute" — arguably, the best network tandem since *pod-nuh* and Ol' Diz.

It commenced April 9 vs. Montreal at the Ravine, with "easy listening, as is always the case with Scully," said Craig, "who managed to live up to his reputation as a peerless baseball play-by-play man." Joe added, "He controlled the flow to perfection. I thought it went beautifully." Once, having tried to say, "Hot shot hit foul," Vin found "it didn't quite come out that way." His job: make 1983 come out as NBC's Art Watson hoped.

In June, Reagan named his all-time play-by-playmen: "[WBBM's] Pat Flanagan," inventing the re-creation, "[CBS's] Ted Husing, and no list of all-time greats would be complete without Vin." On July 6 the All-Star Game sloshed to a 13-3 Americans rout. "Know what this game reminds me of?" said Scully. "A fat man's softball game played for a keg of beer." The first inning braved three errors: "a real Halloween inning," said Joe, asking that the announcement "This game is the property of Major League Baseball" be waived because no one would want it.

Scully noted a pitcher retiring "55 of 58 batters who faced him." Garagiola: "Why wouldn't you try to sign those other three guys?" A large hurler relieved. "He's an 8 on a seismograph," said Joe. "His birthday is Monday, Tuesday, and Wednesday." A bearded infielder resembled Don Knotts, not Charles Atlas. The Franchise: "He looks as if he fell off a box of cough drops." Garagiola: "If he shaves, he only weighs 91 pounds."

Vin told of Babe Ruth batting *righty* in 1923, Mike Schmidt hitting left-handed in college, and sub–Mendoza Line Reggie Jackson making an All-Star Game. One player wore jewelry around his neck. To Scully, "he looks as if he just came from Westminster Abbey." Vin looked like George VI vs. Gowdy, Koufax, and Wills: for a generation too young to know Allen, Wolff, or Nelson, the first network Voice to make baseball breathe, dance, *sing*. Jim Murray critiqued the Mid-Summer Classic, likening The Franchise to The Babe.

"It took baseball in its wisdom 10 years to turn Babe Ruth, the most perfect hitting machine of all time, from a pitcher into a slugger. It took a football season to figure out Marcus Allen wasn't a blocking back and to hand him the football. And it took network television forever to get the message that Vin Scully should do major league baseball and stop fooling around. It wasn't that Scully was inept at other sports. It was just that he was miscast. It was like Errol Flynn playing a faithful old sidekick. Scully could do golf and do it well. Rembrandt could probably paint soup cans or barn doors, if it came to that. Hemingway could probably write the weather. Horowitz could probably play the harmonica. But what a waste!

"Nobody understands baseball the way Vin Scully does. He knows it for the laid-back, relatively relaxed sport it is. Scully is the world's best at filling the dull times by spinning anecdotes of the 100-year lore of the game. He can make you forget you're watching a 13-3 game, as we were Wednesday night at Chicago, and take you with him to a time and place where you are suddenly watching Babe Ruth steal home. He is like a marvelous raconteur who can make you forget you're in a dungeon. He can make baseball seem like Camelot and not Jersey City," having learned "at the knee of Branch Rickey at the time he was most impressionable, a young, ambitious, career-oriented student out of Fordham."

Scully "will tell you why a batter should try to hit to right with a man on first and none out," Murray wrote. "'The first baseman has to stay on the bag to keep the runner close, the second baseman has to cheat a step toward second in the steal or a double play. There's a hole there you could dock ships.'" Pairing Joe G. and Vin "was an inspired piece of casting, not quite like Burns and Allen or the Sunshine Boys but a matchup quite as important to baseball as Ruth and Gehrig or Tinker and Evers and Chance.

"It was originally thought that was a lot of ego for one stage, or one microphone, but the two have locked into place like tongue in groove, or, in this case, tongue in cheek. Garagiola is the locker-room wit, the jokester from the team bus. Scully brings out the best in him and he brings out the best in Scully." On local radio, Vin brought out the best in *it*.

"IN THE 1980s AND 1990s, as the baseball broadcasting industry changed to cater to viewers' shortening attention spans, Scully refused to budge," observed *Scribner*. "While most broadcasts featured teams of two or three announcers, [Vin] usually insisted on working alone, arguing that it made for better communication with the audience." He termed "my approach to broadcasting . . . like I'm talking to a friend," there being much to talk about in 1982.

On Opening Day, Steve Sax, dumping Lopes, almost tripped taking his position. Recovering, he hit .282, made the All-Star team, and became Rookie of the Year. Garvey played his 1,000th straight game. Counting in the counting house: The Dodgers drew 3,608,881, more than they had, or would till 2006. The behind-by-10-games Bums beat Atlanta eight straight to share the league's first-place West saddle. Closing Day at the Stick evoked 1951 and 1962. "We're playing the Giants," mused Doggett, "and if we win there's a playoff with the Braves." The needle stuck: Joe Morgan's homer eliminated L.A.

Next year Dodger Blues shook Garvey, Russell, Cey, and Baker: traded or released. Holdover Monday mimicked Lasorda in the dugout: strutting, arms on knees, hands on hips. On September 30 Diamond Vision showed Atlanta-San Diego. "So the Braves have battled long and hard," Vin said as their last hitter swung. "And there's a ball to [Padres pitcher Gary] Lucas. The throw to first. And it's all over. And the Dodgers are the National League Western champions," losing the LCS—Scully's first network TV playoff—to Philadelphia. "High Hopes" was Harry Kalas's theme song. In 1983 Vin's buoyed NBC.

"It's about time people recognize we're more important than the players," Jack Buck told the *Times* of Scully's reported $2 million national/ local pact. "How old is Vin, anyway, about 78 [*sic*, 55]? Doesn't he just work the games that Valenzuela pitches?" Jack had recently described his schedule to a football player: 215 games on Cardinals wireless, CBS Radio, and NFL TV. The player replied, allegedly, "That's pretty good considering there are only 385 days in a year."' Buck laughed: "And that was a *smart* football player. Seriously, I say good for Vin."

On July 24, Kansas City's George Brett dinged, was ruled out for illegal bat pine tar, then left his dugout like a lynx on speed. For the first time, an American League head (Lee MacPhail) overturned an umpire (Tim McClelland). The tater counted: Royals, 5-4. The "pine tar" game resumed August 18, Hal McRae's out ending K.C.'s ninth. Dan Quisenberry retired New York 1-2-3. Scully "had a pungent reaction to Yankee bushawh," wrote *Newsday*'s Stan Isaacs. One *Game* Joe read a Stripes release charging $2.50 to see the last four outs (1,245 paid). "Could I have that when you are

finished?" said Scully. "I'd like it for my garden to help the roses grow."
Another Saturday, he called Toronto's gaunt, hairy Doyle Alexander "[a]
guy who looks like he spent a lot of time on a raft."

Despite Vin, *Game*'s network rating fell to 5.9. "No close [1983] division
races," he said more correctly than defensively. Worse, many bigs markets
preferred Saturday local coverage. At the time, Scully's audience seemed
a 1970s lookalike. That fall, ABC's World Series starred a Scully then-
soundalike.

THOMAS WOLFE WROTE, "Almost everything I know about spring is
in" baseball. Flatbush expedited Al Michaels's knowledge. "Even then,
New York had a budget crisis," he laughed, "so my school day went only
until noon." Next class: 1:30 P.M.'s opening pitch. Al's real school was
Ebbets Field.

"A quarter and a G.O.—General Organization—card bought a left-
field seat," Michaels said. Each weekend his clan sat behind the plate.
"My first remembrance of life is looking down in the booth at the back
of Red Barber's head and saying, 'What a job! Can you imagine seeing
every game for free?'" At five, Al picked "my career. I grew up on Barber.
Scully succeeds him. Best two Voices, and I get 'em both." By quirk, his
agent-dad moved to L.A. in 1958. Al majored in Arizona State University
radio/TV, later re-creating the PCL Hawaii Islanders. "It all depended on a
press box guy to send balls and strikes." In November 1970, Michaels, 24,
swapped Oahu for Ohio.

The 1972 Reds won Cincinnati's sixth pennant. Al aired his first
Classic—or Scully's eighth? "When he is sitting in your living room
talking about the nation's best-known baseball broadcaster," wrote Wells
Twombly, "he sounds identical." A decade later another writer noted
baseball's "two national TV voices [having] supposedly interchangeable
voices." Michaels denied trying to echo Vin: "When I discovered I sounded
like him I stopped listening." Celebrity, in turn, began.

Al joined ABC, then the Jints. In 1980 he aired his second hockey
game, since no Arledge had done even one. "Do you believe in miracles?
Yes!" Al yelped of the Winter Olympics' Miracle of Lake Placid. Punier
was *Monday Night Baseball*'s backup berth: its hitch, "a football guy
[Keith Jackson] on baseball!" bawled *TV Guide*. "It was no secret that Al
was miffed that network execs took their sweet time making him No. 1

announcer." Debuting June 6, 1983, he did next year's All-Star Game: to Craig, "a TV treat because it presented a rare chance for those without cable to see ballplayers known ordinarily via box scores."

Slow in coming, ABC baseball slowly went away. "ABC pays baseball not to make it televise the regular season," the columnist perceived. "The network only wants the sport for October, anyway." Vin and Al split the 1983–89 Oktoberfest, *USA Today* naming Michaels, Jim Palmer, and Tim McCarver the bigs's "best team": Costas-Kubek, No 2; Scully-Garagiola third. "The overall team rating drops because Garagiola, in his twenty-seventh year, doesn't appear to have kept up with today's game as much as the other analysts," huffed TV critic Rudy Martzke, mind-blind to baseball's play-by-play core. Joe, Vin countered, "had worked, like me, to emphasize the we and not the I."

Local radio/TV forged baseball's current. Network galoots formed its surface: murky as recently as 1982. Up close or far away, the river now seemed clear, sun dancing off a wave. That was Scully. By 1984 it ran through higher ground.

For THE FIRST TIME *Game of the Week* blared exclusivity: No team could broadcast locally before 4 P.M. eastern time. "The blackout," hoped NBC's Tom Merritt, "will help us pick up viewers who might watch a Yanks game in New York," spurning, say, the Peacocks' Cardinals-Reds. NBC upped publicity. Camera coverage shone. Above all, "Scully will be the Saturday afternoon national TV voice of baseball for everyone," Craig mused, "except those watching NBC's backup": *Game* again as a five-star inn.

Joe liked his suite. "I think it will be a whole lot easier. Last year, it was, 'Would the two giant egos clash?'" In 1984 a bitter and backbiting Howard Cosell wanted Vin gone. "Scully has been a ratings disaster at CBS and NBC," the aging diva said. In fact, *Game*'s Nielsen audience rose to 6.4. "If there is a message in ratings information," wrote the *Baltimore Sun*'s Bill Carter, "it is that baseball has come back with a vengeance as a TV sport," trouncing bowling and tennis, the Masters, and United States Football League. To NBC, the hike showed Vin's trickle-down effect.

On April 7 he did Detroit's first no-no since 1958: Jack Morris, at Comiskey Park. "Got him swinging, and he has his no-hitter!" Scully piped as Ron Kittle K'd. Another Saturday the Red Sox dinged. "So Rice hits a long out, and Tony Armas hits one out long!" Harwell's "Tigers" became only the fourth team to lead its league or division each day: "The first-place Bengals," said The Franchise, "are clawing up a storm." A first baseman muffed a throw. Antipodally, "Gil Hodges' big hands made his glove as handy as Michael Jackson's." Righty Alejandro Pena's "stuff is as good as Mario Soto's but Alejandro . . . marches to a different Walkman." Camp Scully seemed Athena. Or was that the 1984 Fall Occasion? It is still hard to tell.

"NBC's coverage of the [Detroit-San Diego] World Series was a pinnacle for televised sport," wrote a critic. "Never before has a continuing story been told so well, not only in pictures, but commentary." Fourteen-camera coverage included instant replay, close up (eyeing runners, off first), and extra motion (Super Duper, baring a ball's seam and path). It played Alan Trammell's long-ball solo; Kirk Gibson's aria, going deep; and Padres' skipper Dick Williams's dirge, telling reliever Andy Hawkins, "We've got a long way to go."

Garagiola's eighth Series was arguably his best. One moment, he likened Ruppert Jones's stance to "a hula dancer on a Don Ho record." Another, he unnerved a viewer by predicting a Padres pitchout.

"How did you know that?" gushed Vin.

"The fist," the ex-catcher said. The pitchout sign hadn't changed since before Joe made the bigs.

Harry Coyle, who had seen it all, hadn't. "Uncanny," said NBC's post-1946 director. "[Garagiola'd] say the batter wiggled, so we'd put the camera on him and the runner proved him right."

Joe's Straight Man became The Main Man: to Craig, "the star broad-caster of the Series. When five games are condensed into six days and nights, Scully's standards can be taken for granted. That does not lessen them."

Tim Lollar was "trying to keep San Diego from disappearing without leaving an oil slick." Lance Parrish dinged Goose Gossage: "With the clocking of the [speed] gun, the Goose has been clocked." Sundown bred "a spider web of light"; San Diego "set the Tigers' lead a-glimmering"; a grounder "knocked the letters off [Detroit's Lou Whitaker's shirt]." Mickey Lolich won thrice in 1968. The ex-titan now sat in a Bob Uecker seat. "*Sic transit gloria,*" Scully mused. "Thus goes the glory." He even lip-read Sparky Anderson: "We've got to get these guys early [or face the bullpen]." Lasorda, Vin added, "is the easiest guy in baseball to read."

In 1974 Vin had hushed on Aaron's 715th homer. A decade later the Padres' Kurt Bevacqua went Series yard. "For one minute, as the replay showed Bevacqua turning around in a circle and jumping for joy, [Scully] didn't say a word," the *Washington Post* observed. Din dissolved to break, "with absolutely nothing said." If silence is golden, Vin had become a vein.

LEAVE IT TO SCULLY to be a period piece—and piece of each October. "The average baseball fan will always remember those players who flourished when he was a kid," he told 1984's *USA Today*. Was the pastime's time past? "Oh, no, I think it's the best game. By that, I mean it's a game that everyone can honestly relate to," everyone having played.

Why had he and Garagiola clicked? "First of all, our roles are defined. There's no competition at all. Both of us have been in the business long enough that we're not reaching anymore."

Name a sport he wouldn't/couldn't do. "Horse racing would scare me to death because I have a color astigmatism. Maybe if there were just two horses in the race and one was black and one was white, I might get it right. But I marvel at how fellows do an absolutely accurate call, with all those horses, and maybe do eight or nine races a day. That would terrify me. The other sports I feel in my heart I could serviceably handle."

That July Dodger Stadium helped handle the Summer Olympics. Next June Guerrero tied Duke Snider for most franchise homers in a month—15. Orel Hershiser cooked a 19-3 menu. Lasorda was "on a seafood diet. I eat all the food I can see." If 1985 players struck, Vin wanted Tom "to go on a hunger strike. Write a book, and make it edible." On October 2 an Angeleno savored Cincy's 5-4 loss to San Diego. "It is all over!" Scully bayed, the O'Malleys clinching the West. "They play the rest of this [Dodgers] game for laughs."

LCS Game 4 parroted comedy and ignominy. "Talk about things you don't expect," Vin said of Vince Coleman mauled by a tarpaulin machine. "It almost devoured him. I happened to be in the park early, and heard him cry." A day later Cardinals mate Ozzie Smith hit "at quarter to six, St. Louis time, lights on since the start of the game," in a 2-all ninth inning, having never homered batting left in 2,967 at-bats. L.A.'s Tom Niedenfuer liked to "rear back and fire," said Joe, "throw as hard as you can for as long as you can." Smith swung at his 1-2 pitch. Scully: "That's driven to deep right field! Back goes [Mike] Marshall! Gone!" Forty-three seconds later, say good-bye/pay some bills. "The Lite Beer for Miller MVP, needless to say, is Ozzie Smith."

Oz moved West. Behind, 3 games to 2, the Dodgers led, 5-4, in a one-out and two Birds–on ninth. Scully again lip-synched Lasorda: "'Do I walk him [Jack Clark] and pitch to that so-and-so [slugging Andy Van Slyke]?' . . . That's what he just muttered in the dugout—a rhetorical question. He's not going to walk him." Niedenfuer fired. "And he hits one to deep left field and that one is gone!" Transplanted Okies cheered the Cards. "And Lasorda got the answer to his rhetorical question—something about 'should I walk this guy and pitch to that so-and-so.' Well, he didn't walk him." Vin's fillip sang a grace note: "Look at who is out there at home plate," greeting Clark. "Vince Coleman. Number 29."

Validation. "The [Dodgers'] Bard of the Base Paths's fame has grown considerably, in part because he [does] baseball's *Game of the Week* for NBC as well as Dodger games," wrote Jimmy Weinstein. Scully was now "a surprisingly well-known public figure. In hotel lobbies, in airport waiting rooms, boarding the Dodger bus on the way to a game, getting out of the bus on arrival at the ballpark or jumping into a cab when leaving the stadium, Scully is besieged by well-wishers." To Craig, The Franchise was "indisputably America's most prominent baseball broadcaster. Whether he is the best baseball announcer depends on the ear of each listener, but surely, by any standard, he ranks with the elite."

Inevitably, some found him an acquired taste. One *Game* Vin noted missing daughter Erin's graduation. Elkhart, Indiana, *Sporting News* reader R. T. Trombly fumed. "He should be kissing NBC's feet for his cushy job." In Rocky Mountain, North Carolina, Carl Harris "had trouble enjoying the game unless I turn off the audio and just look. Scully talks so much that even Garagiola has trouble getting a word in." Vin could learn "from WTBS announcers [Ernie Johnson, Skip Caray, and Pete Van Wieren]—less talk, more fun, and let watchers enjoy the game."

Craig did, enjoying Scully's "often-ironic anecdotes . . . he never endures a slip of the tongue. If you are about to challenge him on a state of fact, don't." The *Globe*man's regret was "not [hearing] Vin regularly on radio, the best test of a baseball announcer. From most accounts, those of us who live in the Midwest, South, and East are missing [his] best." A West Coaster said that "his regard surged after he moved to the East and heard other announcers. 'Scully broadcast with such a naturalness. I thought everyone else could do it, and did.'" Sadder but wiser, he felt like the Red Sox since the last full year of World War I.

The Olde Towne Team had won its last World Series in September 1918, then lost a pennant or Series on the last or next-to-last day of 1946, 1948, 1949, 1967, 1972, 1975, 1977, and 1978. Murphy's Law (if something can go wrong, it will) trumped the Law of Averages (life is fair; things even out). In 1986 the postseason, said *Newsweek*'s Pete Axthelm, left "you breathless." Not even the unspeakable left Scully speechless.

"BASEBALL AT ITS PINNACLE," Axthelm wrote, mixed two grand League Championship Series: Sox vs. California; Mets vs. Houston. Boston then met "a team [whose] MTV video has more stars than Hands Across America," said the *Post*, "which is another reason they present opponents with special problems." The Amazins' won 108 games, beat Houston in an LCS McCarver termed "the most tiring thing I have ever been part of as a spectator or a player," and were a 2½ to 1 Classic favorite.

The Shuttle Series began October 18, Bruce Hurst becoming Boston's first post-Ruth lefty to win a Series game (1-0). Next night the Townies sprayed Shea Stadium with 18 hits (9-3), flying home up, 2-0. Pol Tip O'Neill threw out the third-match ball. Len Dykstra went yard on Oil Can Boyd's third pitch: Mets, 7-1. Headlined *Newsday*: "Catching Up!" A day later Gary Carter dinged twice. "High drive into left field!" Vin said. "Rice is looking up! She is gone!" Then: "And he's hit *another* one! A towering smash! . . . And that one went *over* the Screen!"

Ted Williams tossed Game 5's opener: still lanky as a pelican, elegant like a stallion, and jittery as a colt. Red Sox stars seemed aligned: Hurst, winning, 4-2. "Is this the threshold of a dream or the eve of destruction?" the *Globe*'s Dan Shaughnessy wondered. "Are baseball's heartbreak kids finally going to keep a promise, or are they just setting you up for one final apocalyptic, cataclysmic fall?" The Sox replaned for Queens, Scully nearing his NBC then-summit. Marty Barrett's 13th Series hit scored "[Spike] Owen. And the Sox are on top, 2 to 0." A 4-6-3 Boston double play tied Set 6 at 2. Barrett scored on a ground out force attempt: "The run is in!" —3-2. As in a farce, scenes portend.

Jim Rice, lumbering, tried to score on a single. "To [Gary] Carter! He is out at the plate!" A blister on Roger Clemens's pitching hand forced Calvin Schiraldi to relieve. Bases full, Bill Buckner arced to center—"one pitch [Jesse Orosco's first] and a big out"—stranding Billy Bucks's sixth, seventh, and eighth runners. In the eighth inning, Carter hit with one out, sacks jammed, and "a turn of the screw, as far as tension is concerned." The catcher "lined to left! Right at Rice. Tagging up is Mazzilli to score!" — 3-all. Dave Henderson then hit a 10th-inning "drive to left field! And this one is gone!" striking *Newsday*'s billboard. He reached the dugout as the clock struck midnight. Boston scored again: insurance, having paid a 68-year premium.

With two Mets out, the scoreboard blazed, "Congratulations Boston Red Sox." The Series trophy and 20 cases of Great Western champagne filled their clubhouse. "If you want to make God laugh," Vin would say, "tell him your plans." Ahead, 5-3, Boston did. One out would win the Classic. All year Dave Stapleton had replaced Buckner with the Sox ahead. Inexplicably, manager John McNamara kept Bucks at first. Carter got a hit, "the Mets . . . still alive." Kevin Mitchell singled to center: "Suddenly, the tying runs are aboard." Ray Knight went to 0-2, then swung. "And that's going to be a hit into center field," scoring Carter, "and the tying run is at third in Kevin Mitchell!"

A friend told writer Peter Gammons: "Just when we thought that we had been freed at last, they're going to create a way to again break our hearts that goes beyond our wildest imagination." The Olde Towne Team led, 5-4. Earlier, Vin had said, "Oh, are they up Saturday night at Shea." Literally, it now swayed, "really put through the ringer." McNamara yanked Schiraldi for hard-luck Bob Stanley, whose seventh toss to Mookie Wilson—13th to win the Series—knifed off Rich Gedman's glove. "And it's going to go to the backstop! Here comes Mitchell to score the tying run!" Wilson fouled off two more pitches. "So the winning run is at second base with two out! Three and two to Mookie Wilson! . . . little roller up along first . . . behind the bag. . . . It gets through Buckner! Here comes Knight! And the Mets win it!" Scully's usually singsong voice throbbed, rocked, alight with feel. It is how millions will always remember him.

Later, George Vecsey noted "Vin saying he'd heard a first in the press box: New York writers cheering for the home team. Except that it was horror, not excitement. Buckner screwing up our leads meant we had to rewrite our column." The *Times*'s columnist felt the "misinterpretation" proof of man's imperfection—"maybe the only time Vin was wrong." The wrongness of things gripped Red Sox Nation. "The Mets are not only alive," Scully resumed, "they are well, and they will play the Red Sox in Game 7 tomorrow." Knight smiled: "After they lost the sixth, you knew the end."

The final was rained out Sunday. Next night, Keith Hernandez's sixth-inning, one-out, bases-full, down 3-0, two-run single, mused Vin, "turned the Series around." The Sox "always lose in the end [here, 8-5]," read the *Post*, "but in ways that are so imaginative and heart-rending as to be more memorable than victory." Barrett faced Orosco in the ninth. "Got him with a strikeout!" said Scully, exhausted and inexhaustible. Having covered his Every Year Is Next Year Dodgers, Dick Young hailed a dream-stuff fall: "The four divisional races were a drag. Not one hot finish. Then, two breath-holding playoffs and one excruciating seesaw World Series. Always, it seems, the game has something to redeem it. As The Natural said, contemplating the end of his career: 'God, I love baseball.'"

To many, Scully had *become* it: his voice, apart from name, meaning autumn. Most were pleased. A few wished he had never left the Ravine.

"THE CAN'T WIN situation fell with fury upon Vin Scully during the Mets-Red Sox Series," Craig remarked. "He was accused by partisans in both cities of rooting against their clubs." NBC's Boston affiliate WBZ-TV got 738 complaints; New York's WNBC, 1,128. "Those calls apparently were just a sampling of the feelings of others. I received a flurry of letters and hallway comments complaining about Scully. Stan Isaacs, the sports TV critic for *Newsday*, received the same kind of response, in reverse."

Location was "paramount to interpretation of Scully's words and inflections," the Hub columnist wrote. Four neutral-city Peacock polls found Vin fair. "Curt Gowdy dealt with [this] bias charge when he was NBC's top announcer on the NFL, baseball, and the Rose Bowl by rooting for a standoff of complaints. 'I knew that some of the fans rooted extremely hard, so I had to expect complaints,' Scully said. 'But if it was evenly divided, I felt I was calling it down the middle.'" Metsies recoiled at Games 1-2. "When they rebounded and won the next two games at Fenway Park, it made for unpleasant listening in Boston. When Scully subsequently described the three final games . . . the hook of suspicion went deeper."

After Game 6, Vin "was subjected to scattered insults from fans departing the stadium. Where there should have been happy faces after the Mets' final triumph, there were angry ones": arrogant, ignorant toughs stalking the Peacocks' booth. "Scully has been a baseball broadcaster for 37 years, the last 28 as Voice of the [L.A.] Dodgers, where his objectivity, an article of faith with him, could be verified by fans who grew up listening. Yet fans in Boston and New York believed that not only was he rooting against their team, so strongly was he that he could not conceal the fact."

In Syracuse, New York, Metsophile Peter King knew better, hosting a WHEN Radio call-in show. A phoner regularly played Vin's "little roller up along first" before hanging up: Peter, unlike Townie co-host Phil Markert, crowed. One spring, sunning at Dodgertown, he saw The Franchise. "I tell my story, saying, 'You may think this is way out of left field, but it would mean so much to my partner if you could tape a version where Buckner gets the ball.'" King gulped—ducked—unsure what Vin would say.

"I can't do it right now," Scully said, "but meet me in the press box after the third inning. I'll come out, and we'll do it," which they did. "He said, 'Tell me your friend's name,' then aired a preamble, alluding to Phil and other tormented Sox fans, ending, 'And Buckner catches the ball and the Red Sox go on to win!'"—alas, not till 2004 and 2007.

No post-1986 audience has approached Game 7's 38.9 rating (percent of all TV households) and 55 share (percent of sets in use): "fourth-highest rating of all time for a World Series game," said NBC Sports Research's Greg Seamans, "and most-watched World Series game of all time, with 34 million households." The Mets-Sox Classic averaged a 28.6 rating and 45 share—about 25 million households per minute. Joe Castiglione was not among them: a mourner, not viewer, be.

PERSPECTIVE IS ALL, a teacher told me. By 35, Vin could forget a Dodgers loss. "Earlier I'd get involved. Now I feel I have very good control of my emotions. I can turn a game off, once I get home." By contrast, long after a "little roller," Castiglione, then 39, took Red Sox defeat hard. "My partner is sitting here," Bob Starr revealed, "looking like he's been harpooned."

The born-in-Connecticut Yankee attended Colgate, discovered Fenway in 1967, and traded the interlocking *NY* for Old English *B*. "A good year to switch loyalty," he noted: No Evil Empire matched The Impossible Dream. Joe got an M.A. at Syracuse, covered the *Edmund Fitzgerald*'s sinking, aired the fellow-wreck Indians, and joined Milwaukee in strike-stained 1981. "The Brewers win the second half! The Brewers win the second half!" said Castiglione, like Russ Hodges. Cheeseheads still chant between bowling, brats, and beer.

Growing up, baseball had meant TV. "If the Yankees were at home, they were on Channel 11," said Joe. "I vaguely remember Vin with the Dodgers on Channel 9, not knowing he was just in his 20s. Even then, the diction, language, the melodic voice." In 1983 the ex-college disc jockey— "Give me the Rolling Stones, the Kinks, the Animals, and my favorite, Motown Sounds"—joined Boston's Ken Coleman, stuck between Perry Como and Patti Page. "Like the Red Sox [also Brooklyn] fan, Ken liked things as they were."

In 1986, sallying to Shea, Mr. C. pinched himself: a Classic with The Classic. "Before interleague play [1997], you'd only see the other league's guys at a Series or spring training." Coleman's 1989 heart attack left Castiglione to solo. "We played the Dodgers one exhibition, which went 15 innings. Vin did a couple: cordial, no airs. Some old-time guys go on tangents. Only Scully sustains a broadcast by himself." The jock Voice tells a pro: "'You don't know baseball, never played it.' Vin did, and knows it—too much down time to fake."

Joe never faked forgetting the unforgettable. "My only negative memory of Scully: 'It gets through Buckner! The Mets win it!'" In the runway, he heard a roar, "ran up the ramp to the field, then heard Vin on NBC: A passion to his voice—but restraint to his call." Castiglione thought of Scully "calling him 'Billy Bucks,' and liking him 'cause he was a gamer."

Three days later, entering the Sox skipper's office, Joe again recalled The Franchise. "Why me? I go to church," pleaded McNamara, like Scully, a lifetime congregant. "I don't understand why this had to happen." Vin knew enough not to ask—and that topping 1986 would rival an elephant passing through the eye of a needle. Good Book, great year.

By now, baseball hyped cross licensing, property brand, and consumer analysis. None distilled its non-mud wrestling nub: Hit to right, throw inside, know your game, and sell.

I liked how Byrum Saam hyped Phillies cigars; Lindsey Nelson, Miss Rheingold; Bob Elson, General Finance Co.'s Friendly Bob Adams. I liked how Jimmy Dudley hailed, "Hey, Mabel, Black Label"; Mel Allen said, "Grab yourself a Ballantine!"; and Bob Prince guzzled Iron City. Among other things, Vin sold Farmer John's sausage. "It's 3:30 A.M.," said Jon Miller. "The lights are off. Vin wakes up, he's hungry, puts his bathrobe on, and wanders toward the refrigerator. Does he always talk this way? 'Good evening, wherever I am. Can't wait for some Farmer John's.'"

In April 1987 the Dodgers' VP of player personnel couldn't wait for his 45th bigs year, explaining to ABC TV's *Nightline* the paucity of black officials. "It's just that they may not have the necessities," said Al Campanis, later admitting, "I blew it." His longtime pal—said Vin, "Al didn't have a racist bone in his body"—hoped the fury would blow over. Instead, it blew Campanis down. Doggett's same-year exit was voluntary. Replacing him: Porter, as number two. Data was Ross's marrow. Scully lilted from Camus to Cey. Each man's solo status evoked the past: "Red taught me to tell someone what's going on," Vin said. "I just want to keep him interested and up-to-date. And it has to happen naturally—your relationship with the person listening."

On NBC the person listening was Joe. "Go back and tabulate," said Scotty Connal. "Of every 10 words in a *Game*, Vin might say eight. Slugfest or pitcher's duel, he was there to talk." If 1968 was the Year of the Pitcher, 1987 meant Going Yard. Exception: its All-Star Game. "So Ozzie Virgil at second base, and of course, he's the big man," Scully said in a scoreless 13th inning. "Hubie Brooks at first. Two and 0—line drive into left-center field. That's a base hit—and it will go to the wall! In comes Virgil! In comes Brooks, [Tim] Raines to third, and he's in there with a slide!": National League, 2-0.

On September 27, *Game*'s split screen bared a first: two games concurrently telecast hundreds of miles apart. Another: Vin, apologizing for claiming fan interference in the LCS opener. "He thought someone'd tried to catch it," said writer Rob Rains, "when actually the ball bounced into a basket atop the [Busch Stadium] wall: an automatic ground-rule double." Unconcerned, Ron Bergman wrote a column: "The Greatest of Them All." Red hair had grayed, but "Scully looks dapper and fit. As so many of his show brethren in nearby Hollywood, including old friend and former neighbor Nancy Davis Reagan, Scully is a trifle shy about his age," admitting to "mid-50s. My mother's 85 and she looks 60."

Vin prized humanity, imagining talking to one person. "It's just that I've never envisioned who that one person is. I don't try to broadcast. I just try to have a conversation." Priority: His sole baseball art, Bob Verdi wrote, was of the Polo Grounds the night before its razing. Formality: Verdi visited Vin's hotel room July 4, 1986. The room service waiter delivered a cheese and fruit platter. "Scully sat, his white shirt crisp, his necktie knotted explicitly, his notes and scorebooks nearby. Clearly, no holiday was being observed in Suite 938."

What was: an evolving, if not changing, of the guard.

FROM 1976 TO 2008, the Pirates' Lanny Frattare tended to Southwest Pennsylvania's melting pot: Slavs, Poles, blacks, and Germans. Vin's voice was rich and clear. The Buccaneer's was low and calm. "On *Game of the Week*, Scully taught how to try to invest each day with a freshness, which isn't easy," he said, seeking to gussy up even a routine grounder in the hole. From 1983 to 1989, *Game's* backup Voice did, too.

In 1993 the Smithsonian Institution honored Jack Buck. "I thought Howard Cosell was history's most successful sportscaster, but Bob has surpassed them all," he told the Museum of American History, many in the crowd nodding. "And at his age [then 41], brother, I've got older neckties." Costas grew up in Queens, attended Syracuse, left CBS TV for NBC, and marked turning 30 by getting *Game*. The wunderkind hoped to grow old, doing ball.

"*Game* was a clearinghouse," Bob observed. "Didn't matter where you were, tune in to share a baseball feel." To illustrate, conjure June 23, 1984, at Wrigley Field. Spying Costas, cabbies still yell, "'Hey, the [Ryne] Sandberg Game!' That's what they call it, and it's almost a quarter-century ago." At one point St. Louis led, 9-3. The Cubs trailed, 9-8, in the ninth. Relieving: Bruce Sutter, yoking Joe Page and Dick Radatz; "at this time in his life," said Costas, "absolutely unhittable." Sandberg drove over the ivy in left-center field.

Next inning the Cards recut an 11-9 lead. After Bob Dernier's walk, Ryne again went deep—"identical spot, his fifth hit!" Bob cried. "The same fan could have caught it!" Millions gasped. *Game* and Wrigley shook. Film's *The Natural* had opened in May. "That's the real Roy Hobbs because this can't be happening! We're sitting here, and it doesn't make any difference if it's 1984 or '54—just freeze this and don't change a thing!"

It became "a telephone game [finally, Cubs, 12-11] where you call around the country. 'Are you watching? Channel 4, quick.' Absent *Game*, that can't happen outside post-season. You don't have the stage."

Intent on "always carrying a religious artifact in my wallet," Bob once lost his dog-eared 1958 Mickey Mantle All-Star card. *Gamers* sent 50 Micks. In Milwaukee, Saturday meant Bob's "Secret Stadium" bratwurst sauce. "The formula's in a vault," he confessed. "It tastes like another planet." Bratwursts' arrival signaled an official game. "Tony and I had to alternate talking because one of us always had a mouthful. This became [so] legendary" that the Brewers sent huge vats to Costas's St. Louis home.

"I think my humor loosened Tony," he said, some preferring it to Vin's musings and Joe's asides. "A classic case of opposites attract," said Coyle: Costas, glib and hip; Kubek, intense and gangling. One viewer challenged Bob to a bratwurst-eating contest. "Ma Pesh," the Peacock smiled. "Stevens Point, Wisconsin. Sends me his picture: bib overalls, looks 430 pounds, and claims he holds the record for County Stadium brat consumption"— Orioles-Brewers, August 1972—shocking, said Pesh, since he had never eaten well vs. Baltimore.

In Detroit, Reggie Jackson cleared the roof. Next up, whistling, he pantomimed for Costas. "Reggie says that he'll enter the box, call time to pretend to tie his shoe, and let us discuss the homer and show his replay." Jackson singled, touched his helmet, and pointed to the booth. "'Hey,' Reggie said, as if to add, 'it's all a great show,'" having not even seen 1988's.

In 1998 Costas appeared in the movie *There's Something about Mary*. For Scully, there was something about each 1980s' even year. 1980: Dodger Stadium's first All-Star Game. 1982: Cooperstown, then NBC. 1984: Vin's ooh-aah Series. 1986: "And the Mets win it!" 1988: Vowing to "see things with my eyes," Scully showed a soupçon of his soul.

On August 9 the Peacocks aired Wrigley Field's night inaugural. The Confines were rarely friendlier: Cubs, 6-4. L.A. finished 1-10 in the regular season against New York. The LCS became an antigen: ex-Brooks in seven. On October 15 a Series suggestive of 14 years earlier opened vs. Oakland at Dodger Stadium. Happily, network Voices were as far from 1974's as Mary Martin from Madonna. Joining Vin was CBS Radio's Buck.

From 1954 to 1958, Jack rode Anheuser-Busch's Redbirds wave of loyalty. In 1959 he tried to help fill a void: Dodgers/Jints road coverage on WOR New York. "I'd do 'em, then rejoin the Cardinals. The response was bananas, but the Yanks bitched about territorial rights," limiting the series to a season. Ultimately, the Bums and Swifties matched strength in, among other years, 1942, 1946, 1949, and 1963. "Each wins two pennants," said Buck. "A pitch either way, and one wins all, or none."

As we have seen, the 1985 LCS knit another thread. "Smith corks one into deep right, down the line!" bayed Buck. "It may go! Go crazy, folks! Go crazy! It's a home run, and the Cardinals have won the game, 3-2, on a home run by the Wizard!" Jack Clark's next-set drive gave St. Louis its 14th flag. "Swing and a long one into left field! Adios! Good-bye! It may be that's the winner! A three-run homer . . . and the Cardinals lead by the score of 7 to 5!" That winter Jack's home phone message included each call.

Buck did CBS's 1976 All-Star Game, 1979–82 LCS, and 1983–89 Classic. "When Vin was available, we used him," said Dick Brescia. "When he wasn't [NBC TV], we'd call Jack." Return to 1988's Series opener, fictive even now. Pregame starred the then-youngest National Sportscaster of the Year. "Hi, everybody, it's Bob Costas, along with Vin Scully and Joe Garagiola, set to bring you the Oakland Athletics against the Los Angeles Dodgers." Injury had shelved Kirk Gibson, soon voted league MVP. "He can't push off [with the back leg] and he can't land [on the front]," said Vin. L.A. began by shelving the A's record (104-58) and odds (2-1).

"Fastball. Hit [by Mickey Hatcher] into left field and deep," said Scully in the opener. "Back goes Parker! Way back! It is gone!": 2-0. Later Jose Canseco hit. "And there's a drive to center! Back goes Shelby! To the wall! It is gone! Grand-slam home run!" The camera showed Lasorda, arms crossed, "sitting quietly, and that's quite a trick." By the eighth, it was no trick to see Costas planning post-game in a runway. "Kirk is . . . supposedly unable to pinch-hit," said Bob, seeing him in the trainer's room. Vin scanned the bench. "Is Gibson in the dugout? And the answer would appear to be no."

Michael Weisman was NBC executive producer. "Because of Vin, several times we panned the dugout looking [for Gibson], which heightened the drama." Icing a knee, Kirk heard Scully's verdict: "The man the Dodgers need is Kirk Gibson, and he's not even in uniform. The man who is the spearhead of the Dodger offense throughout the year, who saved them in the League Championship Series, will not see any action tonight, for sure." No. 23 rose; said, "My ass"; and put on Dodger blue.

Soon Gibson began hitting off a tee. "Go get Tommy," he told batboy Mitch Poole.

Arriving, Lasorda met deliverance. "Skip," said Kirk, "I think I can pinch-hit."

"OK," gaped Major Tom, "but you hang back, sit here, don't go in the dugout," build surprise. "If we get to the ninth spot [in the ninth inning], we'll go."

Dennis Eckersley walked Mike Davis. Eyeing a monitor, Scully said, "And look who's coming up! . . . All year long they looked to him [Gibson] to light the fire and all year he answered the demands, until he was physically unable to start tonight with two bad legs . . . and with two out, you talk about a roll of the dice, this is it! Four-three, A's, ninth inning. Not a bad opening act." Limping to the plate like Walter Brennan, Gibson swung like Hank Aguirre. "Fouled away . . . oh and 1," Vin said. "Fouled away again. . . . Little nubber foul, and it had to be an effort to run *that* far. . . . So the Dodgers trying to capture lightning right now."

Buck drew Columbia's denouement. "And a fly ball to deep right field! This is going to be a home run! Unbelievable! A home run for Gibson! And the Dodgers have won the game, 5 to 4. *I don't believe what I just saw!*" In 1940, Winston Churchill vowed "that if the British Empire and the Commonwealth last for a thousand years, men will say, 'This was their finest hour.'" Vin's reconvened: "Three and two. Sax waiting on deck, but the game right now is at the plate. . . . High fly ball into right field! *She is gone!*" Neither viewers, gawking, nor Scully, speaking, grasped what they were seeing. Sixty-seven seconds later: "In a year that has been so *improbable*, the *impossible* has happened!"

Later The Franchise asked, "Where did *that* come from?" of "improbable . . . impossible." Major Tom levitated; Gibson pumped fists like pistons; a 60-year-old male turned 10. "What an opening act, huh?" Scully said, in orange shirt, white collar, red tie, and flushed face. "And I think we've got a leading man, and many of 'em, between now and the end of this great 1988 World Series." It was not a great World Series. It was, however, grand.

Shocked, Vin literally could not sit down. "Whoever the good Lord has for a scriptwriter," said Lasorda, "I'm giving him a raise." Bob was content to give a hand. "If you compare the two calls, maybe Buck's is a bit more dramatic—after all, radio—but what separates Vin from the rest is the overall sound of the broadcast: how he sets tempo, the prologue, impossible to top." That night Weisman and producer David Neal got the tape, "stayed up past morning at Paramount Studios, then took the piece by police escort to Dodger Stadium," said Costas, completing it at airtime.

Their elegiac feature linked Kirk to—what else?—*The Natural*.

MICKEY HATCHER WAS a natural, too. At one time or another, he had lost a baseball in a domed ceiling, tried to catch a ball dropped from its roof, and on St. Patrick's Day painted his face, neck, arms, and hands green. His Game 2 single bred a 2-0 Dodgers lead. Mike Marshall then went yard. "High fly ball into deep left field! Back goes Parker! . . . Gone!" Inning nine wrote "a case of everybody up. . . . And now, the chant [of] '*Or-el*! *Or-el*!' One ball, 2 strikes. Got him!" Game 3 briefly checked momentum. "High drive up the alley, in left-center field, and this one is going to be gone! [A's winning, 2-1] Home run, [Mark] McGwire. And the kid from Southern California breathing life into Northern California!"

Directing, Coyle maestroed his 36th and final Series, including five of TV baseball's seven greatest games: Larsen, Bill Mazeroski, Carlton Fisk's touché, Billy Bucks, and Gibson—others, CBS's Bobby Thomson and ABC's Bucky Dent—vending a game more ballet than cutting edge. Harry's favorite park was Fenway's ricocheted balls and low camera shots and web of blocks and nooks and planes. Like Brando, the Ravine was a contender. "It means Dodgers—and the Dodgers mean TV baseball."

Coyle termed "my job function to give new [directing] kids something to shoot at." By Game 4, Vin's 1988 "walking wounded" seemed full of holes. Costas scored "the weakest-hitting club ever to play in the World Series versus one of the greatest." The weakest won, 4-3, leading Lasorda to thank Bob for "fueling the troops."

Costas: "Just happy to help out."

Tom: "I'll call you when we need you again." He didn't.

Next night Hatcher homered. Mickey then slid "on his landing gear" into first base—and one Davis, L.A.'s Mike, rocked another, Storm, for a two-run blast. "So Davis, who hit only two during the year, hits one in the

World Series!" Vin said. "Hatcher, who hit *one* during the *year*, hits *two* in the *World Series*."

In the ninth, up 5-2, Hershiser faced Tony Phillips. "Got him! They've done it! Like the 1969 Mets, it's the Impossible Dream revisited." Churchill said, "To jaw-jaw is always better than to war-war." Vin's jaw dropped as it seldom had, or would.

A DECADE LATER GIBSON's otherworldly belt was voted Southern California's "greatest sports moment." Mid to late 1980s NBC may have been baseball's greatest network. *TV Guide*'s bigs poll of local Voices named Vin best "national play-by-playman"; Costas-Kubek, "pairing." Who could imagine shorting baseball's billboard? Orioles mandarin Edward Bennett Williams knew. "What's dumber than the dumbest football owner?" said the ex-Redskins boss. "The smartest baseball owner."

Robert Redford said as Hobbs: "I hadn't seen it [shooting] coming." NBC had telecast the sport since 1939. Surely any partner—ABC, rumored CBS—would augment *Game*. "Why kill it?" said Costas, blindsided. "Baseball could'a kept us and CBS—we'd have our weekly series—but [Commissioner Peter] Ueberroth only cared about cash." In late 1988, caring only about October, Columbia paid $1.04 billion for 1990–93 exclusivity. "It announces a hit and miss 12-game [regular-season] schedule," said Bob. "Then an outcry, and big deal, they make it 16." No longer would Saturday afternoon hinge on pulling up *Game*'s chair.

A good deal helps each party. This deal meant "I wouldn't see a game for a month," said Peacock Marv Albert, "not knowing when it was off, not caring when it came back on." A CBS exec brandished a Cardinals hat at a 1988 Christmas party. By 1992 he wore a cap styled "One More Year." Just 13 percent in a Harris poll named baseball their favorite sport. *Game*'s ratings fell to under 40 percent of Scully's. You could see Cher, tour Tibet, or visit Arthur Murray's, but not watch network ball.

Its withdrawal began with Joe G. resigning—"I was trying to renegotiate my contract, and they left me twisting"—to rejoin 1989's *Today*. "Not believing [NBC's exit]," Kubek went back to a future where he never expected to reside. Joining the Yankees' Madison Square Garden network, Tony retired in 1995, leaving a final $525,000 on the table. "I hate the greed, the nastiness—what the game's become," he said. What *Game*'s loss meant became clear.

Its "passing ends a great American institution," said Scully. "It is sad. I really and truly feel that. It will leave a vast window . . . where people will not get major league baseball and I think that's a tragedy." Leaving as an institution, Vin evoked the hypothetical: what might have been, since it *had*. Scully had become a model, Costas hoping to succeed him. "I was happy on backup, but of course the primary game was a goal. Vin just wouldn't cooperate," Bob laughed in 1992. "He never lost his talent. Whatever else I did, I'd never have left the series."

The night of its demise, Bob called from St. Louis: 36, seeming 63. *Game*'s end wrote the Law of Unintended Consequences. Leapfrogging sport, he found the water fine: *Dateline, Now, Meet the Press*, and *Later with Bob Costas*, virtually retiring the Emmy Award. To *USA Today*'s Rachel Schuster, none invoked "the special homey feeling of watching *Game*. What are we going to do on Saturday afternoons next year when CBS isn't showing a game? Mow the lawn? Balance the checkbook? The options are limitless, none of them fulfilling."

For a decade baseball tried to rationalize the irrational. Local would replace network TV. Pigs would fly, the earth turn flat, and cows jump over the moon. *Insight* magazine scored "the network deprivation." The *Washington Post* attacked "nothing short of an abomination." In the Bush White House, I scored the bigs's Reverse Midas Touch. Their dirty linen didn't wash.

Eventually, even baseball ceased defending the indefensible. By 1997 Ueberroth's PR man served his fourth Commissioner. Richard Levin's letter to me ended: "You were right all along."

By HIS OWN YARDSTICK, Don Drysdale pitched in more than three dozen *Game*s. "I hate all hitters," he said. "I start a game mad and I stay that way until it's over." The 1956–69 pitcher hunted heads. The 1970–93 Voice was content not to turn them. "I'm not bigger than the game, just part of it," Don said. Big D (6-foot-6) as Gentle Ben? Absurd, but true.

Circa 1952: Van Nuys, a small farming town in the San Fernando Valley. Don, 16, and friend Robert Redford pitch hay, load squash and onions, and put ball above classmate Diane Baker. Redford played infield/outfield. Drysdale manned second base. Next year Van Nuys's American League Post 193 pitcher failed to show. Its manager petitioned sonny: "Dad told me to get the ball over," said Big D, who did at Bakersfield, Montreal, and Flatbush—then L.A. In 1959 he led the league in Ks, shutouts, and hit batsmen. When Warren Giles fined him for head-hunting, Don tried to pay in pennies, writing his own ticket after 1962.

"That year it all came together," mused John Roseboro. "The curve, speed, control." Tall, dark, and handsome led sport in TV spots. Was he stopper, matinee idol, or son of a bitch? Big D never felt he had to choose. In one year or another Drysdale had a 2.18 ERA, hit seven homers, and opened a Series (1965). "Koufax would have," he said, "but begged off due to Yom Kippur."

L.A. trailed, 7-1, as Alston yanked him.

"Bet you wish I was Jewish," Don gibed.

To Vin, "Off-field Don was a walking party, a pixie, he wanted to have fun. Pitching, he was the guy you'd want in a big game." In his next life, not every game was big. Retiring, he left a Hidden Hills ranch near Los Angeles for Expos English CBC-TV, training daily with a recorder. By 1973 Don joined Angels radio. "He talks good," said skipper Gene Mauch, "particularly for a guy who spent most of his life with two fingers in his mouth."

In 1978 ABC gave him *Monday Night Baseball, Superstars,* and *Wide World of Sports,* finding Don not harsh or stagy—a fact Southern California liked. "My model's Vinny," he confessed. "I talk about inside things, like he does, but without the style." ABC released, then rehired, him. Big D divorced, joined the White Sox, then met ex-All-American hoops player Ann Meyers, who mistook him for Don Meredith. They married and had three children: To his shock, Drysdale became a Ward Cleaver dad. In 1988 he became Scully's partner. "Never happier," said Meyers. "Working where his memories were, with Vinny, away from network TV, his life picture-perfect."

That August, Orel Hershiser began a bigs record 59 straight scoreless innings. Broadcaster and executioner: On September 28, Vin called Big D's 1968 record's end. "Eugene O'Neill wrote a great line," he said in San Diego. "'There's no present and there's no future. There's only the past, over and over again.' And that's what we're looking at"—the past, 20 years earlier, "and we're looking at it again." Orel threw. "A high fly ball to right! Gonzalez backs up! . . . And Hershiser has the record!" Also airing it: a Voice whose past, like Big D's, "over and over again" intersected Vin's.

"I once worried about 'Colemanisms,'" said 1960 CBS, 1963–69 Yankees, 1970–71 Angels, and 1972–79 and 1981 Padres Voice Jerry Coleman, "but now I figure they add to my sex appeal." Jesus Alou is "in the on-deck circus." Cy Younger Randy Jones was "the left-hander with the Karl Marx hairdo." Hail evolution, homering. "Sometimes big trees grow out of acorns," said the ex-Stripes infielder. "I think I heard that from a squirrel." Most broadcasters blur. Like Vin, Jerry penned identity. "He'd be excellent in any event," said Costas. "Goofs make him unforgettable."

"Here's [John Grubb] under the warning track." A hitter lined "up the alley. . . . Oh, it's foul." Coleman denied saying, "'Rich Folkers is throwing up in the bullpen.' I said, 'He's throwing them up.'" Undeniable: "This is the only afternoon day game in the National League"; Pete Rose "has three thousand hits and 3,014 overall"; and "They throw Winfield out at second, and he's safe."

Joining Yanks radio/video, Jerry had never kept score. In fall 1963 New York scored vs. Vin's Dodgers in only three of 36 innings. The Californians thereafter kept company. 1983: Scully/Coleman did the LCS on NBC/CBS, respectively. 1984 and 1988: Each called the Series. 1988: Circles overlapped. The last 10 scoreless innings of Hershiser's record pricked the Pads. "There's a drive to right field!" said Jerry. "He's going to put it away! Oh, doctor! History was born right here at San Diego!"

Big D nabbed Orel in the dugout. "Oh, I'll tell ya, congratulations," he said, joking that at least Hershiser had kept it in the family.

NORMALLY, THE FRANCHISE missed a Dodgers weekend to prepare and cover *Game*. In 1989 Drysdale's laryngitis choked routine. On Friday, June 2, Vin did L.A.-Houston, then flew a Lear jet to St. Louis, landing at 1 A.M. At 9 he awoke for Cardinals-Cubs, whose 10-inning Saturday set took 3 hours, 19 minutes. "It made things a little hairy, but this was nothing compared to some jobs I've had," Vin said, silver's stench still sharp. By 7 P.M., O'Malley's Lear returned to Texas. "I walked into the booth as the National Anthem was being played. When it ended, I was able to say, 'Welcome to the Astrodome,'" not pulling away his Dodgers chair until 2:50 A.M.

"By the 20th inning, Fernando had a first baseman's mitt on. The next thing I knew, third baseman Jeff Hamilton was pitching, [first baseman] Eddie Murray was at third, and Valenzuela at first." Ernie Banks said famously, "Let's play two." Scully thought: "Well, we were playing 2½." *Times*man Mike Downey wrote: "It went on and on. Then on some more. It was the longest night game in National League history. It took 22 innings, 7 hours, 14 minutes, and 44 players to complete": Astros, 5-4. "And it kicked off the longest weekend since Ray Milland's."

Vin got to bed after 4. Nine hours later Sunday's sequel began. "When the Astros' Craig Biggio hit a two-out, ninth-inning home run to tie it, I thought, 'I can't believe it. We're going to have more baseball'": Houston, 7-6, in 13 innings. Saturday was "OK. Sunday they brought me some hot soup," relaxing muscles in his throat. "The old joke about giving some-one chicken soup, it works"—ibid., air-conditioning. "Sunday, going indoors helped. If it had been 95 degrees, 90 percent humidity, that would have been tough." Instead, "I felt up," the crowd alive. "That gets your adrenaline flowing, although I think I'll sleep well tonight."

In all, Vin did 45 innings in two cities, four games, and 27 hours. "When you do something that you love, you can really go a long way. I never felt real tired, like I was in trouble. I guess that's one for the history books." Downey composed a coda. "If that wasn't service beyond the call of duty, Scully then flew to Atlanta for 18 more innings on June 5. Vin, we hereby award thee the Purple Lozenge. Well done."

ON JANUARY 20, 1989, Reagan, 77, left the presidency, normally making the complex simple. On July 11 he guested on NBC's All-Star Game, obsessing on statistic. "I've been out of work for six months," the Gipper said, "and maybe there's a future here." Stan Isaacs noted Vin's yen to work alone: "The unkind assessment of [Reagan's] celebrity gig is that [Scully] came close to his preference." That month *Game* took Vin to Boston. "I can't help it. I keep remembering that dark day when I began at Fenway Park in 1949. Now all I see are luxury boxes." Austere was Ross Porter's play-by-play.

Scully waived the Dodgers' August trip to Montreal: Drysdale stayed home, his wife about to give birth. "I'm by myself," said Porter, "and depending on statistics. Much of the audience knows as much as you do, if not more. You can't sit on past preparation." L.A. won a game, 1-0, on Rick Dempsey's 22nd-inning dinger. Time: 5 hours, 14 minutes. Stats rarely seemed so shrewd.

"I got back to the hotel," Ross stated, "and the voice seemed a little tired [like the 77-83 Dodgers]." Vin said you could tell a good vs. bad season by the number of off-season black-tie soirees: "This year the only invitation we received was the opening of a pet shop in La Puente." Porter's 2001 plight was rougher: a cerebral spinal fluid condition remanding him to the Internet. "I couldn't broadcast, but could always do research." The Stat Man often said: "You can't get behind or down on the game." In 2003 the Dodgers hired Lon Rosen, Magic Johnson's ex-agent, who, finding Ross unedgy, got down on *him*.

On October 10, 2004, Porter did the Division Series final, "thanking Dodgers fans in the sixth inning," said Ben Platt, "for listening all these years." Vin aired the seventh, later learning of the speech. "Ross said good-bye?" he asked Ben, surprised. "I don't think anything's been decided." Axed, Porter was named top 2004 radio play-by-playman and to the Southern California Broadcasters Association Hall of Fame. "I have not had this feeling since Jerry left us," said Scully. "Ross would never make noise. He would never object. He would never bring the spotlight." Two years later Porter had not revisited the Ravine or "even listened to a second of a Dodgers broadcast." His ouster was "a jarring development in my life": worse, hearing it from a reporter.

Ross repaired to Stillpoint Family Resources, founded by his oldest son, raising money for clans of children with special needs. Like Vin, he had the same birthday and mid-teen bulk of grandkids. One, John Michael, was born with Down syndrome and a heart defect. "We play a little game," Grandpa later said. "I say Dodgers, and John Michael says Angels. Then I say Angels, and he says the other."

The Stat Man had found life after play-by-play—also, the futility of being graded vs. Scully on the curve.

ON SEPTEMBER 30, 1989, Costas-Kubek aired the Peacocks' last *Game*. Next month Scully and ex-Met Tom Seaver did their final LCS. It began with Vin, on the corner of Addison and Clark, lauding "this dowager queen, dressed in basic black and pearls, seventy-five years old, proud head held high and not a hair out of place, awaiting yet another destiny— another time for Mr. Right." Behind stood Wrigley Field, about to host the opener. "She dreams as old ladies will of men gone long ago. Joe Tinker. Johnny Evers. Frank Chance. And of those of recent vintage like her man Ernie. And the Lion. And Sweet Billy Williams," loving the Confines' ivy, brick, bluegrass, drop-dead closeness, and animal cracker size. "And she thinks wistfully of what might have been, and the pain is still fresh and new, and her eyes fill, her lips tremble, and she shakes her head ever so slightly. And then she sighs, pulls her shawl tightly around her frail shoulders, and thinks—this time it will be better."

It wasn't. Vin's boyhood team led the Cubs, 3 games to 1, as Jint Will Clark faced Mitch Williams. "I guess we figured it should come down to this," Scully said in a bases-full 1-all eighth. "In every big series there comes a time when it becomes difficult to breathe, difficult to swallow." Clark worked a 1-2 count. "Line drive, base hit into center field! In comes one [run], in comes Butler, going to third is Thompson!" Final: 3-2

On October 17 it was clear and warm—"by local [San Francisco] notion," Al Michaels said, "earthquake weather"—as Vin's ex-sound-alike began ABC's A's-Giants World Series pregame show. At 5:04 P.M., PDT, bawling, "We're having an [7.1 Richter scale] earthquake!" he hit the floor. Ruptured gas lines lit the marina. Part of the Nimitz Freeway collapsed. A Bay Bridge span section hit another level. Sixty-seven died.

By contrast, losing baseball should have seemed a lark. "[Yet] it was tough," Michaels said, "because baseball was such an early stepchild at ABC and had come such a long way." In 1994–95, he joined ABC/NBC's 12-game/absent till July/no day or national coverage The Baseball Network, trying vaguely to replace Game. "That's baseball, America's regional pastime," wrote Sports Illustrated in October 1995. "Such an abomination is The Baseball Network that in Seattle, where people don't cross against a red light on the emptiest of streets, fans booed whenever the Kingdome P.A. made mention."

Ultimately, Michaels retrieved hockey, basketball, ABC's Monday Night Football, once spurned by Scully, and NBC's Sunday Night Football, its audience dwarfing Game's. In 1990 Vin read "a line that 'someday' is not a day of the week. I'm not going to file things away, where 'someday' we'll do this.'" Liking NBC, he loved his wife and children more. The Peacocks offered a full golf schedule: "in all, 14 tournaments. But when I got to thinking about it, each tournament now runs with cable, and that means about five days away from home."

Multiply 14 by five: nearly two and a half months a year. "I'd been there before," countered Vin, proposing a partial slate. "It's not something they were looking for, and that's fine. NBC has been great for me. I'll miss them. I really loved working for those guys." He still had the Dodgers, giving what the network couldn't: time. Little hinted that Scully's was running out.

10

FROM THIS MOMENT ON
(1990–1997)

In 1990 CBS Television began bigs exclusivity. "It pays a bundle to get baseball," said Jack Craig, "names Brent Musburger to play-by-play, then finds that ad sales stink." In late March, the mikeman changeth. Replacing Brent, Jack Buck wrongly seemed a sure bet to gild balls and strikes.

"CBS couldn't grasp that baseball needs description," Buck rued. "They knew that football stars analysts. So they said, 'Let [analyst] Tim McCarver run the show'—as if every pitch deserved scrutiny, which it doesn't." As we have seen, regular-season coverage was the bug. Wrote *Sports Illustrated*: "CBS stands for 'Covers Baseball Sporadically.'" Rued Buck: "We never got a chance to fit."

In 1989, Pete Rose, pleading nolo contendere to gambling, was banned lifetime from baseball by Ueberroth's successor, A. Bartlett Giamatti. Next year's die came up seven. Cincinnati won the West, beating Pittsburgh in the LCS. The defending champion A's still appeared a dynasty—till Eric Davis smacked a World Series hellion. "Back goes McGee! . . . To the wall! It's gone!" said Buck. The Reds won twice at home, then 8-3 in Oakland.

NBC TV's ex-Series prosopopoeia was now CBS Radio's. "We got Vin for Buck," joked sports director Frank Murphy, succeeding Dick Brescia. "Give quality, get quality." In 1985, Columbia inked a five-year, $32 million pact. Rights doubled in 1990 for 20 Sundays, four holidays, and 26-set Saturday *Game*; Hall of Fame induction; preseason, All-Star, and Series preview; and Scully's Summer and Fall Classic.

"So Jose Canseco taps slowly to third," said Game 4's Vin. "And the Reds are one out from one of the great and shocking moments in baseball history. It was David and Goliath all over again." Carney Lansford batted. "And Myers' fastball is popped up! Back of first—Todd Benzinger in fair ground! And the Cincinnati Reds are champions of the baseball world!" sweeping "the lordly Oakland A's four straight." The only dynasty Scully knew was "a Chinese white wine."

VIN HAD ALREADY aired Masters victories by Jack Nicklaus, Raymond Floyd, Tom Watson (twice), Gary Player, Fuzzy Zoeller, Seve Ballesteros, and Craig Stadler, five holes in one, and 13 no-hitters. On June 29 he called another. "The strike two pitch" to Pedro Guerrero "is hit back to the mound. Dribbling to second! Samuel at the bag! Throws to first! Double play! Fernando Valenzuela has pitched a no-hitter. . . . If you have a sombrero, throw it to the sky!" Some felt it scripted. "Believe me, you can't work that way," Scully demurred. "That would remove all the spontaneity. Something always comes to mind."

Jon Miller's mind had been on baseball since age 9. Raised in Half Moon Bay, California, he played the board game *Strat-O-Matic*, miming the public address Voice, organist ("dum-dum-dum," in key), crowd (blowing, like wind), and often Scully from the Ravine. "Friends'd say, 'Let's hit the wave.' I'd say, 'I got a big series coming up—first place for grabs.'" Mrs. Miller wanted to grab Jon around the neck. Hearing him through the bedroom door, friends asked, "Who *is* this?'" Mom denied knowing him. "It sounds, though, like he has a bronchial condition."

At 10, Miller saw his first game at Candlestick. Los Angeles outhit Frisco, 15-12, but lost, 19-8. Billy O'Dell threw a complete game. Three Giants homered. Attendance was 32,189. "Other than that I don't remember a thing," he said, sitting with Dad and a radio in the upper deck. "I looked down at the booth with binoculars, like being backstage. I was hearing and watching what Russ and Lon [Simmons] were saying."

To Jon, 1962 became "my coming of age as a fan," its Khyber Pass the final week. San Francisco played at day. "I'd hear Russ, then he'd re-create the Dodgers at night." Scully could be heard on distant KFI Radio. "I'm thinking, 'Gee, this guy's not very good compared with Russ!'" the soothsayer smiled. "Giants keep winning, Dodgers losing. I'm sitting in a car, on a hill to help reception, switching back and forth!"

On September 30 the San Francisco 49ers played at Kezar Stadium. "The crowd's going nuts hearing baseball. The football guys wonder what's going on." Jints win at home. On P.A., Hodges then re-creates L.A.'s playoff-forcing loss. In the Series, Miller sat in a dentist's chair for Willie McCovey's last-out smash. "Given the pain, how appropriate that I almost bit my dentist's finger."

In 1973, A's owner Charles O. Finley signed the College of San Mateo graduate. Next year Jon visited Baltimore. "I'd grown up on Chuck Thompson doing CBS football. Now I'm amazed: He's doing the O's." That fall another mentor did the Series. "I say, 'A curve, 2-1.' Vinny's much more elegant. 'It's on the way, currrve hiighh.'" Laughing, he mimicked Scully. "'Two-and-one, and it's interesting to note that as Molière said in Seventeenth Century Paris.' Whoever heard of baseball in the Seventeenth Century? Yet people go bonkers about Vinny quoting Molière!"

Ultimately, Jon went bonkers over Scully. "He's so great that young broadcasters emulate him. I hear them around the country and it's unmistakable—'the 1-1 pitch, looww.' Even abroad you can't escape him," Miller said, reliving a jaunt to Japan. "One reason I went was to hear the Yomiuri Giants' Yoncharo Assami. I'd heard of Assami-son but never heard him, can't wait." On TV, Jon did a double take. "*He's* doing Scully. '*Atashiwa Carokwa in stadium neormas. Hagima Mashde doseruski llloowww.*' I go to Caracas. They're doing Vin in *Spanish!*"

Miller joined the Rangers, Red Sox, Orioles, and 1990's ESPN Television. "Coverage went to cable [four-year $400 million] because CBS didn't want a *Game*. We did," succeeding NBC: Jon, in effect, Scully. "The weekend's over, you come back from the beach, and there *Sunday Night Baseball* is." ESPN forecast a 5.0 1990 Nielsen rating. Instead, *Sunday* averaged 3.0. That fall baseball's then-official magazine interviewed Vin about a month, not a day.

WHO WAS MR. OCTOBER? asked *The Show*. "That was a nice catch phrase for Reggie Jackson, but I don't know if it really applies to any one man," said Scully. "I have never really believed there was a Mr. October." Whose October's Song clanged? "Maybe it's too easy, because it's so fresh in my mind, but I think of Andre Dawson. He's a remarkable talent. In 1981 he was the big star with Montreal, and in the Championship Series against the Dodgers he hit .150. Then eight years later, he plays [in the LCS, hitting .105] for the Cubs against the Giants."

Did Classic coverage reflect a skin-deep age? "I'm convinced that society, government, and countries get what they want. The evolution of the media coverage is obviously selling newspapers, sports shows, etc. . . . I don't know what it does to players, whether they are exhausted and X-rayed to the point where they want to join a Trappist monastery."

Postseason: Scully opposed an expanded playoff. As Barber cautioned, "'You would . . . water down your wine.'"

Designated hitter: "The fairest way is what we have now. If you are playing in the American League, the [league] should not be penalized."

Which year meant most, Vin calling each since 1950? His first two, decided the final day. "The fans love it [postseason], but those ties in the standings at the end of 154 or 162 games meant something." For Scully, something still meant October 3, 1951. "The [Polo Grounds'] visiting clubhouse and Giants clubhouse were separated by the hallway. The Dodgers ordered all the champagne and shrimp you needed to celebrate." The Shot made "the caterers in the Dodgers clubhouse immediately push everything across the hall into the Giants clubhouse. When the Giants arrived, they were thrilled to think the Giants management was so optimistic to have all the stuff there, but it was by way of the Dodgers." Across the hall, "there wasn't a sound. But you could hear the Giants' screams."

On ESPN, you heard Miller win a cable ACE Award. "I am incredibly honored to win this award with this room full of talented people," he said at the Beverly Wilshire Hotel. "What am I? I go to games and my best lines are, 'low, ball one,' or probably the line I'm most proud of—'line drive, foul.'" Don't talk money. "'I'm an artiste, you know.'"

By contrast, CBS's "dream season dissolved," said TV Guide, "as the pennant races heated up" and Buck lightly called singer Bobby Vinton Polish for mangling the National Anthem in the 1991 LCS. "The irony," said son Joe, "was that he's trying to help the guy."

Jack found a footprint on his Pittsburgh hotel pillow. Next day CBS director Ted Shaker spotted him in the lobby. "You're in trouble," he snapped, walking away. Mercifully, Buck was fired after airing, like Vin, 1991's Worst-to-First Classic.

THE TWINS AND BRAVES placed last in 1990. Next fall Minnesota took a 2-0 game Series lead. Atlanta's Mark Lemke batted in 4-all Game 3.

"Slapped to left field. Base hit!" said Scully. "Here comes Gladden's throw! Here comes Justice! He scores! And the Braves win it—their first victory of the World Series!" Two more followed: also, Kirby Puckett's sixth-match catch and clout. "The two-one [11th frame] pitch to the Minnesota center fielder. It's driven to deep left-center field! Back goes Keith Mitchell! It is gone!": 3-2. The Metrodome was alive with music; the Twinkies lived.

Atlanta's Lonnie Smith's single began the final's scoreless eighth. On a double, infielders Greg Gagne and Chuck Knoblauch, deking Smith, helped him slow, stop at third, and die. "After eight full innings of play, Atlanta nothing, Minnesota nothing," said Vin, drained. "I *think* we'll be back in just a moment." In the 10th, "[Gene] Larkin, the left-hand hitter, up there. Bases loaded, one out, and the game on the line. . . . You can taste the pressure here in the Dome as Alejandro [Pena] straightens up. And the pitch to Larkin. Swung on—a high fly ball into left-center! The run will score! The ball will bounce for a single! And the Minnesota Twins are the champions of the world!"

In 1992 Eric Karros launched L.A.'s record four straight Rookies of the Year, preceding Mike Piazza, Raul Mondesi, and Hideo Nomo. At 65, 1950's rookie rarely mentioned retirement. "Andre Dawson has a bruised knee and is listed as day-to-day," Vin said. "Aren't we all?" A decade earlier Ravine arrivals on Souvenir-Baseball Radio-Night got a baseball-shaped transistor. "Every radio was on," wrote Eric Neel. "The stadium was like your living room, rich with his voice. And I remember thinking then that it's Vin who unites us—culture, class, and race be damned." In 1991 a black motorist, Rodney King, was beaten by mostly white L.A. cops, who, in turn, were tried for brutality. On April 29, 1992, the verdict reared: not guilty. Directly South L.A. began to burn.

Pulled from his vehicle, white truck driver Reginald Denny was beaten by a mob, the assault rebroadcast on TV. Giving the lineup, Vin saw fire on a Dodger Stadium monitor. Neel had been "at stop lights and in unfriendly bars, restaurants, gas stations, gyms, and liquor stores where Vin's name [was] nothing less than a shibboleth." No name could douse this rage. Scully "was extremely aware of the obligation I had not only to broadcast the game, but my obligation to maintain the safety of . . . people at the ballpark or panic. So I said nothing. It was very painful." Some picture baseball imitating life. Might it help by *avoiding* life? "I really think that my job is to hold on to some degree of normalcy. The ball game goes on, life goes on. It's some small consolation."

On October 22 consolation crashed: Barber dead, at 84. In Toronto, Vin schooled for that night's Series. "I could almost hear him telling me, 'Vinny, don't spend any time during the game talking about me. The people have not tuned in to hear about me. You want to talk about me, talk after and before the game. But when you go into that booth you do the game.'" The game went on; *life* went on. In 1993 Miami, life meant a bigs first Opening Day.

Vin once told a South Floridian: "I give your five-day roll-on about two hours." April 5 was better. Charlie Hough threw the Marlins' first pitch a foot outside to lead off Dodger Jose Offerman. Umpire Frank Pulli called a strike as 42,530 roared. Hough flung another, wider. Again, Pulli struck. "Anywhere the pitch was," said Marlins announcer Joe Angel, "Frank was going to inaugurate this place [Joe Robbie Stadium] with a strikeout."

Offerman fanned. Next month the Ravine had its first perfect (9-0) homestand. Equally mint was Closing Day.

ON SUNDAY MORNING, October 3, 1993, the Braves and Giants shared a 103-58 record. Next year the new wild card swelled postseason. "Too late for us," joked Jints skipper Dusty Baker. "Whoever lost last day goes home." Like 1951, 1962, and 1982, the Stonehams and O'Malleys closed the year. Inverting history, L.A. led, 7-1. "Bottom of the eighth," said Vin. "Crowd doing a little hand-clapping, trying to get something started." Rookie Piazza had earlier rocked his 43th dinger. "[Now] it's a high fly to right field. . . . Miracle of miracles! He's hit *another* one!" For Piazza—also, Frisco, losing, 12-1—"what a way to say good-bye."

LA Weekly's Ruben Martinez liked Vin saying, "Wellll, *hellllo* everybody, and a very pleasant evening to you wherever you may be. On a beauuuutiful night at Dodger Stadium.'" Rapport was the effect and aim. "At the ballpark, you could hear him call the game while walking through the parking lot or standing in line for a coke." Back home, Ruben heard The Portable Vinny in the kitchen till 9 P.M. "My parents would tuck me in, then I'd sneak back to the kitchen, snatch the radio, run back to my room and place it under my pillow."

A child has enough of Pop, say, by 12 (with luck, he reconsiders). Martinez couldn't get enough of Vin. At 16 he got a driver's license, "and the chance to be transported from smog and freeway traffic to the ballpark. And while there've been plenty of opportunities to tune in Scully and the Dodgers on TV over the years, it's still the radio version that is my favorite." George Will called baseball proof of God's existence. Ruben was "more secular than devout. Baseball was my religion. . . . Scully [was] my priest," eager to convert.

To Vin, football was faceless: "They wear big helmets and masks." Basketball, frantic: "Too much going on at once. The bodies get all tangled up." Baseball was exact: "You can hit a ground ball to the third baseman, and no matter how fast you can run, he'll beat you at first base" because bases were 90, not 85 or 58 feet, apart. "The dimensions are perfect. Not almost perfect, they're perfect," making baseball fixed and spatial, easy to engage and eye. "When you come out to see Eric Davis or Darryl Strawberry or whoever, you never lose sight of any of them, nobody's in your way."

Football was collective; baseball, individual. "There's no way there could ever be a Fernando in football, just no way," Scully said. "But in baseball, Fernando . . . was a religious experience. You'd see parents, obviously poor, with their little youngsters, by the hand, using him as inspiration."

Most faith values life. Vin's "constant companion" devalued it. In 1992–93 the Dodgers' Campanella, pitcher Tim Crews, team executive Ike Ikuhara, and son of traveling secretary Bill DeLury died. On July 3, 1993, Drysdale, 56, had a fatal heart attack in Montreal, where 37 years earlier he roomed with Tom Lasorda. Red-eyed, Scully opened that night's game from Olympic Stadium. "Never have I been asked to make an announcement that hurts me as much as this one. And I say it to you as best I can with a broken heart."

Don returned to a California so different from the Van Nuys of his youth that it is hard to believe that it existed. A memorial service lured a coalition of the loving. Hershiser termed Drysdale "a modern-day hero." Dick Enberg, speaking, wept. A 1973 eulogy to Lyndon Johnson ended: "He first saw light here. He last felt life here. May he now find peace here." Big D's biggest game lay ahead.

THAT OCTOBER A LISTENER MUSED: "Vin Scully on the radio, the TV muted out. The World Series doesn't get easier unless you are there with a Walkman." Life doesn't get harder than January 22, 1994. Scully's oldest son Michael, an engineering supervisor for Arco Oil's Four Corners Pipe Line Inc., took a helicopter to patrol an oil pipeline, checking for earthquake damage. It crashed, killing him at 33. Again Vin found strength in faith— "It helped me, overwhelmingly"—and work. "I threw myself back in. I consider myself very fortunate to be able to do something I enjoy so much." Scully enjoyed the baseball of his youth, increasingly hard to find.

"How come the '94 strike didn't come later?" asked Major Tom. "We were in first when it happened!" The stoppage began August 12. In September baseball canceled its first Series since 1904. On January 22, 1995, the New York Chapter of the Baseball Writers Association gave Scully the William J. Slocum Award for long and meritorious service to baseball. "Long, yes," he said. "Meritorious? I've been lucky." Some felt baseball's luck had run out with greedy players, agents, and owners. Ironically, Vin found the strike a winnowing force for good.

"Sitting around for [1994's] 40 days or so [234, counting 1995] taught me a lesson." Golf got old. "Then I'd have lunch with the guys and that got old." Soon even the hardware store looked good. "'Oh, my gosh, imagine if this was it.' It made me realize if I retired I'd be bored. I found that I'm not the type to just sit on the porch and watch the sun set." Scully's first post-strike game began: "After being away, I've come to the realization that I need you more than you need me." He returned to something upon which the sun rarely rose.

On June 4, 1990, L.A.'s Ramon Martinez had tied Mr. K by K-ing 18 Braves. In July 1995 he threw Vin's bigs radio/TV record 18th no-hitter, including three perfect games. Bob Murphy had aired 34 years sans Mets no-no: "I can't imagine anyone coming close to that number." The ex-banjo hitter blamed it all on Fordham. "I was so lousy the idea of no-hits follows me." Actually, the last out did.

Scully aired the end of all but one—his *first*—no-hitter: Boston's Vern Bickford's August 11, 1950. Next was Carl Erskine vs. visiting Chicago June 19, 1952. Vin entered the dugout before Oisk began warming up. "He had a ball in his hand and was flipping it up and down. Finally, he looked at it, saying, 'I wonder what this little ball has in store for me today.'" Before being knocked out, pitcher Willard Ramsdell walked in the third: "the Cubs' only base runner," said Vin. "Happy [Felton] planned to have him as his post-game interview, paying $50, if Erskine got his no-hitter."

*Long Island Press*man Jack Lang recalls Ramsdell, watching a TV in the ninth-inning clubhouse, "rooting for Erskine to get the no-hitter against his team."

Oisk's wasn't taped. "None of mine were," said Scully, "until that ninth inning of Sandy's fourth one, as I was trying to figure out what to say that he would want to hear 30 years later. That's when I decided to use the date and time." The year of Martinez's no-hitter Vin got an Emmy for Lifetime Achievement from the National Academy of Television Arts and Sciences—and joined the Hall of Fame's Frick Award broadcast committee. "He keeps wanting to replay the 1966 Series," joked the Orioles' Chuck Thompson, a fellow member. "That's one vote we won't recount."

Vin liked consensus. "Forget the glitz," Al Campanis said. "It's tradition that matters when you think of the Dodgers." A visit meant the Dodger Dog, traffic arriving late and leaving early, and peanut vendors tossing bags like Magic Johnson in the paint. A Brooklyn-L.A. players mural draped the outfield wall. Another link: the managing instructor and scout who signed Fernando, among others.

In 1979 Bob Welch began struggling: lost speed, sore arm, or both? Campanis approached Mike Brito: "What you are doing tonight?"

"Nothing special. Why?"

"I want you to go down to field level," said Al, putting Mike behind the plate in a dugout box.

Using a radar gun, Brito found that Welch's fastball was five miles per hour slower. "From now on," Campanis ordered, "whenever we're at home, you go down there and time him." The Straw Hat Man became baseball's first Radar Man. "You see him on TV," said Scully, "cigar in one hand, gun the other."

Above all, Dodgers unanimity meant Vin.

Brooklyn-born Jean Picker Firstenberg followed The Franchise to become 1980–2006 Director and Chief Executive Officer of the American Film Institute. "I was raised on Barber. Vin not only rose to his heights, but spoke more poetically."

In 1955, Hamilton, Ontario's Doug Gamble, 11, left school, saw a drug store "where the owner had hung a sign, 'Final score, Dodgers 2, Yankees 0,'" and flew home. In 1980 he moved to California, later to write for Bob Hope, Phyllis Diller, and Ronald Reagan. "If there were a Mount Rushmore for baseball broadcasters, Scully's face would be on it."

Norman Augustine led Lockheed Martin Corporation, became under secretary of the army, and headed the Boy Scouts of America: "Vin so stirred in my imagination that after carefully scoring some 300 games I could produce my now widely unremembered copyrighted calculator for baseball managers."

To *Miami Herald* columnist Dan Le Batard, baseball wasn't "black-and-white nostalgia or families gathered around a crackling radio or Hemingway's old fisherman romanticizing about The Great DiMaggio" but "Ivan Rodriguez, coming out of the crouch, Greg Maddux versus Tony Gwynn, and Nolan Ryan versus anyone." Most of all, wrote the 30-something, it meant Scully.

The object of his devotion flashed a from, but rarely of, Hollywood smile. "I love tradition," Vin said. "It's slightly disconcerting to have been around long enough to become one."

GAME OF THE WEEK's tradition crashed in 1990. Six years later it faintly reemerged, Fox Television becoming baseball's new network: to some, flaunting 20/20 sight; others, hubris sans vision.

Fox's Voice was the World Series' youngest since 1953's 25-year-old Vin. "When I think of who went before," said Joe Buck, 27, "it sends chills up your spine." The 1996 Classic opened with the first National Leaguer to ding twice in his first two ups. "Wa-a-ay back!" cried CBS Radio's Scully. "The kid [Braves' Andruw Jones] has hit *another* one!" Afterward, calling home, Joe heard Dad ask, "What time is the game on?" Actually, Jack heard each word. The Series' 17.4 Nielsen rating tripled Fox's average. "That's why we got into baseball [for $120 million a year]," huffed President David Hill.

Buck *fils* admired Pop's old friend. "I'm stunned every time how prepared Vin is. He's got stories on visiting players that the guys he's speaking about don't know themselves," siring "a consistency of tone and spirit in broadcast after broadcast." To Joe, Scully "sounds the same as he did when I was a kid watching the *Game of the Week*." Buck had grown up. Had *Game*?

Initially, Joe called Dad's sport "my stock market, my assembly line, my court case, my operating table." Stock rose when in 2002 the busy camper replaced Fox's Pat Summerall. "Curt Gowdy and Al Michaels are the only other broadcasters ever to have been their networks' No. 1

Voice for baseball and football simultaneously," said *Sports Illustrated*, noting Joe's same-week Division Series, pro football, and local Cardinals schedule—"juggling them, marriage, kids, and my side job as a clown," he laughed—eager to seem New Age in a less *Simpsons* than *Waltons* sport.

In 2004, the magazine asked if the wiz kid and/or wise guy preferred nepotism or birthright. "Nepotism. It pisses people off a lot more." (Fancy Vin saying that.) "I don't think I'm destined for 10 more years in baseball," Joe told the *New York Times*. "The *Game* isn't what it was." (Or that.) "I put a lot of work into baseball, but you don't get the payoff as you get from a great football game." Scully would agree when Dodger Stadium was renamed for Barry Bonds.

NBC's weekly *Game* was national, Fox's regional and random: start around Memorial Day, fade after Labor Day. "Vin does nine innings every night," Buck said. "I can't imagine . . . even imagine wanting to do that." Each September Fox did baseball only once or twice, Joe often missing. Ultimately, he spurned some *post*season coverage. "Joe'd rather do the NFL [*regular* season]!" barbed an ex-Fox Voice. "Its baseball guy, on *sabbatical*! Who'd tolerate it?" The question was rhetorical.

Gowdy telecast each 1966–74 *Game*: also, a record 12 World Series. In 2008 Buck's TV 11th tied Vin and Mel. By contrast, one year his regular-season eight games in 19 weeks ended August 4, trailing partner McCarver and other Foxers Thom Brennaman, Kenny Albert, Dick Stockton, and Matt Vasgersian. Shakespeare wrote, *As You Like It*. Fox's one-size-fits-all broadcaster liked to be away.

*Times*man Richard Sandomir questioned Joe's respect for the baseball customer. "If you or the casual fan doesn't want to consider me the No. 1 baseball announcer at Fox," Buck jabbed, "it's not my concern. I don't know why it would matter." What did: Like 1980s' Vin, Jon Miller did a 2007 140-set net/local schedule. Buck's 18 included just 10 Cardinal games (vs. 2000's 120).

"Remember Gowdy," the once-Fox announcer said. "Vin was so popular partly because Curt'd seemed to downplay baseball." Joe, he barbed, *stiffed* it: little identity, baseball as afterthought, forced dialogue with Tim. NBC had loved the game. Fox tolerated it. Scully grew up with Tyrone Power. Buck kept a life-sized cutout of Mike Myers as Austin Powers. The Franchise read poetry. Buck liked acerbity. Baseball grabbed both early. It never let Vin go.

In 2008, conceding preference for TV's *The Bachelorette* vs. baseball, Buck beaned the latter on ESPN Radio. "I'm realistic," he said of football's prepotency. Baseball "takes forever"; therefore, Everyman "doesn't have the patience to put into it"; thus, "it's asking a lot to watch." Culturally, his view had merit. Personally, Buck seemed a Gen-X talisman. Everything came back to him.

"If he's going to do baseball, stop trashing it," the ex-Foxer said. "If not, leave. Stop cheating fans who pay his salary." At least Fox began a 2007 each-Saturday *Game*, retrieving a decade-old Bud Selig vow. Ratings hit a seven-year high.

"People come to me all the time and say how they miss it," Scully had said in 1999, "and I guess me." Continuity works. Imagine.

ACQUIRING BASEBALL, Hill yelped, "No more dead guys!"—sinking, among others, Babe Ruth and Mickey Mantle. By 1996 the Brooklyn anecdotist whom Vin replaced in 1950 was 78. "One good thing about you," Jack Buck told Ernie Harwell, "is that you don't die young."

Ernie fused "two for the price of one!"; "lonnng gone!"; and "he played every hop perfectly except the last" till Michigan football coach-turned-Tigers president Bo Schembechler canned him in 1990. The Detroit *Free Press* screamed: "A Gentleman Wronged." T-shirts blared, "Say It Ain't So, Bo!" At the White House, he met President George H. W. Bush, who grasped the Importance of being Ernie. "Someone said I was lucky," said Harwell, rehired in 1992. "They pointed out usually you have to die before people say nice things about you."

In June 1996, CBS's *Game* from Atlanta starred three for the price of one: for those of you scoring, 6-4-3. "In my forty-seven years, that's the first Dodgers triple play I've ever seen," said Scully. "I've seen lots by the opponents, but this is numero uno." Off-air, Ernie whispered, "I saw their last in 1949." Vin, noting how "sitting next to me is the man who announced that triple play," asked if *it* was scored 6-4-3. Harwell laughed: "I don't right remember."

An Angeleno remembered Lasorda, retiring in 1996 of a heart attack, and interleague play, debuting June 12, 1997, at Oakland: A's, 5-4. "Maybe the game needs something like this," said Vin, a self-styled "traditionalist. The appeal of natural rivalries like the Mets and Yankees or White Sox and Cubs is probably too great to overlook." On TV's *The Simpsons*,

Harry Shearer impersonated him voicing the Springfield Isotopes. *The X-Files* creator Chris Carter named characters Dana Scully and Agent John Doggett in the men's honor. Another honor had been long delayed.

In 1997 baseball retired No. 42 on the anniversary of Robinson's 1947 bigs debut: to Vin, as Roger Kahn once wrote, tying "sweetest song and saddest thought." In 1951 he had hosted a seminar at the Catskills resort Grossinger's. For the heck of it, the ex-hockey forward decided to ice skate. Jackie and wife Rachel, "large with child," Scully said, asked to go along. Tying laces, The Pioneer told The Franchise, "I'll race you for five bucks."

"Gee, Jack, I didn't know you skated," Vin said.

"I've never been on skates in my life," said Jackie, ankles turned in.

"Jack," said Scully, trying to be fair, "there's no way you can beat me."

A photo shows them, knees bent, facing the camera. Robinson looks ready to dance off first. "Maybe you'll beat me, and that's how *I'm going to learn*." Said Vin: "That's what made him great. To Jackie, his competitive spirit would overcome how he had never been on skates."

In 1950, selling to O'Malley, Branch Rickey asked: "Comest thou [reporters] here to see the reed driven in the wind?" Robinson was a rock, not reed. Segregation split sites like Greensboro and Winston-Salem. Then-Giants prospect Bill White had his bus stoned in rural Virginia. Robbie braved "colored only" restrooms and hotels. Each year the Dodgers barnstormed from Vero Beach to Brooklyn, absorbing the South's small towns, red clay, and witching power. Joyful blacks packed each park. Jackie feared some getting tanked.

"I was struck by his maturity and responsibility," said Scully. "Every now and then you would see him castigate a fan about unseemly behavior. So he was playing, he had everything else to contend with, and he was also trying to explain that his presence was not a reason to get drunk. That was part of the extra baggage he carried with him and he carried it remarkably well."

One hot day in Philadelphia, Vin was "sweating bullets" after the game. Outside the clubhouse, a fan sliced two large watermelons to cool each player on the bus. "Jackie came out and the guy handed him a slice. He was all set to explode because he thought this was some insensitive jive, when he realized the guys were all hollering and laughing, showing him they all had the watermelon. Even me, a red-haired Irishman!"

Robinson, Vin said, could "be relaxed and charming." The uniform made him over. "Jackie was probably one of the few people in this world who excelled when he was angry." After a pitcher tried to hit him, Robinson walked, stealing second, third, and home. Once Scully asked Maury Wills why he never tried to steal home. The Mouse That Roared explained that he feared failure.

"That never, ever went through Jackie's mind," said Vin. "So when you realize all the things he went through, and how intelligent and sensitive he was, he truly was the right man for a most difficult job." Without Rickey, there was no Jackie Robinson. Without The Pioneer, there arguably was no Rosa Parks.

ABOUT THIS TIME baseball began righting another wrong. In 1991 Montreal's Dennis Martinez pitched the Ravine's first road-team perfect game. "On the field, you saw Hispanic names," said Scully. When would the bigs, above? Columbian Edgar Renteria's single won the 1997 World Series. "An Hispanic hits it," recalled Jaime Jarrin. "I call it. Our [Latina Broadcasting Company] audience of 35 million heard it," as many as heard Vin on CBS. Thirty-five Hispanics did the majors vs. eight a decade earlier.

Next year Jarrin became Cooperstown's third Hispanic Voice (others: Buck Canel and Rafael Ramirez) and fourth Dodger (joining Barber, Harwell, and Vin). "As I'm taking the call of my selection," he told XM Radio, "my wife began to cry." Emotion hit hubby Induction Week. "Only if you're there can you feel how the impact registers." Later, son Jorge— "The Captain"—began covering traffic for English and Spanish radio, a ball in his office bearing Dad's and Scully's name. L.A. remains the sole broadcast team with two active Famers.

"If Jaime wore a uniform," said Peter O'Malley, "we'd retire the number." In a sense, he did: 110. "That's the percent you must devote yourself to your profession," Jarrin vowed. "You have to rise above bigotry to be regarded as an equal. I hope people see someone in me who came to this country without knowing the language, but through hard work and responsibility was able to go places." The Cuban patriot José Martí said, "I am America's son. To her I belong." For decades Jaime belonged to baseball. Belatedly, baseball belongs to him.

By 2007, 17 of 30 teams strutted a Spanish-speaking network: Julio Gonzalez, Hector Martinez, Gustavo Moreno, and Jaime's partner, Pepe Yñiguez, among others, reaching up to 52 million people. In 1958, "probably one in 10 Dodger fans at the park was Hispanic," said Jarrin. "Now it's four in 10," the fastest-growing U.S. minority bulging *beisbol*'s public between and beyond the lines.

"Tomorrow lies as much with them," said Peter Gammons, "as with white suburbs of *Ozzie and Harriet*." For Jarrin, that meant going back to Los Angeles's eighteenth century future as a Spanish colony. The Spanish *Mi casa es su casa* means "My house is your house." No longer do Hispanics enter from baseball's back porch. In 1997 technology entered through The Franchise's front door.

BEN PLATT WAS BORN AS 1962's Dodgers snatched defeat from the jaws of victory. "I've been listening to Vin since I came out of the womb," he laughed. "There's been a confluence since then." In 1972 Ben's mother, Mimi, died of a rare lung disease called obliterative bronchiolitis. "When things were down, my older brother Marc and I'd listen to Vin," in their bunk bed, over KFI or KABC. "If the game was quick, we'd hear the post-game till 10." Lights out. Sweet dreams. "A few games were on TV, which meant they were special." Mostly, Vin meant radio.

In 1993 Platt joined the Dodgers' fan magazine *The Big Blue Review*. His second story detailed Rick Monday, succeeding Drysdale: Lasorda mimic, ex-Padres Voice, and future Emmy honoree and *Tales from the Dodger Dugout* author. Platt's must-source was his boyhood Voice. "It's my second trip to the press box. Vin's on a radio break, and I've never met him. I ask if he'd give me a couple quotes. Gracious as ever, he missed Don." In 1996 the team asked Ben to create its official website. The Webmaster spoke to "Vin and Ross and Jaime and Rick. Rick was interested." Vin "was Vin."

Did Wordsworth need a backspace? "Oh, it's computer stuff," said Scully, pleasantly. "That's nice," but unnecessary: Vin did his own research. "Each year the Dodgers got him each club's media guide," said Platt, "and out-of-town newspapers and magazines." Scully's aim was making a player special. "He'd read a paper, get out his scissors, and cut out any little bit he could turn into a story. Then he'd insert that nugget in the Dodgers' or other team's media guide, and he did this for all the teams." Multi-stop browsing fueled one-stop telling.

Cautiously, Ben began touting the Internet's utility. "Mr. Scully, it has all of that stuff available. Instead of ink all over your hands, I can show you a faster way."

"'Ben,' he told me, 'I've been doing this for 47 years. The system seems to be working.' And he was *right*. His system *did* work. The trick was to convince him that this way might work even better."

One day, Vin phoned out of the blue. A son-in-law had given him a computer: Could Platt install it? "I go to his home, put the computer up, show how to start it, put the phone in the jack," and left. That October, team photographer John Soohoo showed Ben the media darkroom used by visiting photographers to process photos: "in a digital age, not used much any more." Platt got Barry Stockhamer, VP, Marketing, to make it an Internet office. "It was behind the dining area, near a restroom, in the press box. We fixed it up, put in phone lines, it became the hub."

April 1, 1997. Opening Day at the Ravine. Leaving the bathroom, Scully spies the tyro. "Oh, I see this is where you're going to be."

"It's good stuff," said Ben. "If I can help you, let me know."

"Fine," Vin said, reverting to the system.

Curt Schilling opened for Philadelphia, Platt accessing the *American Journalism Review*—AJR.org—linked "to every program in the country," including the *Philadelphia Inquirer*, CBS SportsLine, Phillies website, and ESPN.com. In five minutes, Ben found 50 pages, approached Scully, and gave him the material.

"What's this?" Vin said.

"Everything you need to do a game."

A half century earlier, Scully had a personal telegrapher as a stringer for the *Times*. Now, intrigued, the ex-techie read Platt's mass. Ben's career flashed before his eyes. Slowly, *Vin's* eyes widened. Finally: "Ben, this must have taken you hours."

"No, about five minutes. It took me twice that long to print it."

"This is fantastic," said Scully, mentally reaching for his scissors. A day later The Franchise called.

"Yes, Mr. Scully," said Platt.

"Call me Vin. This might be a time to start using my computer. Could you come out here tomorrow?"

NEXT DAY BEN LINKED a computer and DSL line, including bookmarks in Fastball.com, newspaper programs, and major sports sites. For three months, "I'd go over for an hour or two, two or three times weekly." Scully phoned almost daily. "What does this mean, how do I do that?" He requested a scanner, learned about a floppy disc, tried one slot, then tried another. Lewis Carroll wrote of "curiouser and curiouser." A computer was "curiouser" to virtually anyone over 35. "I'm sure it was tortuous," Platt guessed. "But Vin stuck it out because he saw the potential." At 69, The Franchise, hooked up, was hooked.

As a boy, Vin read a tiny New Jersey paper. The adult told Ben: "I wonder if it's still there." Finding it, Scully used scissors to cut and paste. Later, learning to revise, Vin never revised what he wanted. In 1950, 11 English-language dailies fed the Apple. "I'd get material there, then walk into the booth and the statistician would give me a yellow pad with the lineup and next to that would be the player's average, his home runs, and RBI. That was it." Now Vin—"Internet dumb," he mocked—used a computer and Ravine hardware. "No crutch," said Platt, "but to research strange interleague teams, help prepare what he needed": that "one little jewel about a person to open a window of a person's understanding."

Porter's statistics in an inning might dwarf Scully's in a game. "I'd print 100 pages, and he'd reduce it to two," said Ben, "then weave it into the larger picture." Vin had read Ahab and Ishmael. Finding that "a guy liked Melville, he'd do two innings there. He'd look for gems, was a diamond-hunter," ultimately adding a small laptop "that could be slipped in his bag." Platt's 1999 article, "Dodgers in Cyberspace," noted L.A. not meeting the Mets till August. "Yet in May, in two hours, I did all the research I needed," said Scully. "It's like the old story about penguins, learning more than you ever wanted to. Luckily I don't have an addictive personality because I could see going in there for information and never coming out."

Vin went there for *"This Day In Baseball* [from CBS SportsLine, now Baseballlibrary.com] because every now and then there's something precious I can use during a game." Next: The Franchise read the rival team's hometown paper. Finally: "I get a team report from the *Sporting News* on-line, maybe go to Fastball.com, then maybe read a couple of columns on-line. I'd print everything," said Platt. "Vin just devoured it."

In 2000, the History Channel began the Internet's *This Day in Dodgers History*, compiled by Ben and team staffers. "Vin still has the originals. Every fifth inning we'd do this. It was great: The history of the Dodgers read by the one guy who's seen more of it than anyone." That year they were mentally eliminated by Labor Day. "There was nothing to talk about, so Vin'd say, 'Ok, let's see what else is left.' He'd cite an event, which given his baseball grasp would segue to a dozen more."

Meanwhile, Dodgers.com folded into mlb.com. Manning each team's website, baseball began viewing Platt as more than another pretty key. "I became a national correspondent. Vin'd call me on the road, maybe with a computer question." TV floor director Boyd Robertson and producer/cameraman Rob Menschel became computer-literate. "They were there, could sit at the laptop, did what I used to do."

Ben smiled, wryly. "Vin's very computer savvy now. It just shows his desire to keep on top of things." Can't teach a dog new tricks? You could if it's a purebred. Scully's "Internet dumb" seems as long ago as Ebbets Field.

By 1997, CBS RADIO had forged the bigs's largest network since Mutual's 1950s 500-outlet titan. Inverting Fox TV, it put *baseball* spots on *football* inventory, plugging regular and postseason coverage. "We thought a lot about the sport," said Frank Murphy, "and encouraged our affiliates to, which helped outlet clearance [98 percent for *Game*]."

Then, in August, ESPN shockingly outbid CBS for 1998–2002 exclusivity—"They paid a bundle [$40 million]," said Murphy. "That mattered far more than PR or clearance"—soon approaching Vin *and* Jon Miller about the 1998 World Series. "What better way to start our coverage?" said general manager Drew Hayes. "We are working to bring Jon and Vin together as the voices of two generations," ignoring how the plan might leave one generation's Voice cold.

CBS's 1997 and last Series matched Marlins-Indians. In October, sitting in his 100th city's 1,000th hotel room, Vin thought, "and it was really for the first time, 'I don't want to be here.' That's when I knew I should get out of that. When you get that feeling, you should take a hike." Sandomir mused how Scully "is calling his last World Series on radio, so turn your television set off. You should settle in with Vin, whose mastery of language, history, and facts is unmatched. There is comfort in listening as he composes a kind of music in the vibrant cadences of a singsong voice nurtured in northern Manhattan."

Cliché says that "only Nixon" could have visited the People's Republic of China in 1972. In 1997 only Scully could link Jaret Wright and an earlier Cleveland pitcher tugging at his cap: Bob Lemon's 1949 near no-hitter vs. Boston interrupted, said Vin, by Red Sox manager Joe McCarthy's claim that "whitened from wear, his cap was no longer standard." Only Scully: The mother of Marlins pitcher Livan Hernandez had left Cuba to see sonny pitch. Vin explained why: Alberto Juantorena, Cuba's 1976 Olympics gold medal runner, was a 1997 government official.

Jacobs Field's odd infield dirt color led Scully to fess cheating on a Navy World War II color blindness test. A pastiche of broken bats conjured the 1941 song "Celery Stalks at Midnight." The Franchise described his padded garb—"and I'm stunning in my ski cap"—while working with the window open. Next night he conceded having sung off-air Broadway's "I'm love-ly, ab-so-lute-ly lovely," adding "confession is good for the soul—we've closed the windows because we were freezing to death."

Warmth oozed from yarn, not hype. Ex-Reds manager Rogers Hornsby never left his dugout, Vin told a listener. "When a time came to change pitchers he would whistle, like you're whistling for a cab. The pitcher would look over, and he'd go, 'You're outta there!' Can you imagine what that would do to the modern psyche of these young high-priced players?"

In Game 3, a blown catch galvanized baseball's ultimate grammarian. Fordham's Jack Coffey was "very much a literate man," said Scully. "And we had a ballgame where our shortstop and second baseman settled under a pop fly. The shortstop said, 'I got it. I got it. I got it.'" Inning over, "We all came in the dugout, and Jack called the team together. He said, 'Now look—I realize you're playing baseball. But remember, you are representing an institution of higher education.'"

The head Ram butted lousy grammar. "It is not 'I got it. I got it. I got it.' It is 'I have it. I have it. I have it.'"

Scully laughed. "And I swear to you, a couple of days later. Pop fly, shortstop: 'I have it! I have it! I have it!' He dropped it. I swear."

CBS Radio had sworn by Vin. Could Vin swear by ESPN? "I still love the challenge of informing and entertaining," Scully informed the *New York Times*, "but for the 20 hours before each game, it's excruciating. All I do is go to my room, to the ballpark, and back to my room. I don't go to parties. I'm saying, 'The meter is running.'"

To Vin, the Series had once been bigger than Ike, brassier than Uncle Miltie, more boffo than *Our Miss Brooks*. Now it meant "two weeks away, where I don't want to be." In March 1998 he retired from network radio.

"I DECIDED I'D RATHER have clean and clear sailing October to do whatever I wanted. I couldn't answer, 'Why am I here?'" Scully said, distaste less for baseball—"What has it meant? Other than my family, it has been my life"—than time "apart from home." Another family was about to stop minding the Dodgers' jibs.

O'Malley had confessed to being married to his job. "You can say that about a lot of people," said Vin, almost wed to the O'Malleys. "Walter was very gregarious, a happy, loving man, with that white cigarette holder, the twinkling eyes—*avuncular*, like a father to me," once twitting his baseball son. "We had a broadcasting team in those days. There was a skinny young guy that was on that team. Red-haired fellow. Whatever happened to that redhead?" A 1955 photo vaunts Vin kissing Walter's daughter Terry's forehead at Brooklyn's Hotel Bossert post–Game 7 fete. She was "like a sister to me," he said now, "Peter a brother in the sense that we have been together so long. We roomed together when the Dodgers toured Japan. Today, we share a lot of insights—quiet thoughts we might not share with others."

By the early '60s, O'Malley *père* felt that American big business would one day run baseball. U.S. Steel, he told Vin, might own the Pirates. "Here, as always, Walter was ahead of the curve," said Scully. "It's strange it came to pass and it affected his son, but I'm sure Peter, who was brought up at his father's knee, also heard the same thing and finally realized what was happening."

On Saturday, January 4, 1997, Peter asked Vin to meet next morning at Dodger Stadium. Scully "knew it had to be something very important." Arriving, he found an empty Ravine. "Peter and I may have been the only people there that day. We sat in his office and talked for at least two hours. We spent two hours talking about life in general and all other good things." O'Malley revealed that he and Terry were putting the Dodgers up for sale. "He went through the reasons for selling. Life is so short you want your friends to be happy, and he felt this was a wise decision. I said, 'If that's what you want to do, I'm happy for you.'" Vin was not happy for himself.

Driving home, "I felt like I had been kicked in the stomach as it all started to register. I suddenly had a tremendous sense of loss, of closure, of a major portion of my life." In time, he became Brooklyn's last bond. "The Dodgers without the O'Malleys," Vin shook his head. "It was [as] hard to imagine" as the Dodgers without Scully.

11

STARDUST (1998–)

"Some guys are lucky," said Cubs post-1995 radio's Pat Hughes. "They get a once-in-a-lifetime year." The '69 Amazins' amazed Lindsey Nelson. Baseball swung to 1998's Mark McGwire–Sammy Sosa homerthon. "Baseball's been very, very good to me," yapped Senor Sammy. Nineteen fifty-one was very good to Vin.

"You think of Bobby Thomson, Russ Hodges," Hughes said a half century later. "I think of Vin," 23, standing behind Barber as The Flying Scotsman swung. Red eyed left-fielder Andy Pafko, running out of yard. Scully typically eyed detail: "I happened to see Ralph Branca's fiancée, in a first-base box," pull out a handkerchief, dry her eyes, and replace it in her purse. "Who else would notice *that*?" laughed Pat. "What's changed in almost sixty years?"

Like Vin, Hughes, born in San Jose, 48 miles from San Francisco, grew up a Jintsophile. Demographics is called destiny. Proximity was to Pat. "I'd hang around Candlestick Park, and for some reason the Cubs clubhouse was always open. One day I snuck in. Billy Williams. Ron Santo. Ernie Banks had such huge hands. I remember him shaking my hand and squeezing it." Soon radio's future Mr. Cub squeezed for The Show.

At 15, Pat and brother Mark stole into Candlestick's press box, having heard Vin "over KFI for years." Spying an open door, they saw the man, "whom I already was in awe of, at work on TV." Scully smiled: "Hey, boys, how are you?" Vin did a Union 76 spot, winked at the monitor, and "never shooed us off." In 1983, Pat, 28, cracked bigs radio at Minnesota, joining Milwaukee a year later. "Mr. Baseball! Try reinventing [Brewers Voice] Bob Uecker's wheel." A decade later The Game needed to reinvent its own.

In a 1994 CBS poll, 39 percent liked baseball vs. 1990's 61 percent. The imminent players' lockout showed a sport not content to leave bad enough alone. "Some timing," said Pat, moving to Chicago. "Baseball had become the Flying Dutchman." The Franchise's port wed authenticity ("Ironically, we all fight the urge to mimic him"), longevity ("With a losing team, by July you say, 'What'll I talk about today?' Not Vin"), and probity.

Hughes approached him before a game. "A hundred years from now, what'll people remember you for?"

"Not the honors or titles," said the Voice that *L.A. Times* magazine dubbed "the most trusted man" in Los Angeles. "I hope two things. First, that I was accurate, and two, that I was fair."

It is fair to say that 1998 revived The Game. "What a record-assaulting, home run–blasting summer," *Sports Illustrated* wrote. The Great Race vs. Ruth and Roger Maris fueled a Greater Feud. "Forget Red Sox-Yankees," Pat said (also Jints-Dodgers). "A greater rivalry is Cardinals-Cubs. In St. Louis, fans cheered Sosa. Chicago went bananas when McGwire found Waveland Avenue." The Race would have stirred, in any case. Cubs-Cardinals made it throb.

"Daily the pressure rose," said Hughes, fretting over No. 62. "It's okay to plan a few words," warned 715's Milo Hamilton, "but you have to sound extemporaneous." Vin would add professional: i.e., restrained. Singer Rosemary Clooney advised nephew George to "pull back a little." Stengel told players: "Not too easy, not too hard." Strangely, Santo preferred an 0-2 pitch. "Other times I'd try to kill the ball, and miss or pop it up. When I was disciplined I was better." To Pat, 1965's Perfect Game tied vocabulary ("baseball's best"), discretion (neither a flacker nor rooter be), structure ("Vin's stories have a beginning, middle, and end"), and timing of a comic. "So smooth. He'll pause, build suspense, then a punch-line—boom."

It helped to have the league's best save-the-Confines stage. "To me, Dodger Stadium is palm trees, wonderfully kept-up, and being in the next booth from Vin." On September 8, 1998, Busch Stadium sufficed. At 8:18 central time, its then-Bunyan lashed Steve Trachsel's first pitch. "Drives one to deep left—this could be—it's a home run! Number 62 for Mark

McGwire!" Pat roared. "A slice of history and a magical moment in St. Louis. A line drive home run to left for Mark McGwire of the St. Louis Cardinals!" —his riposte to Gibson's top-this poke.

Mark hugged his mates and 10-year-old son at the plate. Sosa clasped him near the first-base line. The Cardinals' Joe Buck and Mike Shannon also cut "a slice of history," Hughes's being more replayed. The Cubs, being the Cubs, soon again turned Cubsward. "Not much to talk about," Pat said. "You just remember Sparky Anderson," Vin's 1979–82 CBS Radio analyst. "'Yesterday doesn't matter,' he said. 'In baseball you have to go out and prove yourself each day.'"

Like 1980s Vin, Hughes aired each inning of every game. In 2005 he began a CD series, *Hall of Fame Baseball Voices*. "If I did Scully's, I'd add cover pictures of Ella Fitzgerald, Wayne Gretzky, best of the best." Especially winsome: Vin's "audio-video" effect—"total recall. Mentally he files everything"—on a Dodgers simulcast. "Does radio and TV at once. Saves me the trouble of flipping back and forth."

In 1992 Pat muted sound, watched the screen, and heard Scully call Toronto's Devon White's leaping, rolling Series catch. "The detail was amazing, runners returning to their bases." Color man Johnny Bench sat, stunned. "Vinny, have you seen this game before?" he said, finally. Vinny had.

In *Casablanca*, Bogart tells Bergman, "We'll always have Paris." Pat will always have The Race. Vin is content to be called accurate and fair.

In March 1998 the O'Malleys sold the Dodgers to media czar Rupert Murdoch. "Vin Scully will be a Dodger as long as he wants to be," vowed Fox TV's Vince Wladika. Ed Hookstratten cautioned that Vin signed a new deal each year. Wrote Larry Stewart, "The sale of the Dodgers by the O'Malley family, the whole process from beginning to end, has hit him hard. 'I've said it before and I'll say it again,' Scully said. 'This is a time of great sadness for me.'"

The new Dodgers' owner junked organ music, ordered blue game jerseys, and turned "a holy relic into a hot potato," the *Los Angeles Times*'s Bill Plaschke said. Scully radiated cool. Alejandro Pena threw a ball through catcher Jack Fimple's glove. "We had a report that Mike Brito caught Pena at 97 miles an hour on the radar gun," Scully said. A revision lowered it to 96. "Either way, you're going to get pulled over." Daniel Boone with a

Louisville Slugger "spit on his hands as he [Pedro Guerrero] always does
. . . like a big man getting ready to chop down a tree." Noted Vin: "The
word-picture works on any medium," including a film whose title could
have signed his name.

In December 1998 Scully was hired for Kevin Costner's Universal
Pictures *For Love of the Game*. "A star is born: Vin Scully," said *USA Today*.
Amused, The Franchise told "the entertainment industry [it] has nothing
to fear from my participation in the [1999] movie, which I did because
of my friendship with Kevin and my own love of the game." Like Vin,
having played it, Costner profiled the Tigers' Billy Chapel (in baseball's
first single-game flick) hurling a no-hitter (Vin did Detroit's last [Jack
Morris's] on 1984 NBC) vs. the Yankees! (revenge for 1941, 1947, 1949,
1952, 1953, 1956, 1977, and 1978) to end a 19-year career.

Off-season production braved a Bronx chill, not cheer. "The director
[Sam Raimi] shot [The Stadium's] action as if he was directing a TV
presentation of the game," said Scully, "so there's shots from center field
with Kevin pitching," tutored by two Davids, the Yanks' Wells and Cone,
themselves each tossing a perfect game. Before the latter's, Yogi Berra
crouched for Don Larsen's pregame pitch. "Mr. Larsen," Cone asked,
recalling 1956, "are you going to jump into Yogi's arms?" Larsen laughed.
"You got it backward. *He* jumped into *mine*." Berra gave his glove to Joe
Girardi, who used it for *Cone*'s perfect game vs. Montreal.

"Only in baseball," Vin would tell you. "Yogi, Larsen, me, it's '56
again. I love the history"—and Costner's arm. "When I say he throws a
fastball, you'll see movement on his ball." To him, the extras—Class-C
players—were as real. "They made the plays in a real game that you'll
see in the movie." Its spine was play-by-play: Thus, Scully shot scenes
separately. "I didn't want a script. Kevin never saw my stuff till editing.
[Film and then-Fox analyst] Steve Lyons and I looked at a TV screen of the
game. We just did our thing as if we were on the air."

Keeping his "day job," Vin denied "an Academy Award speech in my
future or, I suspect, even another acting role. I had a lot of fun, but I was
basically playing myself." It was the only character he knew *how* to play,
said Scully. He knew priorities. too.

BEN PLATT JOKES that if he wrote a baseball book, Vin's chapter would be
titled "God Has Red Hair." It would reveal a flaw: "Vin likes kids," Ben

kids us not. "Critics actually think we have too many TV shots of kids as a new inning starts." The flaw was intentional. "'Find me a picture of a kid,' Vin'll tell a cameraman. So we find one, in his parent's arms, and Vin'll say, 'And there he is, sleeping the sleep of a good child.'" In Hollywood, a tyke steals the scene. At Dodger Stadium, he's good for business.

"Unlike a lot of creative types," Platt said, "Vin grasps the bottom line." The hoops junkie was a friend of Los Angeles Lakers coach Jerry West. "That didn't stop him from rooting against his team," knowing how Dodgers attendance fell if the NBAers made the playoff. "Maybe 2,000 people'd stay home to watch basketball on TV." In the pressroom, Vin watched Kobe Bryant hit a shot. "Look at that!" someone bayed. Looking, Scully didn't like what he saw. "Darn. This isn't good for Peter."

October 24, 1999: On a night the World Series' lights go on in Georgia, Vin presents MasterCard's Major League Baseball All-Century Team before Game 2. Earlier honorees gather in the anteroom. Except for Ted Williams, Scully has aired each. Koufax is voted left-handed starting pitcher, the irony pleasing the emcee. "I was there the day he tried out for the Dodgers," Vin tells Ben before the game. "I broadcast every game he pitched. And here I am introducing him as an All-Century pitcher." The Franchise scans the room. "These players are like sign posts of passage of my life."

September 24, 2000: A vote of American Sportscasters Association members names Vin "Sportscaster of the Twentieth Century," routing Cosell, Allen, Gowdy, Enberg, Barber, and Harwell. Regular season ending, love bathes the Ravine. ASA president Lou Schwartz presents a McNamee-era bronze mike. "Amazing. I've been at a lot of events, but none like this. Every time I mentioned Vin's name, the place exploded." Later, Diamond Vision replays Scully's speech, 46,393 chanting, "Vinny! Vinny!" He ends: "And now, if you don't mind, it's time—it's *time*—for *Dodgers* baseball," perspective still leading off.

To Fox, that meant "changing anything and everything at the drop of a bat," Mike Penner wrote. "Managers, general managers, division-winning rosters, uniform exteriors, stadium interiors," ditching dugout boxes. Only Scully's "tenor remains the same; the cadence . . . unchanged." If Reggie Jackson was Mr. October, Scully owned April–September. "Enjoy him while you can." Dodger Stadium enjoyed its one hundred millionth visitor. Unfazed, the 2000 Giants opened the bigs's first privately funded baseball-only park since O'Malley's. Pacific Bell Park filled a waterfront site off China Basin. Dogs trained by Don Novello, *Saturday Night Live*'s Father Guido Sarducci, rescued dingers from the drink. A right-field sign totaled home drives to the channel: Barry Bonds was first to dent (Willie) McCovey's Cove.

"What a great sight," Scully said in its opening series. "To look out there and see all the yachts [and kayaks and fishing boats and freights], and the people sprawled out on their decks with their TV and drinks, it was unbelievable"—a floating right-field sports bar. Brooklyn had never been like this.

By CONTRAST, Fordham had changed little since Mom strolled Vin across the Rose Hill campus. The baseball field abutted football's. V-shaped stands fringed the plot. Beyond first base lay a batting cage, like bullpens at Ebbets Field.

The effect was familial. The family, though, had changed. Vin's classmates often wore a coat and tie, had a crew cut, smoked a pipe. Today's wore grunge, treating attitude as adjective. Scully spoke to each.

Knowing that "it will bring back memories," Scully gave Fordham's 155th commencement speech May 20, 2000. "I had never given one. They happen in May and June, which, since it's baseball season, means you can't get away." When university president the Reverend Joseph O'Hare invited Vin, "I initially asked him if I couldn't just get the degree." The 1999 speaker had been ex-U.S. Senator George Mitchell. "I was hoping the same people who listened to Mitchell wouldn't hear me because they'd get the bends." Instead, they got a man who said "it's best to know your subject, and I know myself very well."

Class of '49 began with what he *wasn't*—a scientist, general, or educator: "I would like to take this moment to declare that I am a candidate for the United States Senate representing the State of New York," Vin twitted Rudolph Giuliani and Hillary Clinton—then noted what he *was*: "It's only me and I am one of you. I walked the halls you walked. I sat in the same classrooms. I took the same notes and sweated out the final exams; drank coffee in the café; and played sports on your grassy fields. I hit a home run here: Jack Coffey Field, against CCNY, the only one I ever hit." Rose Hill tied a mother's carriage, teacher's hand, and baseball: above all, radio.

Corinthians touts "faith, hope, and charity." To Scully, Fordham meant "home, and love, and hope": home, 1940–49; love, "closest and dearest friends"; hope, "dreams." They could humble, even teach. In 1956 Ralph Branca's father-in-law arranged an audience at the Vatican, Vin explained. "Beside herself," Bridget begged, "'Oh, Vincent, when the time comes, please remember what he [Pope Pius XII] said.'"

Vin promised, only to hear the pontiff speak in German, French, and Italian. Eying Ralph, Pius said in English: "Where are you from, my son?"

"New Rochelle, New York, Your Holiness," Branca said. Wife Ann asked, "Will you bless our family, Your Holiness?" He nodded, moving on.

Scully was next, having absorbed Bridget's admonition. "Are you with them?" was all Pius asked.

Having made the audience laugh, Vin assured the graduating class of today being "with them." The world, he said, "will try very hard to clutter your lives and minds." Scully's road map differed: simplify, clarify. "Leave some pauses and some gaps so that you can do something spontaneously rather than just being led by the arm. Don't let the winds blow your dreams away . . . or steal you of your faith in God." Follow the Ten Commandments. "Build a better . . . moral climate." Be a bobbed cork: Pushed down, bound up. "Sometimes even your wildest dreams can come true."

He spoke for 19 minutes. Giving an honorary doctorate of human letters, honoris causa, Michael T. Gillan, dean of Fordham College of Liberal Studies, cited sixteenth- and seventeenth-century Jesuit scholars lauding "eloquentia perfecta . . . which connotes a mastery of expression that is informed by good judgment and consistent principles. Those Jesuit schoolmasters of another age, if they had known anything about baseball, would certainly have approved the rhetorical gifts of the man who has been the voice of the Dodgers for the past 51 years, Vincent E. Scully"—at Rose Hill, still "one of you."

IN 1950 SCULLY JOINED a peerless Apple colony of future Hall of Famers: Barber, Giants' Harwell and Hodges, and Yanks' Allen, Dean, and Gowdy. Sixties and '70s L.A. was a close-run thing, Salon.com's Gary Kaufman wrote in 1999: "a lucky time and place for a kid who liked to listen to sports on the radio. We had Scully doing the Dodgers, Enberg doing the Angels and Rams, the colorful, vocabulary-investing Chick Hearn doing the Lakers, and Bob Miller, less famous than the others, somehow making hockey action make sense on the radio for the Kings." It was easy to get spoiled.

On December 4, 2000, Fox Sports Net 2's *Carl's Jr. Sports Roundtable* aired Miller, Hearn, and Scully's first show together: their then-120 play-by-play years half as old as the Republic. "On practically any night of the year," said the *Times*'s J. A. Adande, "we [can] tune into a local team broadcast and hear the best in the business," teaching icing, the zone press, and infield fly. "But as special as it is to have these Hall of Famers all working simultaneously in the same city, it's even more rare for the three of them to be in the same place at the same time": adding Jarrin, a nonpareil four.

To Adande, Vin still meant "summer days at the beach. I think of . . . the smell of suntan lotion and the sound of . . . Scully's voice," the latter earning a final quarter-century selah. In 1984, Vin introduced Danny Kaye at the Kennedy Center. "I had to walk down center stage before the most prestigious audience in the world and give a speech about [Kaye getting a Lifetime Achievement Award]." Other honors: 1987, Ronald Reagan Media Award. 1991–92: NASS and ASA, respectively, Hall of Fame. 1995: National Radio Hall of Fame; Fordham's first Arthur Daley Alumnus Memorial Award; Bogota, New Jersey, baseball field named for Vin; and National Academy of Television Arts and Sciences Lifetime Achievement Sports Emmy. 1997: Academy tribute and Southern California Sports Broadcasters Hall of Fame. 2000: ASA Century's Best Sportscaster. 2007-present: old (28th time, California Sportscaster of the Year) and new (seventh, eighth, and ninth Halls [Fordham Prep, Sports Broadcasting, and National Association of Broadcasting] and two lifetime achievement awards [Golden Mike and John R. Wooden]). "Any time I can have my name linked with John's," Scully said, "I'm way ahead of the game." In 2009, the American Sportscasters Association named Vin "Top Sportscaster of All-Time."

Saturday, April 21, 2001: The Ravine press box takes The Franchise's name 51 years after Vin's first homecast (naturally, Giants-Dodgers). "It takes a certain amount of persistence to be Vin Scully, the prepared broadcaster, each night," said *Times* columnist T. J. Simers. "Outside his broadcasting booth there is a line of people hoping to catch a glimpse." The "cult [was] here to pay homage to him once again. They unveiled a pair of impressive 'Vin Scully Press Box' signs—if only his vocabulary could rub off on some of us writing inside."

Several tried. Michael Knisley defined *euphony*: "Listening to Scully is pleasant enough, but as long as the Dodgers keep Hiram Bocachica on the roster, it's pure bliss." Bill Plaschke put on life's must-do list "see[ing] Vin talk. Fly to Southern California, rent a car, drive up and down the freeway for three innings, and see for yourself." Team president Bob Graziano felt "Vinny has the same impact on my boys now as he did on me when I was young." The impactor wasn't sure. "To be absolutely honest, when I was asked about the naming of the press box proposal, I was honored, but I wanted to decline. The press box is sacrosanct for the writers—it's not the place to have a broadcaster's name."

New "Walk of Fame" artwork honored Cooperstown's Murray, Bob Hunter, Ross Newhan, and radio's Jarrin. "Any time you walk by and see the name Scully on the press box, it should be representative of all those years and all those writers," mused Vin. A coast away baseball returned to Flatbush, the Class-A Cyclones packing a beachfront bijou. Joan Hodges became a regular. Like Bedford Avenue, hitters eyed the boardwalk. Born in Jamaica, Queens, George Vecsey loved Brooklyn's venue: "KeySpan Park," he wrote, "a spiritual retreat where fans of a certain age daydream of . . . the good old days."

Opening Day was June 25, 2001. We remember a bad day 78 days later.

SCULLY'S SISTER'S SON, Dan McLaughlin, was an attorney on the 52nd floor of New York's Twin Towers. Usually at work by 8:30 A.M., he decided first to vote in New York's September 11 primary. "He was late, thus fortunate," said his uncle. "For anyone who had anyone in that part of New York, it definitely brought it closer to home," like another date of infamy. "When Pearl Harbor occurred, I'd turned 14 the prior week. All we had was radio, and you had to wait until [next day] Monday to see pictures, and then maybe in a week, you went to the movies to see newsreels." By contrast, "when President Kennedy was assassinated, the country wouldn't let go of the mood that TV helped create."

On September 17 the Dodgers played their first game post-9/11. George W. Bush's pregame video preceded Scully on KTLA and at the park. Vin then spoke, calming, mending. "All of us have experienced a litany of emotion whether it would be shock, disbelief, and horror followed by grief, mourning, and anger," began L.A.'s captain/chaplain. "All of us have indeed lost a lot. We have lost thousands of lives. We have lost some of our self-confidence. We have lost some of our freedom. And, certainly, we have lost a way of life."

Bush had asked America to "go back to work." Baseball, Vin said, "gets up out of the dirt, brushes itself off, and will follow his command, hoping in some small way to inspire the nation to do the same," steadying a shaken craft. Cops and firefighters had become a 9/11 buoy. "We look to our own backyard to honor the men and women who selflessly put their lives in danger." Two officers got the Los Angeles Police Department's Medal of Valor, the Ravine chanting, "USA!" Scully led a moment of silence. "God Bless America" followed, a huge flag lovingly unfurled. "I was a very ordinary person asked to say some things at a very difficult time," Vin said. Even "Take Me Out to the Ballgame" seemed hymn, not ode.

"The mood was down, but at the same time, people there wanted to see a game. Slowly, you could see people were more into it. After a while I finally noticed a lighter mood in the park." Semanticist, "not a psychologist, just an announcer, I'm not making some great proclamation. I like people to think of me as a friend. The nicest thing I've had people say to me is, 'You know, when I hear your voice I think of some nights with my mom and dad barbecuing in the back yard,' or 'I remember a summer vacation.' If it helps to bridge a nightmare into some normalcy, I'm pleased to serve as that bridge."

On October 4, 2001, Barry Bonds whacked McGwire-tying homer 70 at Houston. A day later he faced L.A.'s Chan Ho Park. "The 1-0 pitch on the way," Vin said. "The fastball hit into deep right field. It is away back—and gone! There it is! Number 71." Next March the team's official website polled fans' favorite Dodger. Scully topped Lasorda, Koufax, Valenzuela, and Garvey. "The favorite Los Angeles Dodger," said the *New York Times*, "has never gotten a hit, thrown a pitch, or filled out a lineup card." Vin's public was his shield.

In 2002 Howard Rosenberg satirically likened him to Russ Hodges. Letters to the *L.A. Times* editor bristled. "Listening to Scully," one read, "is as close to God as you can get without dying." A native Flatbusher nodded. "First time I went to a baseball game, my father took me to Ebbets

Field," Charley Steiner said in the book, *What Baseball Means to Me*. "First time I had a game on radio was probably '56. I was six. And that first voice I heard on the radio in my mom's kitchen was Vin's." Like Scully, he loved the crowd. "My eyes and ears grew about as big as the tubes in back of our big brown Zenith." Learning that play-by-play was "Vin's job—his *job*?!"—Charley knew "what I wanted to do with my life."

Mom was a sweet, lovely woman, but not exactly a fan. In 1957 she bought Steiner a mitt. "Every kid remembers his first glove, almost as fondly as his first love," said Charley. Ma assumed that, being left-handed, sonny's glove should fit that hand. "She gets a right-handed glove. For the first couple of weeks of my ballplaying life I'm trying to throw with my right hand," tossing "like a ballerina. Believe me, I knew where my future lay, and it wasn't on the field."

Steiner's first fungo game began a block from his house. "Donnie Sorensen, an experienced veteran of nine," said to hit the ball, run to first base (elm tree), second (towel), and third (another elm), then dash home (cardboard). Charley was nothing if not literal, racing for the tree, towel, tree, and "home. I mean *home*. All the way to my *house*! I couldn't figure why everyone was chasing after me, laughing, screaming, and telling me I was running the wrong way."

Not homeless, the Flatbusher soon was teamless. "When you're eight, you don't give a damn about business. Los Angeles might as well have been Saturn, it was so far away." He tried pinstripes and piano: a last lesson October 13, 1960. "My teacher wouldn't let me out, despite it being Game 7 of the Pirates-Yankees Series. She looked at me and, in broken English, asked, 'What's the World Series?'" Bill Mazeroski cost Charley a $1 bet. "Not only was that a monthly allowance, but my piano career came to an end. Maz swings, and I'm playing 'On Top of Old Smokey.'"

Steiner entered Bradley University, sold an underground paper in Haight-Ashbury, parlayed with Abbie Hoffman, and at Woodstock mixed mud and drugs. The Boomer's prism refracted Vin's. "We were right about the war in Viet Nam—how wrong it was. We were right about civil rights, right about questioning authority." He aired the New York Jets, USFL New Jersey Generals, and ESPN TV boxing and *SportsCenter*. In 1998 radio's *Sunday Night Baseball* dawned. "I knew I'd arrived," said Charley, "when I saw the bases." They did not include a cardboard, towel, or tree.

In 2002 he joined the Yankees, wasting three years as water to broadcaster John Sterling's oil. Paroled, Steiner became Vin's second in 2005. "Talk about your karma," he said on National Public Radio's affiliate *Perspectives*. "I go back to my Brooklyn home, to the living room with the radio, and say, 'Mom, remember how I'd listen to a guy do the Dodger games? Remember how I wanted to broadcast the first time I heard his voice? I'm going to L.A. I'm working with *him*.'"

At that moment, his cell phone rang. "It's Vin, congratulating me for coming West." Stunned, Charley looked at his mom, having lent new nuance to coming home.

STEINER LIKENED "broadcasting in the booth next to Vin" to playing pepper with the Babe. "He's the only guy who could do it [solo]. That voice. His timing. Plus, he is never flustered," Charley said. "There isn't going to be another Vin. To me, he's The Man": also to the "grandfather and grandson working the jigsaw in a Long Beach garage," wrote Eric Neel, "with the folks tuning at the Short Stop bar on Sunset Boulevard, with a family listening to a radio beside a campfire up in Yosemite, with anyone who's ever heard him, really, because he's just ridiculously good at what he does."

Frank McCourt agreed, buying the team in 2004. Plaschke warned: "If he even thinks about messing with Vin Scully." McCourt didn't, not crazy like a Fox. At the time, "someone suggested that I was a bridge," said Vin—that term again—"for the team from Brooklyn to Los Angeles and now from one ownership to another. So I guess I'm an additional bridge to . . . McCourt." He accompanied the New Englander to Boston: Scully's first regular-season game "seen simply as a spectator." The Yanks visited the Ravine, their first stop since 1981: "It wasn't so much the rivalry as bringing back my childhood, where the romance began." The 1984 Dodgers had telecast 46 games. In 2004, Fox Sports Net 2's and KCOP's coverage tripled to 144. Vin's 110 included all home, West Division road, Eastern interleague, and Halos Freeway Series.

"A few years ago," he said, "I asked [then-Dodgers head] Bob Daly that since most Fox games in the East began at 4 o'clock in the afternoon and 10 in the morning, and our audience then wasn't that big, would they mind letting me stay in the West, and they said OK. Basically it gives me more time at home"—except that The City wanted more of Vin's time on new flagship KFWB 980. "At least stay longer," cajoled Tom Hoffarth, "coming back to the end of the games to call what turn out to be the climactic moments. The problem is his doing [all nine innings on] television."

Since 2000 Vin had simulcast innings 1–3 on radio, preempting other mikemen. "When I first started, I had some fears and trepidation," he noted, "but I realized that Chick Hearn, God bless him, did the simulcast for so many years that people accept it." Houston columnist David Barron wasn't "quite sure how to describe what he does other than to say he calls radio and TV at the same time and does both justice."

McCourt kept the simulcast, video's irresistible force long ago decking radio's immovable object. On October 2, 2004, hoping to clinch the West, L.A. scored thrice in the ninth inning to tie the Giants. Bases full, Steve Finley needed just a sacrifice fly. Instead, "high fly ball into deep right field!" Scully said on wireless. "*Wherever* it goes, the Dodgers have won . . . and it's a grand slam home run!" Vin's style changed little on radio vs. TV.

Bobby Bonilla seemed to be "playing underwater." Terrmel Sledge's first name rose from Dad's fusing Terrence and Melvin. Oscar Robles singled a bouncing pitch, like stickball played in Brooklyn. Ramon Ortiz's first mitt was a folded-over slab of cardboard, Mom using old dresses to stitch together baseball pants. "He puts the game in human terms," said Jon Miller. "This is not mythology. These are flesh-and-blood human beings. And when we're mindful of that, we feel more connected to the game."

In March 2005 Steiner began his "second or third" week with Scully. That winter hurricanes had battered Vero. "All of a sudden," said Charley, "Vin starts doing this incredible three-to-four-minute rhapsody about the nearby palm trees." Old stands collapsed; newer were left intact; saplings were severed. Scully paused. "And isn't that what spring training is all about?" Steiner stared. "Damn!" he softly said. "That's why he's Vin Scully—and that's why I'm sitting here listening." Charley got up, left the booth, and, dazed, shook his head.

That August, Vin emceed the golden anniversary of Brooklyn's out-of-body title, introducing the '55ers—Podres, the Duke, Oisk, Mr. K—"very close pals of mine," he said. "I was about the same age as most of them. Plus, that was the day of roommates. Just a totally different time." Scully never left the booth—"I didn't want to take a bow. It's their day"—yet became "the star of the ceremony," wrote Adande. "When Scully was introduced, the cheer . . . was as loud as anything heard all day."

Vin's same-day FSN West 2 game tracked baseball's half-century trek from two-camera black-and-white to gaudy-graphic color. Next month Neel etched broadcasting's Grand-Not-Yet-Old Man. "Vin strolls into the Dodger Stadium press box that bears his name, does a little vaudevillian shuffle, and says, 'Ta-da!'" Scully's Westlake Village home lay 30 miles away. An hour late, after two hours on a freeway, he arrived riffing *My Fair Lady*'s "I've grown accustomed to the pace" and apologizing for the delay. "I left yesterday . . . from Bolivia." Amazingly, you could now hear him in La Paz.

XM Satellite Radio began airing each bigs home game April 3, 2005. For a fee, a listener anywhere could access Vin. "Many are people who may have seen him on TV," said XM director of corporate affairs David Butler, "or who are baseball fans who have heard about the legend of Vin Scully but had never had the luxury to hear him call a game on radio." Simulcasting "mutes [Vin's] poetry in deference to the power of the visual image," wrote the *Washington Post*'s Dave Sheinin. "[Still it meant] 81 opportunities to carve out your little slice of baseball heaven."

The Internet carved, too. MLB.com's *Gameday Audio* subscription package even bared Scully archives. "Hi, everybody" segued via "Dodgers lead, 1-0" to what Vin spied during break. "A little boy sitting in his dad's lap. Another youngster, maybe six years old with a glove. And another one, a restless two-and-a-half to three, a little towhead. [Chuckle.] So you look around the stands and you see kids of all ages, sizes, and shapes." Add Fox, DirecTV, "and other baseball packages," he later said, and "I can be spotted anywhere. In the old days, you were known in your area. Today there is no area."

Depending on age, a senior could recall Red; a Baby Boomer, Kirk and *Game*; or Generation Xer or Yer, asking, "You know that old guy who calls the Dodger games?" said Neel. "He's really good." Each heard modern twist ("Swinging and missing and down goes Griffey, credentials and all"), old-time mot ("They also serve who only stand and wait"), and easy as Sunday lilt. "He's seen everything there is," observed Lasorda. "What's going to rattle him? Why would he rush?" —to retire.

"Vinny can't leave," Miller said. "We're not ready. You can't walk away from it when you're the best there ever was." Neel noted Harwell calling "your favorite announcer 'a comfortable slipper' and how someday, when he's gone, a new shoe is going to pinch." Jon was right, Eric knew. "Vinny can't retire. We're not ready"—especially since, as Doug Gamble wrote, "Scully still hasn't reached his personal bottom of the ninth."

WOOING SOME WHO HAD, Vin spoke to *Retiree* magazine in 2005. What would he do, named Commissioner for a day? "This will come as a shock, but the first thing I would do is get rid of 14 teams. I'd get back to eight teams in each league. Not that it will ever happen, but that's what I would do." What was *left* to do? "I don't know. The world just keeps changing," said Scully, having recently voice-overed MLB's video game for Sony PlayStation. "Who'd have believed *that* five years ago?"

How had baseball changed? AstroTurf, the designated hitter, 1957's Continental Shift. What hadn't: baseball as playing cards. "You can't compare it, for instance, with basketball or football." Hoops rivaled 21: two cards. "Hit me. Bingo. You make it or you don't. Constant action. Action. Turnover. A lot of people like 21." Gin rummy was more cerebral. "Some like that. Then there's people who love chess," cheering a hit and run. Another group might attend to get a girl or gassed. "Then somebody hits one over the fence and it's 21 [again]. It's like beauty. It's in the eye of the beholder."

To Vin, the ultimate beholder was the Kindly Light That Led. Asked with whom he would like to lunch, "Well, probably Number One would be Christ," Scully said. "Let's just say I'd rather go one-on-one with Him." Baseball's number one wore blue. Few expected umpires "[to] be as gods," said Parnassus. Scully *did* expect "accuracy. They're paid to be in the right position and they're paid to be patient." Like faith, accuracy could curb imponderable. "The rules can be very complicated. If you don't know all the rules, at least you should have a book and be able to look them up."

Near 79, he still admired Faulkner's "old verities and truths of the heart" that would not deceive. One game in 2006 was not to be believed.

ON SEPTEMBER 18, vying for the Western Division lead, Los Angeles trailed San Diego, 9-5, in the ninth inning. Empty seats specked a Monday night record 55,831 sold-out Ravine. Traffic snarled even earlier than usual. Dodgers leadoffer Jeff Kent went first-pitch deep. "To the track! To the wall! And gone!" Vin said. "And the Dodgers are now down, 9-6."

The exodus continued as J. D. Drew swung. "And another drive to deep right-center and *that* is gone! . . . What is that line? 'Do not go gentle into that good night.' Well, the Dodgers have decided they are *not* going into that good night without howling and kicking." The Padres were not without pitching. Relief's Horatio at the bridge, Trevor Hoffman, entered. Said Scully: "It is Trevor Time!"

TV's *Laugh-In* coined "very interesting." Russell Martin made it fascinating. "A drive into left-center! . . . That ball is carrying into the seats! Three straight home runs!" Cars U-turned. Some seats refilled. The Dodgers were "still a buck short. The folks who hung around to ride it out are in for quite a ride." Behind, 9-8, Marion Anderson connected. "And another drive into high right-center! At the wall, running, and watching it go out!" L.A. had trailed earlier, 4-0. Now, "Believe it or not, four consecutive home runs and the Dodgers have tied it up again!" Girders throbbed. "Can you believe this *inning*? In fact, can you believe this *game*?"

Point: San Diego regained a 10-9, 10th-inning lead. Counterpoint: Kenny Lofton walked in the bottom half, "a rabbit as the tying run." Nomar Garciaparra faced Rudy Seanez. "And a high fly ball to left field! It is away out and gone! The Dodgers win it, 11 to 10! Unbelievable!" Eighty-four seconds later the familiar voice reemerged: "I forgot to tell you, the Dodgers are in first place." Karl Marx called religion the people's opiate. At such a moment, Vin seemed a listener's.

"Truck drivers, English professors, kids with braces on their teeth, even the Little Old Lady from Pasadena like Scully," said Phil Elderkin. Gary Kaufman recollected Cooperstown's multimedia program for Vin's silver anniversary. Phoning, he found "that there was a six-week backup for reference requests, 'but since you're writing about Vin Scully, I can do it right away.'" Steve Bisheff penned "what got the biggest reaction I've ever had" in his 25-year-old *Orange County Register* column. "Take the time now to listen as much as you can. Some day you'll want to tell your grandkids. They'll be all excited about some new announcer they like, and you'll smile and shake your head and give them the only answer you can: 'Ah, but you should have heard Vin Scully,'" his "voice the backdrop of your life."

Eight months before "Trevor Time!" The Franchise signed a three-year pact at a reported near-$3 million per anum: to Adande, "the best Dodger deal in a long time." Improbably, Vin held his first-ever press conference clad in a Dodger blue sports coat, blue hankie in his pocket, light blue shirt, and blue on blue tie. Jarrin hailed "my mentor," who thanked Jaime for "teaching me to say La Jolla and La Cienega." Jamie McCourt said, "[He] brings out the best in us all," even the 2005 second-division Dodgers. Husband Frank "loves how the face, the personality, of the Dodgers is Vin Scully," thanking him for "taking [Jamie's] hand" to make her less nervous the day the McCourts bought the club.

Question and answer began. What was it like to be a city's silhouette? "When I'm looking in the mirror in the morning, I'm not thinking, 'I'm shaving the face of the franchise,'" said Vin. Longevity? "Old friends have pointed out, 'You haven't advanced since 1954.'" Quality? *SI.com*'s Jon Weisman noted "the most common criticism Scully receives today: he makes more flubs than he used to." Vin shrugged: "As a play-by-play announcer, the mind and the tongue might not be as sharp as it was. I still think I do a reasonably good game." Would he retire? "I'll go day to day like the ballplayers." Had he got a raise? "I'm just thankful to get a free seat."

T. J. Simers asked if Scully colored his red hair. Like Pavlov, he told a story. Living to 97, Bridget had red hair late in life before finally going to the bottle. "Not *that* bottle," Vin laughed. "She dyed it, and it turned orange": no bottle for her son. Did The Franchise like names plucked from the back of Dodgers jerseys? No. McCourt said they would return in 2007.

Q & A ended by retrieving late 1957. O'Malley had asked Scully to start "rooting for our club": new coast, new approach. At 30, Vin demurred, knowing himself and his game. "It's all based on trust," he told the Dodgers' sachem. There are worse ways to be recalled.

12

"LET US DEFINE OUR TERMS"

By 2006 ALMOST EVERY DAY was evocative of Scully's past. On October 4 New York and Los Angeles began the National League Division Series. (Mets won.) Two Dodgers were put out on the same play by L.A.-turned-Apple-catcher Paul Lo Duca. "Here comes a throw on that runner and here comes another runner, and Lo Duca is going to tag both of them out and the Dodgers become the Brooklyn Dodgers of old!" waxed Vin, invoking Babe Herman doubling into a double play. "We turn the clock back to the daffy days of the Brooklyn Dodgers." Critics went nuts. What history! What exposition! Only Scully! (Again.)

In *The Making of the President 1960*, Theodore H. White wrote: "By the last weeks of the campaign, those forty or fifty national correspondents who had followed Kennedy since the beginning of his electoral exertions into the November days had become more than a press corps—they had become his friends and, some of them, his most devoted admirers. When the bus or the plane rolled and flew through the night, they sang songs in chorus with the Kennedy staff and felt that they too were marching like soldiers of the Lord to the New Frontier."

To White, JFK was what some reporters wished to be, but weren't—handsome, lilting, elegant. Ibid., Vin's "admirers," swelling since mid-century. Each Irish Brahmin disliked the bogus, was sensitive by nature, and saw humor in absurdity. To Gary Kaufman, damning Scully was like knocking Shakespeare. "You can do it, but you say more about your own foolishness than anything else."

The diplomat and journalist Clare Boothe Luce said that any leader could be described in a sentence. Washington begot his office. Jackson democratized politics. Lincoln saved the union. A sentence can define baseball broadcasters, too. Mel Allen was a play-by-play celebrity. Red Barber was the Southern gentleman. Van Patrick became Falstaff behind the mike. What sentence evokes Scully?

A book of mine etched Allen's rise, ruin, and recovery. Before starting, I knew its arc: Mel had all, lost all, and, incredibly, came back. *Pull Up a Chair* is different. Stephen Ambrose said, "For me, the act of writing is the act of learning." I have tried here to learn how anyone could be so good, so long. Ranking baseball's all-time announcers, I once rated Vin 100 on a 1-100 point scale, his niche a gimme. "Before we talk," Plato wrote, "let us define our terms." What makes Scully, Scully?

Affinity, for one thing: what Whittaker Chambers styled "some quality, deep-going, difficult to identify, in the world's glib way, but good, and meaningful." Kaufman noted Vin's park bench lure: "the guy who enjoys reading crime novels in the hotel and goes to mass on Sundays and loves to steal afternoons in the swimming pool with his grandkids and Sandra," wiling hours "studying player bios and stats because he's never quite shaken the Catholic school sting of a nun's ruler across his knuckles"; the "lanky kid at Fordham who stood in the outfield practicing game calls, never really believing he'd get to announce in the Show. And, even now . . . the little boy from the Bronx who curled up under his parents' radio and listened to the crowd noise of college football games through the speakers."

Privacy, for another. TMZ.com and YouTube reveal more than we need to know. By contrast, Vin would woo, inveigle, but never overwhelm. "Everyone who has listened to Scully feels as if he or she knows him," Paul Oberjuerge wrote. "In fact, he reveals almost nothing of his personal life." As of 2005 Porter had not been inside Vin's home. "It's how he is," Ross mused. "Yet he makes [a fan] feel more important than he is. In all the years I was with him, I never saw him rude." George Vecsey would see Scully, "knowing, but not knowing, him. Always polite, but you wouldn't get into a conversation."

The Dodgers' 1990–2001 broadcast director remembered a day game in Chicago. "We're on Michigan Avenue after dinner," said Brent Shyer, "people coming up. 'Oh, hi, Mr. Scully.' 'Can I take your photo?' Always, 'Hello, sure.'"

A man admitted to "hearing you for years."

Vin brightened: "Oh, you should get a medal!"

An Angeleno confessed to falling asleep to Scully.

"Sure," he laughed. "I've put most of this city to sleep over the years."

Hospitality hid the loneliness of the long-distance speaker. In 1999 Sammy Sosa homered 63 times and led the league in strikeouts. "He pays the bill for those home runs," Scully said, knowing baseball's. "The fact that you're working three hours talking on television doesn't touch that [loneliness], doesn't do a thing." Vin's public—unboutique, largely middle class—grasped his refusal to confide or whine. In turn, under perfect fit, he grasped *its* injury and reticence—nobility, above all.

Reserve bred **proportion**. The 2005 Dodgers hosted Cincy. Preface: "A beautiful sunset coming now. Seventy-three degrees at the start of the game." Backdrop: Ohio was a sauna. "Earlier we were talking about playing in the heat, back in the days before air-conditioning. They say the old-time ballplayers would sometimes go back to the hotel at night and take water and pour it all over the bed and then sleep on a wet mattress." At Milwaukee's Schroeder Hotel, "everyone slept with the doors open, and a lot of guys, I remember, slept on the floor, with their pillows and heads in the doorway, just hoping to catch a bit of air coming down the hallway." Who else could tie the icebox and postmodern world?

Reliability made Scully, Scully. Bill Dickey said of Lou Gehrig: "Every day—any day—he just went out and did his job." By 2007, "if I had to guess," Vin mused, "games that I have absolutely missed because of illness, it would be a handful, maybe five." To actor Robert Wuhl, "the sound of [Vin's] voice, like the sound of your dad coming home and throwing his keys on the kitchen table, is the sound of comfort and security for so many of us." To Eric Neel, Vin was "doing what comes naturally": ticking consistency like a watch.

Credibility made Scully, Scully. On July 31, 2007, one homer shy of Aaron's record 755, Barry Bonds began a three-game Ravine series. "This to me is different," Vin said of less filling vs. still tastes great. "Aaron's [No. 715] was received with great love, affection, adoration. I'm not sure how this one will be received. The story won't be what I say. The story will be what the crowd will say." Scully wasn't "here to root, or disparage. I won't give an opinion. That's not my job." He did predict L.A.'s greeting. "I think it will be mixed," and was. ("So Barry Bonds fouls out, much to the delight of the crowd.")

The series ended with a walk—and whimper. "Fred Lewis, who is basically Barry Bonds's caddy right now, will run for him. So he's done," Scully said. "And what that means: *It* will not happen here. The vigil is over in Dodger Stadium. They will now fold the circus tent, pull out the pegs in the round. The roustabouts will clean out everything, and take the troupe . . . down to San Diego," where No. 25 hit 755. Did Vin even care? "I just do between the lines," he said, Bonds having crossed them.

Music made Scully, Scully. Parkbound, Vin "put on Broadway music, peppy music, I'm singing along, getting up, getting ready." Driving home, he put on "strings, and music that is very soft." Vin "has the most musical voice in baseball," Kaufman wrote, "not the clipped, old-time-radio cadence of most broadcasters who date back to the '50s and beyond. Although his timbre is thin"—a "musical Irish" tenor—"everything is smooth and rounded. The melody rises and falls on the tide of the game."

Bill Cosby knew, one night leaving for an airport 40 miles away. "World Series," he told the driver. "Turn the radio on." Riding, he heard "a voice that is as wonderful and as welcoming as anyone that I love in my family." Arriving, the actor hesitated to leave his car: "To heck with the flight, just sit here and listen." Cosby hummed along, approximating pitch and tone. Duke Snider felt they would captivate a kindergartner. "Have Vin read a phone book over the P.A. at recess. I think they would stop play in the sand box . . . on the merry-go-round. Vin has that presence": time-out, meet tune in.

"It's not just a marvelous catch; it's a *maaaaarvelous* catch," wrote Ruben Martinez. To Brad Buchholz, Vin's inflection said more—"Swung on, a *hiiigh* drive. . . . Walker goes a-*way* back! To the *waaal* . . . she is *gone!*"—than "anyone's in the business. Scully adores the dash. He loves punctuation. He paints with silent space"—also, bending vowels and simile and allusion. "The words *Wilver Stargell* delight him. To him they are instruments of music." Scully played his in the office, kitchen, yard.

"I'll sing anywhere," Vin said, recording for Sandra "The Wind Beneath My Wings." In 1998, chiming "Take Me Out to the Ballgame," he honored the pied piper of Wrigley's Seventh-Inning Stretch. "I'm delighted to honor the memory of Harry Caray, and to quote Harry, 'Lemme hear you!' A one, a two, a three," Scully said, mike turned baton. Teenagers swayed. Dads held daughters. "People still call it the best rendition we've ever had," said Pat Hughes. "Smooth, on-key, smiling, so prepared."

In 2007 Jon Weisman compared Vin to before, say, 1970. "Scully's voice in those days was more polished than it is today," he said, hearing tape. "It's silkier. It *glides*. Today you could characterize him as having more of a drawl—not a Southern drawl for the Fordham grad to be sure, but a deeper, richer flavor than he had before."

A crooner once asked Bob Costas, "You know who I'd really like to meet?"

"Who?"

"Vin Scully," said Ray Charles.

"Why?" Bob said, surprised.

"You gotta remember that to me the picture doesn't mean anything," said Charles, blind since seven. "It's all about the sound." In 1992 Vin got the Voice of Vision Award for an "incredible gift of painting vivid word pictures so those without sight can also see Dodger baseball." Would you introduce me? Ray asked Bob.

Costas took him to Dodger Stadium. "Vin was, of course, very gracious, and certainly had an appreciation of who Ray Charles was, his historical standing. But Ray was like a little kid taken to see Santa Claus or something! He was just beside himself. The man was beaming, clapping his hands, throwing his head back in delight." It was, he guessed, "the highlight of Ray's year."

In 1994 they communed on NBC TV's *Now*. Charles aped his favorite Scullyism: "A *hiigh* fly ball into *deeep* right *fieeeld*!" Bob hit the floor. Vin smiled: "Yep, that's my call."

To Barber, the English language was "the most beautiful thing, next to human love, I know." *Language* made Scully, Scully. Rick Monday asked if "English were my second language, because Vin's poetic about even saying hello." A hit over second base between two diving fielders "really did look like a bowling alley." A liner barely missed the third-base bag: "If you sliced meat like that, you'd see right through it." A Saturday afternoon–Sunday night–late-night plane to Denver–Monday schedule became "a long day's journey into night into day"—again O'Neill. Even hairstyle moved the Muse. One day a hirsute player entered the game. "What, ho! What, ho!" Vin hymned. "What men are these, who wear their sideburns like parentheses?" Kaufman blasted "parodying him about spouting flowery language. Other radio announcers tell you what's happening on the field, and you imagine it. With Vin, you see it."

Seeing, Dick Enberg envied. "All those phrases, those wonderful things that he does, go instantly"—he snapped his fingers—"from the brain to the mouth. I'll be listening to him and think, 'Oh, I wish I could call upon that expression the way he does.'" Rockies pitcher Mike DeJean threw a curve "like a kid scaling a stone on a pond." Dante Bichette hit "a blur that finds its way into Eric Karros's mitt." Frozen in midair, shortstop Walt Weiss fired to first "like one of those old, posed quarterback shots." The "phrases are short," wrote Buchholz, "there's always one idea to a sentence," Vin talking seamlessly, tying Durante and Donne.

Knowledge made Scully, Scully. At Fordham, Vin began a lifelong affair with books: "my best friend on road trips." Pillow pals included James Michener's *The Source,* Joseph Heller's *Catch-22,* David Halberstam's *The Powers That Be,* "almost anything" by Roger Angell, *The Glory of Their Times* by Lawrence S. Ritter, and Mark Harris's novel *Bang the Drum Slowly.* Off-season, he and his wife took "exotic vacations," wrote *Scribner,* to Europe, China, Macau, Australia, Israel, and Egypt, among other sites. In season, "I love the tapestry of the game," Vin said. "Let your senses be the teacher."

Check position players. "Their moving around tells you what kind of a hitter it is and how they plan to pitch him." Learn the pitcher's style. "Then, how does he do in his first confrontation with a power hitter? You find how good he is." Birddog the catcher. "A lot of hitters like to peek just before the pitch." Skip the friendly skies. "Whenever a fly ball is hit, the first thing I look at is the outfielder," not the ball. The fan looked "with his heart, and why not? The last thing I would want to convey is, 'Go to the ballpark and do this'! Baloney! I don't want to sound like some stern taskmaster. Holler and have a ball." Not hollering, he did.

Discipline made Scully, Scully. The smoker quit in the 1970s. Recalling Desmond, he rarely drank. "I'd have loved to play golf in the morning and have a beer with the guys," Vin told Ben Platt, "but I won't. I never drink on a game day." He also spurned air-conditioning, "the bane of my existence. Especially if I've gotten hot and perspiring, I can really be in trouble."

Scully "never, ever" used *we* about the Dodgers. Instead, "diligently he intersperses biographical material and anecdotes between pitches," said Dave Sheinin, "information he keeps on notebook pages in front of him." Charlie Slowes watched a Dodgers-Nationals taped telecast. "I spent a lot of time today," he told Vin, "listening to *your* broadcast to learn about *my* team." Scully stilled as nirvana lit Brooklyn, Aaron passed Ruth, and Superman tugged at Gibson's cape. In 2007 reliever Takashi Saito faced the Angels' Vladimir Guerrero: "the kind of [TV] match-up that speaks for itself," wrote Phil Mushnick. "Scully said he wouldn't intrude . . . just allow the audience to watch." For five minutes, as good as his word, Vin didn't say one. Finally Guerrero flied out.

To some, FDR's 12 years as President were insufficient; 12 minutes of George W. Bush, enough. A difference was *wearability*. Recall 1965. "Vin never exhausts his welcome," said Costas. "It isn't just the last pitch of the Koufax game. It's that whole inning, and how he perfectly captures the scene and the passion. Vin never wears out his welcome." Retrieve Gibson, going deep. "He excels at capturing the sense, the atmosphere, the buildup to the moment. Gibson limping out of the dugout, the crowd's reaction, the drama of the situation, the mounting tension. And he has a way of summing things up afterwards that is beautiful" — above all, real.

Reality meant grasping, if not liking, it. "Experience is the hardest teacher," Vin told Fordham's Class of 2000, "because you will get the exam long before you get the lesson." It taught how "it's a mere moment in a man's life between an All-Star Game and an Old-Timers' Day." Quoting Emerson, Scully "knew the depth, the draught of water of every one of his men." An Opening Day 2007 runner embarrassed weak-armed Juan Pierre. "Better get used to it," The Franchise said.

Scully knew who paid the freight. "The object of the game is both to win pennants and attract fans," said Jim Murray, "not necessarily in the order named." He ignored 1981's next-day work stoppage — but not how a listener could buy a next-homestand seat. "When writers rap me for not reporting something controversial, I usually ask them if they would rip their publisher in print if he'd done something wrong." Radio/TV's effect: "I'm extremely conscious of the number of children and young people who listen to Dodger broadcasts. I'll tell them what's happening on the field, but I'm not going to rip some ballplayer's private life in front of them." Above all, our sound bite age: "I can't relate. I realize that attention span is very brief. So I try not to dwell on anything too long."

Even his own children, Dad said, "used to drive me crazy. I'd be picking up my daughters at grammar school, and they'd jump in the car, and no matter what was on the radio, they would hit the button—and then, in five seconds, hit it again. They wouldn't wait! Five seconds! But that's the way we are." Having grown up in Los Angeles, Salon.com's Kaufman recalled the way it was.

"LOTS OF KIDS AT SCHOOL rooted for the Oakland A's or the Pittsburgh Pirates, powerhouses of the day," he wrote of the 1970s. "Those teams won a lot (and had cool caps), but you couldn't go home from school and listen to them on the radio. I was an Angeleno, and Dodger blue all the way." Moving "half a lifetime ago," Gary still missed The Franchise.

Scully meant *empathy*: "introducing a scene by thinking, almost feeling, through the likely emotional register of Teddy Roosevelt's proverbial 'man in the arena,'" Neel mused, citing examples from the ninth inning of Koufax's perfect game. Taking the mound, "tonight, September the ninth, nineteen hundred and sixty-five, he made the toughest walk of his career, *I'm sure*," said Vin. Sandy got two strikes on Joey Amalfitano. "*I would think* that the mound at Dodger Stadium right now is the loneliest place in the world." His one-one fastball sailed on last-batter Harvey Kuenn. "*You can't blame* a man for pushing just a little now." Stepping outside himself, Scully went inside the player.

Intimacy ensued. Garagiola was the sole exception to Vin's one-man rule. In 2007 catcher Guillermo Rodriguez made the Jints after 12 years in the bushes. "If ever a fella paid the bill, here he is." Bills didn't bother pitcher Barry Zito. A two-on jam did. "Now, how would you like to be the catcher? . . . You're going out to talk to a Cy Young Award winner who has a contract worth $126 million, and you're getting paid per day on the minimum in the major leagues, and you go out there and say, 'Listen, son, I want you to do this,'" Scully laughed. "What a spot." James Loney hit into an inning-ending double play: "Obviously, Guillermo Rodriguez came out there and gave Zito the tip." Hideo Nomo was due to bat in a bases-full tie game. "Would *you* let Nomo swing? [With one out] what's the worst thing that can happen?" Announcers talk to one another. Vin talks to us. "He'd rather quote Cole Porter than Eddie Vedder," Buchholz said: apt, given Cole's "I Get a Kick Out of You."

Finally, *history* made Scully, Scully. On November 5, 2007, the Dodgers, minus a title in 19 years, hired an ex-Yankees manager with four in the last 12. A half century earlier the team had left Flatbush. Brooklyn-born Joe Torre—like Vin, a young Jintsophile—now followed, introduced at a press conference-turned-investiture. "[Already] he's an integral part of the Dodger family," Scully said on a blue-draped Ravine platform, distilling a laying on of hands.

January 1, 2008, began L.A.'s golden anniversary. "Fifty years is a big chunk out of anybody's life. You realize that time does fly and where did it go?" Vin said of riding down Colorado Boulevard in Pasadena's 119th Tournament of Roses parade. The 350-member Los Angeles Unified All-District High School Marching Band preceded the team's first float, "Celebrating America's Favorite Pastime." Players including Nomar Garciparra, of nearby Whittier, sat in a dugout. Fireworks lit a Dodgers sign. Jarrin, Fernando, Karros, and Garvey recalled title parades through Center City. "This is a generational float," said Steve, at six a Brooklyn batboy. Bill DeLury, Newk, and Oisk remembered 1955.

More than 500,000 watched on the 5½-mile parade route. A 35-foot-high floral Dodger, wearing No. 50, swung to go "a-way back." Scully and Lasorda sat in the float's grandstand—to Tom, "box seat"—section, waving, pointing, smiling. Behind them, team organist Nancy Bea Hefley serenaded bystanders. Vin recalled 1958. "Opening Day in a parade was a memorable moment when we first came out here. I'll enjoy every minute of this [parade], too. This is a first, for sure."

Fitzgerald wrote, "There are no second acts in America." The Dodgers disagreed. O'Malley's 1956 Orient Express had traveled to Japan. In March 2008 it played China's first baseball exhibition vs. San Diego in the Summer Olympics' Wukesong Stadium. Back home, Los Angeles staged a 50th birthday exhibition vs. Boston—at the Coliseum! "There are generations of Angelenos who have grown up as Dodger fans and never had the opportunity to see a game [there]," McCourt augured "a once-in-a-lifetime" chance. The Associated Press fancied a "field . . . reconfigured as close as possible to the original": a time impossible to relive but not to miss living.

All 90,000 seats sold almost instantly. The Dodgers then asked the Coliseum Commission, city, and fire department, said an official, "if there was any way we could accommodate additional fans." In 1956, 114,000 paid to see an Australian national-American services game in Melbourne. On Saturday, March 29, baseball's largest crowd, 115,300, including standees, jammed the shooting gallery, Ping-Pong parlor, or amusement park—each fit—for "a meaningless game," Vin rhymed, "that is so full of meaning." To McCourt, "It's just breathtaking to see that baseball diamond again carved into the football field."

Permanent seats had reduced left field 50 feet to a Little League 201. To compensate, the screen was raised 18 feet to 60. Outside, a "Baseball Festival" wooed thousands of congregants. Ex-Dodgers manned autograph booths. Live period music featured "California Dreamin'." T-shirts hyped "I Was There." Torre fed the flock: "It's a privilege to share this with the Boston Red Sox," he began. "Excuse me"—smile—"the *World Series* champion Boston Red Sox. For some reason, that doesn't bother me any more." Later, the ex-Brave conjured playing there in 1961. "Man, this place brings back memories."

Like Scully, the new Dodgers' skipper thought the day less waif of a moon than bright noon sun. "Baseball is all about history," Joe said: a Boomer's coming of age. Before the game, the Commission dedicated a bronze plaque at the peristyle entrance, hailing Vin's "six decades and 50th anniversary." Dedicating it to "the 138 million fans who've come to our games since 1958," The Franchise was honored on the field for being "the most beloved figure in Los Angeles since Zorro," wrote Ken Levine of the *Huffington Post*.

Introduced by Charley Steiner, Vin met a din cresting somewhere between Azusa and Yorba Linda. "Aw, c'mon, it's only me," he aw-shucked, looking down, again in blue suit and tie. "We stand on the curb and watch the heroes go by and applaud them." The throng would not stop applauding *him*. Wally Moon tossed out the first pitch; Marilyn McCoo and Billy Davis, Jr., harmonized the National Anthem; and a hardscrabbler relived a foe. "I know the hitters are foaming at the mouth," Don Newcombe steamed. "It's [the screen] a monstrosity. It was a monstrosity then." Steiner hailed "a baseball Woodstock," except that drug smoke yielded to tailgating's smoked ribs.

Boston captain Jason Varitek gave the score: "Dodgers 85, Red Sox 81." (Actually, Sox, 7-4.) Torre's five-man infield affirmed the Coliseum "having room for almost one hundred thousand people and two outfielders." Boston's Kevin Youkilis played Screeno. Shortstop Julio Lugo played a drive off the wall. The throng sang "Take Me Out to the Ballgame," written a century earlier: It sounded like the Mormon Tabernacle Choir. Recalling The Mouse, Big D, the Duke, an adult turned child. Scully felt "a million miles away," working for Channel 9 in the right-field press box, "it [being] . . . impractical to re-create the [1958–61] home plate booth," he told the *Daily News's* Tom Hoffarth.

"It seems freakish now," Vin advised a listener, "but we came here and we played, and in the second year, the games became very exciting and everything was fine. I imagine the players tonight are asking, 'How could they possibly have played here,' but they played here and they played very well." *Times*woman Christine Daniels said, "A city hangs on [his] every word." *Sports Illustrated* announced baseball's "best broadcast team: Scully and Scully." Wrote Richard Hoffer: "Having stitched together all those seasons, all by himself . . . when you say *Dodgers*, you really mean *Vin Scully*," tying the LP and DVD.

On April 26, he gave Pepperdine University's commencement speech. Three days later WFUV Radio, turning 60, threw a bash at Sotheby's Manhattan auction house. In 1956 Ralph Branca had helped Vin be presented to the Pope. Now the ex-Bum pitcher presented Fordham '49 with the first annual Vin Scully Lifetime Achievement Award in Sports Broadcasting. CBS Radio's Charles Osgood '54 got a similar prize in news. "If we're giving awards," said WFUV's Ralph Jennings, "why not name them for the most important news and sports figures at the station?"

ABC's Elizabeth Vargas emceed, oozing edge. Emmylou Harris got the inaugural Sound and Vision Award, singing and surprising. "When I became a big baseball fan decades ago," Nashville's Hall of Famer said, "I would turn down the sound of the television to listen to Vin Scully call the World Series on the radio for many years, because radio is the medium." On June 13 remembrance turned message and messenger: "boats against the current," *The Great Gatsby* read, "born back ceaselessly into the past."

In 1958 John Wooden had met Vin by opening a Brentwood apartment gate. Now they staged "Scully and Wooden: For the Kids" at the 7,100-seat Nokia Theatre/L.A. Live. "The idea began with [the *Times's*] T. J. Simers, who got them to agree," Ben Platt said. "Two local sports legends, combining to fight pediatric cancer." Proceeds benefited Mattel Children's

Hospital of UCLA and ThinkCure, the Dodgers' official charity, for Children's Hospital Los Angeles and City of Hope.

Platt's computer convert helped $25 to $200 tickets go faster than Davey Lopes. "[It's] Father's Day weekend," Scully wrote. "Join us, proud fathers, and help other fathers, and mothers, of course, to save some youngsters with stories about baseball and basketball." Weisman thought "about how long these people have been a part of Los Angeles," yet never having jointly and publicly reminisced. "You just had to be here." For 90 minutes, viewers, many in Dodgers and Bruins shirts and jackets, heard two friends craft good company.

"This is a night that you'll never forget and will never happen again," emcee Simers began, introducing the actors. A standing ovation greeted Scully and the wheelchaired Wooden, then again when they left. Bill Walton recalled the Coach yearly showing how to put on shoes and socks. Wooden, 97, hailed longevity—"Don't let the peaks get too high and the valleys too low"—and the then-playoff Lakers. Vin expressed gratitude, noting a recent Dodgers slump. "All I hear about was the Lakers," he laughed. "Bless you, Lakers."

Was Scully a Dodgers fan? "No. . . . [Especially] Yesterday, I found it was not difficult not to root." Why was he a southpaw? "Nuns would swat my left hand when I used it because back then people didn't think being left-handed was natural. They'd whack me with a ruler." Explain his self-description: "The Great Coverup." As children, "we kind of imagined ourselves, in all honesty, as young brave Indians who would not show emotion." On film, a tortured "Indian would bite on a stick, whatever. That's the way we grew up": stoicism in season.

The Coach and The Franchise traded Lincolnisms. Vin: "A father gives his children the greatest gift by loving their mother." Wooden, joshing Simers: "It is better to keep quiet and let people think you're a fool than to speak up and remove all doubt." The UCLAer compared teams, games, and eras. Scully compared Presidents. Golfing in 1990, he told George H. W. Bush that in the White House "you can say anything you want about your baseball career." Leaving it, "remember, in that [1947 Yale-Fordham] game, we both were oh for three."

His autobiography *An American Life*, Reagan remained an American Original. He and Scully, Vin told Nokia's audience, often returned to Pacific

Palisades from a 1960s night speech and game, respectively. Seeing his car, the Gipper waved Vin over. "How'd we do?" he asked. "We [Dodgers] won," Scully said regularly.

Elected President, Reagan gave the then-CBSer a 1980 Thanksgiving interview: "You know, I'm the one who invented instant replay."

"Really. Tell me about it," Vin urged, not knowing, he added later, that Al Gore would invent the Internet. Reagan relived the 1930s Drake University Relays on WHO Des Moines: Scheduled to speak after the 60-yard dash, Drake's President began talking with runners still in the blocks. Speech over, Reagan had to re-create the race. "No wonder," Scully observed, "he became President someday."

Vin led the crowd in song, credited Fordham's barbershop Shaving Mugs quartet, and noted "questions where there are no answers in this world for finite beings." To one query—"When" would he retire?—the sellout flock roared, "*No, no!*" Scully joked, "Let's talk about the Lakers." Then: "I'm looking forward to at least" 2009. Wooden denied fearing death: "I'll be with [late wife] Nell[ie] again." Vin conceded having pined for song-and-dance: "If I come back, I'd like to come back looking like Cary Grant, dancing like Gene Kelly, and singing like Bing Crosby."

Simers ended on more true confession. Scully named his favorite word (*love*); least favorite word (*hate*); best noise (*stringed music*); worst noise (*chalk on a blackboard*); and favorite cuss word (*darn it*). (Wooden's favorite curse: *Goodness gracious sakes alive.*) How would God greet them? The Coach: "Well done." Scully: "Welcome, my son." *Vitae* and video retrieved a postwar rite of passage. On July 31 the Dodgers passed a Rorschach test, acquiring, depending on your view, a mercurial or psychotic bopper.

Manny Ramirez hit Tinseltown having loafed, feigned injury, huffed "Boston doesn't deserve a player like me," and decked the Red Sox's 64-year-old traveling secretary. "And all eyes are on the newcomer," Scully said of his fellow Washington Heights expatriate. They saw Manny bat .396, slug .743, hit 17 homers in 53 games, and help the ex-O'Malleys erase a 5½-game West deficit. On September 25, St. Louis clubbed Arizona, 12-3, Dodgers clinching. L.A. promptly lost to San Diego, 7-2. Mused Vin: "Who cares?"

The best-of-five Division Series opened at Wrigley Field. Favored: the 97-64 last-Series-title-1908 anyone-can-have-a-bad-century Cubs. WTBS owned TV exclusivity, Scully airing KABC's non-simulcast. Chicago straightaway began stranding runners. "So they wind up the merry-go-round again," Vin prefaced a bases-full, two-out, 3-2 K. Manny homered: Dodgers, 7-2. Next night each encored, 10-3. The series then wayfared to the Ravine.

Optimist: The glass is half full. Pessimist: The glass is half empty. Cubs fan: When's the glass going to spill? Game 3: ninth inning, Alfonso Soriano batting, L.A. up, 3-1. "And the Dodgers are one out away," chimed Vin. "One sweet beautiful marvelous out away. They will take it any way, shape, or form. Strike out, ground ball, fly ball, fair ball, line drive, any way they can get their hands on it. That precious thing called the final out."

Jonathan Broxton worked a 0-2 count. "And now it's not one sweet precious out, it's one sweet precious pitch." Soriano half-swung. "Strike three called—and the Cubs are dead! The Dodgers racing out onto the field, mobbing Broxton. They have done it by sweeping the Cubs! All they kept talking about was '100 years! 100 years! It will finally happen!' Well, it was a disastrous happening for the Cubs and a delicious trio of victories for the Dodgers!" They should have quit while ahead.

Bob Uecker called Philadelphia so hard "people go to the airport to boo bad landings." They booed—and beat, 3-2 and 8-5—the visitors in LCS Games 1-2. At Dodger Stadium, huge letters *THINK BLUE* loomed beyond the outfield. A good thought filled Set 3: Dodgers, 7-2. A sign in their clubhouse had seemed batty in July: "The Road to the World Series Begins Here." L.A.'s ended, losing, 7-5 and 5-1. MannyMania peaked, Ramirez hitting and slugging a postseason record .520 and 1.080, respectively.

"Dodgers grateful for [his] dread[lock]s," *USA Today* punned. Others' gratitude fixed the mike, not field. The "last great constant in the Dodgers picture," Buchholz wrote of Vin. "Beat writers and baseball men literally stop talking when he passes through. He belongs here simply because he *always* has been here. He belongs here because there is a story to be told, and no one [more] entices us to listen to the words": literature in a highlight age; serving the undimmed and undumbed down.

"Perhaps it's because lyricism—and for that matter, radio—is so horribly out of style in Twenty-first Century Information-Age America that we focus all the more intently, nudge, and settle in to really 'listen.'" Listening, you heard a perfect 10.

EPILOGUE

PICK A STUDENT aspiring to radio/TV. Whom should he emulate? Almost every Voice has, if not a vice, some chink. In decline, Mel Allen talked too much. Bob Prince would wander; Ned Martin, misstate; Curt Gowdy, bore. Jack Buck could be flip. Harry Caray morphed into caricature. A tyro should avoid each flaw. Vin had none.

A 1966 book listed *Quotations from Chairman Mao*. A writer might list the Lessons of Chairman Vin. 1) "Remember Polonius," he said of *Hamlet*. "'To thine own self be true.'" Rochester Triple-A general manager Dan Mason got 200 audition tapes for a 2003 vacancy. "I got tired of hearing 'em. Everyone was trying to be Scully." 2) Read. "I can't get through the books I'd like," Vin said, trying. "Fiction, history, politics, mostly non-baseball." We hear Aquinas by design, not chance. 3) Knowing pros and cons maximizes a broadcaster's positive. The successful Voice also minimizes negative.

4) The Puritan Work Ethic works. "I still love Olivier's 'humility to prepare and confidence to pull it off.'" Never profane on air, Scully's four-letter word was *toil*. 5) The greatest sin is not to try and fail—but to fail to try at all. "Push yourself," Scully said in 2006. TV's *It Takes Two* and *The Vin Scully Show* failed, but taught: Losing yourself, you find yourself. 6) Be factually, not politically, correct. In 1998 Vin asked Pat Hughes about "a rather minor statistic" before a game. "He wanted to double-check it. Still a mania about being right." 7) Have somewhere else to go. Balls and strikes fit a 2 to 1 squeaker. At 20-1, "you have to tell a story," Scully said. "Let me interest you, even if the game doesn't."

8) Longevity counts. The Franchise, Ernie Harwell, and Milo Hamilton have worked 166 bigs years, cumulatively. "Walk, exercise, keep up on things," Vin said. "Stay young. I thank God to a) give me

this job at such an early age, and b) allow me to keep it so long and to keep my health." 9) Live/list priorities. "I've always felt [that] I haven't really accomplished anything. What I've done is spend a lifetime talking about the accomplishments of others," said Scully, asked his legacy. "I hope people would consider me a good human being and good husband, father, and grandfather. The last thing would be the fact that I was a pretty good broadcaster."

10) Safe at home beats a little traveling music. Al Helfer, Russ Hodges, and Jim Woods aired 17 teams, among them. Vin bleeds Dodger Blue. "Being with one team built his legacy," said Harwell. 11) Shun tempora. "I'm still very much old-fashioned," Scully said. "A guy who changes to ride one tide may drown in the next." 12) At the same time, be from, not of, the past. In 2007 a foul ball killed a minor-league first-base coach. Before retiring, Vin hoped helmets would be mandatory. "Gosh, those dear dead days beyond recall," a young man sighed in Arthur Miller's *All My Sons*. Scully moved beyond.

The Dodgers' adieu broke Brooklyn's heart. KeySpan Park has not replaced razed-in-1960 Ebbets Field. Dodgertown, to Vin "greatly associated with the Brooklyn Dodgers," but "now far, far away from our fan base," expired in 2008: "the final severing of the umbilical cord with Brooklyn"—all bricks and mortar, gone. That May, Scully hedged on going. "There's a lot of hoopla in this job, but it's lonely for the wife," he told the *New York Times*. "So I want to talk seriously with [Sandra] about her feelings [about retirement]. I want to know what's in her head."

On September 6 Vin reupped for 2009. "I still get goose bumps with an exciting play. So I told Frank [McCourt] that I'll try it for another year." The Franchise will one day retire. His Scully School can live.

ON ELECTION EVE 1960, John F. Kennedy spoke to a packed throng at Boston Garden. Tired, he did dismally. Aide Richard Donahue eyed envious politicians. "You know, they can't understand this," he said. "They think he has a trick. They're listening to him because they think if they can learn it they can be President, too." We have listened to Scully locally or nationally in 1950–57 Brooklyn; 1958 to present Los Angeles; 1970s–90s Atlanta and Spokane on network radio/TV. Absence is said to make the heart grow fonder. Vin's made perspective brighter. "I wish we'd heard him longer," said a friend in rural Ohio. "Then I think, no, if that'd

happened we might have taken him for granted," missing what a writer dubbed "the man inside the radio, even as a boy."

September 1997. Brett Butler pinch-hits in the ninth inning: possibly the cancer victim's last home at-bat. "This is a painful time," says Scully. "As the team is running out of time, his career is running out of time. And this crowd is saluting him." Butler, "visibly affected as he backs out of the box," pauses to palm his batting helmet. "He lifts the helmet, finally . . . and now, very shyly, he puts the helmet back on." More applause. "And now, Butler checks in. Or at least tries to." Sherwood Anderson scripts a hit. Brett pops up. "Life is so cruel. You look up at the sky and say to yourself: Would it have affected matters if You would have let the little guy get one base hit? And the answer is no." Pause. "He fouled out to the catcher."

September 1998. "By the sixth inning the San Gabriel Mountains have turned a rich, deep violet, their outline growing bolder as the golden light of afternoon fades away. The air grows cool," said Brad Buchholz. Scully cites Charles Russell and Frederic Remington, next "a golden path of light," then the "light almost gone—and time [again] running out." The Dodgers bow to Colorado, 10-5, slip-sliding from the pennant race. Organist Nancy Bea Hefley—"summing it up musically, as she always does"—plays "September Song," "especially those [lyrics] that go, 'The days dwindle down to a precious few,'" said Vin, tending each syllable, drawing us in.

March 21, 2007. On local TV, Scully compares the Mets' Jose Reyes to singer John Fogerty's "a brown-eyed handsome man." Reyes legs out a hit, steals second and third base, and makes pitcher Hong-Chih Kuo throw wildly. "That run belongs to Reyes," said Vin. "He reminds me of Jackie Robinson."

April 15, 25 days later. Baseball hails the 60th anniversary of ending its color line. ESPN's *Sunday Night Baseball* airs Dodgers-Padres. A Ravine pregame bash includes each Dodger, on the third base line, wearing Robinson's retired No. 42. Said catcher Russell Martin: "It seems like there were a lot of Jackies out there."

Jennifer Hudson sang the "Star Spangled Banner." Hank Aaron and Frank Robinson threw out a ceremonial first pitch. Clear sky—to Vin, "cerulean blue"—knit the canopy. Joe Morgan, Dave Winfield, and actors Courtney Vance and Marlon Wayans led the company. To Bud Selig, the game's "most powerful moment was . . . Jackie's coming into baseball. . . . Not only is he a baseball Hall of Famer, he's a Hall of Famer for all time."

Don Newcombe, 80, looked ready to dust a batter. Rachel Robinson beamed: at 84, having overcome. Selig presented the Commissioner's Lifetime Achievement Award. A choir chimed "Oh Happy Days," the Robinsons' favorite song. Earlier Vin had been introduced. The din volleyed, rose above the outfield, and crashed against the tiers.

Shyly, baseball's Homer asked the crowd to quiet: embarrassed, lush with memory, fixed on its Lochinvar. Watching, a sense of time stood still: fielder crouched, batter cocked, and pitcher draped against the stands—above all, the hope that you would always pull up a chair.

SOURCES

Brief portions of this book have appeared in slightly different form in *The Voice* and *Voices of The Game* by Curt Smith.

Grateful acknowledgment is made for permission to reprint excerpts from the following:

FDR: A Centenary Remembrance by Joseph Alsop, copyright the Viking Press, 1982. Reprinted by permission of Thames and Hudson Limited.

The Fireside Book of Baseball edited by Charles Einstein, copyright Simon & Schuster, 1956.

Miami and the Siege of Chicago by Norman Mailer, copyright the Viking Press, 1969. Reprinted by permission of Thames and Hudson Limited.

President Kennedy by Richard Reeves, reprinted by permission of Simon & Schuster, 1993.

Rhubarb in the Catbird Seat by Red Barber and Robert Creamer, reprinted by permission of Doubleday and Company, 1968.

The Boys of Summer by Roger Kahn, copyright Harper & Row, 1971.

The Voice of Heaven on Earth by Dave Sheinin, reprinted by permission of the *Washington Post*, July 5, 2005.

When It Was a Game, reprinted by permission of Home Box Office, 1991.

Play-by-play commentaries are used with the permission of the Miley Collection. Grateful acknowledgment is also made to: ABC Television, CBS Radio, Mutual Radio, and NBC Radio and Television.

BIBLIOGRAPHY

Allen, Mel. *It Takes Heart*. With Frank Graham, Jr. New York: Harper & Brothers, 1959.

———. *You Can't Beat the Hours: A Long, Loving Look at Big-league Baseball, Including Some Yankees I Have Known*. With Ed Fitzgerald. New York: Harper & Row, 1964.

Alsop, Joseph. *FDR: A Centenary Remembrance*. New York: Viking Press, 1982.

Barber, Red. *The Broadcasters*. New York: Dial Press, 1970.

Barber, Red, and Robert Creamer. *Rhubarb in the Catbird Seat*. Garden City, New York: Doubleday, 1968.

Buck, Jack. *Jack Buck: "That's a Winner!"* With Rob Rains. Champagne, Illinois: Sagamore Publishing, 1997.

Castiglione, Joe. *Broadcast Rites and Sites: I Saw It on the Radio with the Boston Red Sox*. With Douglas B. Lyons. Lanham, Maryland: Taylor Trade Publishing, 2004.

Cosell, Howard. *Cosell*. With the editorial assistance of Mickey Herskowitz. New York: Playboy Press, 1973.

Costas, Bob. *Fair Ball: A Fan's Case for Baseball*. New York: Random House, 2000.

Creamer, Robert. *Babe: The Legend Comes to Life*. New York: Simon & Schuster, 1974.

D'Agostino, Dennis, and Bonnie Crosby. *Through a Blue Lens: The Brooklyn Dodgers Photography of Barney Stein, 1937–57*. Chicago: Triumph Books, 2007.

Durso, Joseph. *Yankee Stadium: Fifty Years of Drama*. Boston: Houghton Mifflin, 1972.

Finch, Frank. *The Los Angeles Dodgers: The First Twenty Years*. Virginia Beach, Virginia: Jordan & Company, 1977.

Friedlander, Jeremy, ed. *A Baseball Century: The First 100 Years of the National League.* New York: Rutledge Books, 1976.

Gowdy, Curt. *Cowboy at the Mike.* With Al Hirshberg. Garden City, New York: Doubleday, 1966.

Greenwald, Hank. *This Copyrighted Broadcast.* San Francisco: Woodford Press, 1997.

Halberstam, David. *Summer of '49.* New York: William Morrow, 1989.

Harmon, Merle. *Merle Harmon Stories.* With Sam Blair. Arlington, Texas: Reid Publishing, 1998.

Hodges, Russ. *Baseball Complete.* New York: Grosset and Dunlap, 1952.

Hodges, Russ, and Al Hirshberg. *My Giants.* Garden City, New York: Doubleday, 1963.

Holmes, Tommy. *The Dodgers.* New York: Collier Books, 1975.

Kahn, Roger. *The Boys of Summer.* New York: Harper & Row, 1971.

Jackson, Kenneth T., Karen Markoe, and Arnold Markoe, eds. *The Scribner Encyclopedia of American Lives.* New York: Charles Scribner's Sons, 1998.

McNeil, Alex. *Total Television: A Comprehensive Guide to Programming from 1948 to 1980.* New York: Penguin Books, 1980.

Mailer, Norman. *Miami and the Siege of Chicago: An Informal History of the Republican and Democratic Conventions of 1968.* New York: Viking Press, 1969.

Major League Baseball Promotion Corporation. *Baseball: The First 100 Years.* New York: Poretz-Ross Publishers, 1969.

———. *The Game and the Glory.* Englewood Cliffs, New Jersey: Prentice-Hall, 1976.

Manchester, William. *One Brief Shining Moment: Remembering Kennedy.* Boston: Little, Brown and Company, 1983.

Metz, Robert. *CBS: Reflections in a Bloodshot Eye.* New York: Playboy Press, 1975.

Miller, Jon. *Confessions of a Baseball Purist: What's Right, and Wrong, with Baseball, as Seen from the Best Seat in the House.* With Mark Hyman. New York: Simon & Schuster, 1998.

Okrent, Daniel, and Harris Levine, eds., with historical text by David Nemec. *The Ultimate Baseball Book.* Boston: Houghton Mifflin, 1979.

Oliphant, Thomas. *Praying for Gil Hodges: A Memoir of the 1955 World Series and One Family's Love of the Brooklyn Dodgers.* New York: Thomas Dunne Books, 2005.

O'Neill, Terry. *The Game Behind the Game: High Pressure, High Stakes in Television Sports.* New York: Harper & Row, 1989.

Post, Robert C., and Amy Donovan, eds. *Every Four Years*. Washington: Smithsonian Exposition Books, distributed by New York: W. W. Norton and Company, 1980.

Powers, Ron. *SuperTube: The Rise of Television Sports*. New York: Coward-McCann, 1984.

Reeves, Richard. *President Kennedy: Profile of Power*. New York: Simon & Schuster, 1993.

Reeves, Thomas. *A Question of Character: A Life of John F. Kennedy*. New York: Free Press, 1991.

Reidenbaugh, Lowell. *The Sporting News Take Me Out to the Ball Park*. St. Louis: Sporting News Publishing Co., 1983.

Rosenthal, Harold. *The 10 Best Years of Baseball: An Informal History of the Fifties*. New York: Van Nostrand Reinhold Company, 1980.

Schoor, Gene. *A Pictorial History of the Dodgers: From Brooklyn to Los Angeles*. New York: Leisure Press, 1984.

Vecsey, George, ed. *The Way It Was: Great Sports Events from the Past*. New York: Mobil Oil and McGraw-Hill Book Co., 1974.

Vincent, Fay. *The Last Commissioner: A Baseball Valentine*. New York: Simon & Schuster, 2002.

White, Theodore H. *In Search of History: A Personal Adventure*. New York: Harper & Row, 1978.

———.*The Making of the President 1960*. New York: Atheneum, 1961.

Wolff, Bob. *It's Not Who Won or Lost the Game, It's How You Sold the Beer*. South Bend, Indiana: Diamond Communications, 1996.

Wood, Bob. *Dodger Dogs to Fenway Franks: And All the Wieners in Between*. New York: McGraw-Hill Publishing Company, 1988.

INDEX

ABOUT THE AUTHOR

CURT SMITH is America's leading baseball radio/TV historian: to *USA Today*, "the voice of authority on baseball broadcasting." He also wrote more speeches than anyone for President George H. W. Bush. The *New York Times* terms his work "the high point of Bush familial eloquence."

Smith hosts the National Public Radio affiliate *Perspectives* series. He is a columnist for GateHouse Media Inc., Major League Baseball's official website MLBlogs.com, and *Jewish World Review*'s PoliticalMavens.com, and Senior Lecturer of English at New York's University of Rochester.

Pull Up a Chair is Smith's 13th book. Others: *The Voice: Mel Allen's Untold Story, Voices of Summer, What Baseball Means to Me, Storied Stadiums, Our House, Windows on the White House, Of Mikes and Men, The Storytellers, The Red Sox Fan's Little Book of Wisdom, Voices of The Game, Long Time Gone,* and *America's Dizzy Dean*. NBC's Bob Costas says: "Curt Smith stands up for the beauty of words."

Raised in Upstate New York, he was a Gannett Co. reporter and the *Saturday Evening Post* senior editor before joining the Bush White House in 1989. Among speeches for the 41st President were the State of the Union; "Just War" Persian Gulf speech; and address on Pearl Harbor's 50th anniversary. Smith later headed the ex-President's speech staff, writing Bush's moving 2004 eulogy to President Reagan given at Washington's National Cathedral.

Associated Press and the New York State Broadcasters Association have voted his radio commentary "Best in New York State." Smith wrote and coproduced ESPN-TV's *Voices of The Game*. He has helped write ABC/ESPN's *SportsCentury*, hosted Smithsonian Institution and XM Satellite Radio National Baseball Hall of Fame and Museum series, and keynoted events like the prestigious Cooperstown Symposium on Baseball and American Culture.

Smith has written for, among others, the *Boston Globe, Newsweek, New York Daily News,* the *New York Times, Reader's Digest, Sports Illustrated,* and the *Washington Post.* He has appeared on numerous network radio/TV programs, including ABC's *Nightline,* BBC, CBC, *CBS This Morning,* ESPN *SportsCenter,* Fox News Channel, the History Channel, and CNBC, CNN, and MSNBC.

The 1973 State University of New York at Geneseo graduate has been named among the SUNY system's "100 Outstanding Alumni." He is a member of the Judson Welliver Society of former White House speechwriters, Baseball Hall of Fame Ford C. Frick Award broadcast committee, and Museum of Broadcast Communications and National Radio Hall of Fame committee, originating the Franklin D. Roosevelt Award in Political Communication. Smith, wife Sarah, and their two children live in Rochester, New York.